READING SCRIPTURE WITH THE CHURCH FATHERS

CHRISTOPHER A. HALL

InterVarsity Press
Downers Grove, Illinois

InterVarsity Press
P.O. Box 1400, Downers Grove, IL 60515
World Wide Web: www.ivpress.com
E-mail: mail@ivpress.com

InterVarsity Press® is the book-publishing division of InterVarsity Christian Fellowship/USA®, a student movement active on campus at hundreds of universities, colleges and schools of nursing in the United States of America, and a member movement of the International Fellowship of Evangelical Students. For information about local and regional activities, write Public Relations Dept., InterVarsity Christian Fellowship/USA, 6400 Schroeder Rd., P.O. Box 7895, Madison, WI 53707-7895.

Scripture quotations, unless otherwise noted, are from the New Revised Standard Version of the Bible, copyright 1989 by the Division of Christian Education of the National Council of the Churches of Christ in the USA. Used by permission. All rights reserved.

Cover photograph: Scala/Art Resource, N.Y.

ISBN 0-8308-1500-7

Printed in the United States of America ♾

Library of Congress Cataloging-in-Publication Data

Hall, Christopher A. (Christopher Alan), 1950 -
    Reading scripture with the church fathers / Christopher A. Hall.
      p. cm.
    Includes bibliographical references and index.
    ISBN 0-8308-1500-7 (pbk. : alk. paper)
     1. Bible—Criticism, interpretation, etc.—History—Early church,
ca. 30-600. 2. Fathers of the Church. I. Title.
BS500.H27 1998
270.1—dc21
                                 98-23027
                                    CIP

20	19	18	17	16	15	14	13	12	11	10	9	8	7	6	5	4	3	2	1
15	14	13	12	11	10	09	08	07	06	05	04	03	02	01	00	99	98		

To Deb, Nathan, Nathalie and Joshua

Preface

I remember preparing to visit London for the first time. I skimmed the famed city's history, glanced at maps, highlighted sites and imagined how each location would appear in person. When I actually visited London I was not disappointed. It was much as I had imagined it to be on the basis of my limited research. Still, occasional letdowns did occur. For example, I was surprised to discover that Big Ben was so small. The photographs I had seen of Big Ben, perhaps because of camera angle and lighting, portrayed a striking structure dominating its surroundings. The actual clock, impressive though it was, did not compare well with the photographs I had seen. The result for this tourist was a mild sense of disappointment.

I mention this because the same sense of disappointment or even disillusionment can ripple through a reader encountering the church fathers for the first time, particularly if expectations are unrealistic, ill-informed or unfair to the subject at hand. So from the beginning let me tell you what to expect and not to expect in the following pages. This is a book about how Christians, in particular Christians in the first seven centuries of the church's history, have read and interpreted the Bible. It is specifically designed to meet the needs and questions of people who are interested in entering the world of patristic exegesis and need a road map to guide them.

Significant new commentary series devoted to early Christian biblical interpretation, such as the Ancient Christian Commentary on Scripture (ACCS, published by InterVarsity Press), are appearing and provoking much interest. Many people using a series such as the ACCS will find that a guide is helpful as they begin to study the exegesis of the fathers. This is the role I have attempted to assume in this book. My goal is to present as clearly, simply and accurately as possible the methodology and content of patristic biblical interpretation. Why should we bother reading the church fathers? What is a church father? How do the fathers read the Bible? What methodologies and techniques do they employ? What biblical emphases, themes and characters do they tend to notice that modern readers might overlook? How was their reading of Scripture influenced by their own linguistic, political, social and philosophical environment? Where do they shine in their interpretation? Where might they occasionally stumble? How can the fathers help us to read the Bible well today? These and other relevant questions—and hopefully reasonable answers—will occupy much of the text.

Scholars already familiar with the fathers will find little new in this book and perhaps be surprised at what has been omitted. Why, some will ask, are certain fathers absent from the text and others included? My answer is that both space and purpose have limited my discussion and analysis. Some figures that one would listen to carefully in a detailed patristic study will remain largely silent in this introductory text. I have not written in detail, for example, about the contributions of exegetes such as Ambrosiaster and Tyconius, unknown figures for people just beginning to study patristic biblical interpretation but old friends to those who have thoroughly explored the field. Other readers might ask why I have detailed discussion of fathers who did not produce extended line by line commentaries, such as Gregory of Nazianzus, while I largely overlook the riches of the Syriac and Coptic traditions.

My main desire was to introduce and analyze patristic figures whom the church, both East and West, has recognized as illustrating how to read the Bible well and to apply its riches to a variety of needs, issues and circumstances. Thus, my focus will be on the eight great doctors or preeminent teachers of the church: Athanasius, Gregory of Nazianzus, Basil the Great and John Chrysostom in the East; Ambrose, Jerome, Augustine and Gregory the Great in the West.

Some of these fathers wrote extensive biblical commentaries. Others did not. All, however, possessed minds saturated in the biblical narrative. All interpreted the Scripture within and to a wide variety of circumstances and people. At times a father such as Jerome will exegete a biblical text in response to a question posed in a letter by a friend or, occasionally, by an enemy. In addition, Jerome left behind many significant biblical commentaries. Fathers such as Athanasius and Gregory of Nazianzus interpret the Bible within a wider context of theological controversy. Theological treatises rather than biblical commentaries offer the best entrance to their exegesis. As I attempt to show in my discussion of Athanasius, some of the "black dwarf's" best exegesis occurs as he reacts to a specific theological position he views as a threat to the gospel—that of Arius and his followers.

Other significant fathers such as Gregory the Great and John Chrysostom were gifted pastors, interpreting the Bible as they preached faithfully to their congregations in Rome, Antioch and Constantinople. Because their exegesis arises within the context of pastoral issues and concerns it possesses an especially practical character. Neither Gregory nor Chrysostom will allow their audience to study the Scripture at arm's length. Indeed, all the fathers insist that the study of the Bible is not an esoteric, intellectual exercise practiced by the isolated academic.

Instead, the fathers argue that biblical interpretation is an ecclesiastical activity to be practiced in the church and for the church within the context of prayer and worship. It is a communal act rather than a private, individualistic endeavor. The ecclesiastical, communal and devotional nature of patristic exegesis will come as a surprise to many modern students of the Bible, particularly for those trained in the hermeneutical techniques of the modern academy. The fathers are united in their insistence that the text of Scripture opens itself to those who approach it reverently and receptively. In short, the fathers consistently treat the Bible as a holy book whose riches can be mined adequately only by those prepared to honor and obey the message the Scripture contains.

And yet, some will ask, can the insights and interpretive methodology of Christians living hundreds of years in the past remain relevant for the Christian living on the cusp of the second millenium? Can a bridge be built to the world of the fathers? Obviously I believe such a construction project to be a genuine possibility. The first step in bringing these two interpretive worlds together—that of the fathers and of the modern Christian—is to ask how modern Christians tend to read and interpret the Bible. After this preliminary task is completed, the rest of the book will explore the hermeneutical outlook and methodology of the fathers, an interpretive perspective that will readily supplement, support and periodically criticize modern hermeneutical approaches.

O N E

WHY READ
THE FATHERS?

J EROME, AUGUSTINE, BASIL, GREGORY OF NAZIANZUS, JOHN CHRYSOSTOM, Gregory of Nyssa, Athanasius, Origen, Theodore of Mopsuestia, Cyril of Alexandria, Clement of Alexandria, Justin Martyr, Irenaeus, Ambrose, Gregory the Great. For some of us the names are familiar. Perhaps memories of a past Western civilization or church history course come to mind. We have read Augustine's *Confessions* or sections of *The City of God*. Yet the passage of time has blurred our memory or dampened our enthusiasm for the personalities and world of the early church.

Maybe our recollection of past attempts to understand a church father's writing discourages us. We recall the desire to explore an early Christian text, yet remember the terrible dullness of plowing through translations that obscured more than opened patristic perspectives to us. On the one hand, we say to ourselves, surely there is a reason why Augustine's name keeps turning up in print. On the other hand, too often Augustine's writing and world remain hidden to us, veiled behind cultural barriers, hermeneutical idiosyncrasies, incomprehensible translations and confusing theological controversies. The same could be said of lesser-known personalities such as Jerome or Basil.

For others, the church fathers represent a vast unknown, unexplored territory. Questions proliferate. What is a church father? Did all early Christian leaders receive this designation? If not, how did one qualify to be called a father? Why should we take the time to read them? Were they not all wild allegorizers? Did they really understand the gospel? Or did their Greek and Roman background distort the gospel beyond recognition?

Can the Fathers Be Trusted?

Protestant readers might be particularly suspicious at this point. Can the fathers be trusted? Weren't most of them Roman Catholic or Orthodox? Didn't they believe in salvation by works? Isn't their understanding of the gospel more Greek or Roman than Christian? For many inquirers, the image of wild-eyed, legalistic, imbalanced ascetics quickly surfaces, fomenting suspicions.

Indeed, the trustworthiness of the fathers remains a fundamental question for Christians from many different backgrounds. Will the fathers lead us astray? Did they read the Bible well? Or did their own cultural and religious blind spots prevent them from clearly comprehending the heart of the gospel? For many Protestant Christians there is a deep suspicion that the abuses of late medieval Roman Catholicism find their seeds in the thoughts of the fathers themselves. Does not Martin Luther himself question "what good it does to rely on the venerable old Fathers, who have been approved through such a long succession of ages. Were not they too all equally blind, or rather, did they not simply overlook the clearest and most explicit statements of Paul?"[1]

And yet the same Luther who seems ready to discard the fathers consistently interacts with them throughout his work, particularly relying on the insights of Augustine. Perhaps we are more faithful to Luther if we examine carefully his own methodology in reading the Scripture with the fathers. He is not reluctant to criticize them when he feels they are in error. Simultaneously, though, Luther listens carefully to their voices and praises them when he feels they interpret Scripture correctly.

Sola Scriptura?

Many view the church's history from the second to the sixteenth century as a succession of mistakes upon mistakes. For many Protestants much of church history remains a barren wasteland, a desert of error strikingly characterized by the absence of the Holy Spirit's guidance and discernment. Only with the arrival of Luther, Melanchthon, Calvin, Zwingli and Simons was a clear, undiluted, biblically based understanding of the gospel retrieved and revitalized. Does not the Reformers' insistence upon *sola Scriptura* cast grave doubt on the church fathers' marked tendency to read Scripture in light of the church's tradition? Are the Reformers' doubts, on the other hand, centered on the fathers themselves or on how others have interpreted or misinterpreted their teaching?

Take, for example, Luther's comments on 2 Corinthians 3:6 in his treatise *Concerning the Letter and the Spirit*. Paul writes of God, "who has made us competent to be ministers of a new covenant, not of letter but of spirit; for the letter kills, but the Spirit gives life." Luther contends that Origen, Jerome and other "fathers have stretched and misused this passage," while acknowledging they did so "to fend off Jews and heretics, as everyone well knows or is able to know." Hence, they should be excused for their faulty exegesis, but surely not followed in their error. What more particularly seems to aggravate Luther, however, is the inability of his Roman Catholic opponents, such as the theologian Emser, to distinguish between the good the fathers have to offer and the errors they sometimes commit. In Luther's view, Emser and others

> have no judgment with regard to the work and teaching of the fathers; they gobble up everything they find until they obey the fathers only in those things in which the dear fathers slipped as men. And they drop them when they did well, as I could easily prove with regard to all the teachings and lives now held to be the very best.[2]

Luther consistently insists that it "is necessary to compare the fathers' books with Scripture and to judge them according to its light."[3]

The slogan *sola Scriptura*, then, is the frank assertion and admission, as Anthony Lane puts it, "that the church can err."[4] The fathers themselves insisted that the church be held accountable to Scripture. At the same time, *sola Scriptura* has never meant that the only resources the Christian needs to understand God's Word well are the Bible and the Holy Spirit. The ideal of the autonomous interpreter can more easily be laid at the steps of the Enlightenment than the Reformation. Rather, Reformers such as Luther and Calvin wisely considered the history, councils, creeds and tradition of the church, including the fathers' writings, as a rich resource ignored only by the foolish or arrogant.[5]

Indeed, have Christians at any time and in any place ever read the Scripture in a vacuum, hermetically sealed from all historical, linguistic and cultural influences that potentially blur or skew the Bible's message? Is it possible or preferable to follow the advice of Alexander Campbell to "open the New Testament as if mortal man had never seen it before"?[6] Can we so easily escape from the interpretive culture and community in which we have learned to read the Bible? Is the stance of the objective, autonomous observer and interpreter truly attainable? One wonders. And yet many modern people seem instinctively to assume that an objective, highly individualistic interpretive stance and methodology are laudable goals and realistic possibilities. Not infrequently modern Christians, liberal and conservative, view their own interpretive environments as hermeneutical shells in which the air has been systematically filtered from the corrupting influences of the past and present. Exactly how and what one would identify as potential corrupting influences, though, differs for the modern liberal and pietistic Christian mind. Both groups, however, demonstrate a deep wariness of the Christian past. Too often for the Christian liberal the past extends to the emergence of the Enlightenment. Frequently for the Christian pietist it reaches only to the eruption of the Reformation.

The Absence of Memory

Robert Wilken cogently argues that many modern theologians and Christian laypeople find themselves rootless and drifting in a barren secular and ecclesiastical landscape, largely because they have forgotten their Christian past.[7] The modern mind, Wilken believes, has lost any sense of obligation to the past. Instead, many modern thinkers have purposely limited their reliance upon past ideas and traditions, choosing to view autonomous reflection as the heart of rationality. One discovers truth only by purposefully separating oneself from the object of knowledge. For the modern Christian, Wilken contends, this autonomous stance has spawned an unrelenting suspicion of tradition.

Wilken identifies Roman Catholic theologian David Tracy as a case in point. For Tracy,

> The traditional Christian theologian of whatever tradition, preached and practiced a morality of belief in and obedience to the tradition and a

fundamental loyalty to the church-community's beliefs. The modern historian and scientist—whether in natural or social sciences— preaches and practices an exactly contrary morality. For him, one cannot investigate a cognitive claim with intellectual integrity if one insists simultaneously that the claim is believable because tradition has believed it. For the new scientific morality, one's fundamental loyalty as an analyst of any and all cognitive claims is solely to those methodological procedures which the particular scientific community of inquiry in question has developed.[8]

The result, Wilken contends, is a tendency to produce theology in a context (the university) and with a stance (Tracy's autonomous inquiry) that ironically and unnecessarily divorces the theologian from the very religious community in which theological exploration and reflection finds its roots. Wilken observes that while "Christian faith has always been a critical and rational enterprise, and at its best has welcomed the wisdom of the world into the household of faith," the wisest Christian thinkers also recognized they were "bearers of tradition," a tradition founded on Scripture, subjected to critical examination, tested in the lives of "countless men and women," defended against critics, and "elaborated in myriad social and cultural settings."

It is this broader interpretive community that Tracy views with marked suspicion in his quest for autonomous inquiry. Why, Wilken fairly asks, should "one assume, as Tracy apparently does, that reason is to be found only outside of tradition, and that genuine rationality requires 'autonomy.' This premise seems to invite a willful amnesia, a self-imposed affliction that would rob our lives of depth and direction."[9]

A Long Journey Home

Thomas Oden, editor of the Ancient Christian Commentary on Scripture (InterVarsity Press), has written extensively of the tendency of modern people to underestimate the contributions of the past and exaggerate the wisdom of the present. Oden himself, a theologian firmly ensconced in the classical liberal tradition for many years, increasingly recognized in the late sixties that his disrespect for and ignorance of the Christian past had severely warped his own theological, philosophical, historical and political perspective. Oden's spiritual pilgrimage over the past twenty-five years is in many ways an apt illustration of a theologian reawakening from

Wilken's "self-imposed amnesia" and is worth examining in some detail.

Thomas Oden grew up in a home that was deeply rooted in the pietistic tradition and the political ideals of the Democratic Party.[10] Oden's parents combined a devotion to the Scripture and to a deeply personal faith with a commitment to liberal political philosophy and the union movement. Oden took this upbringing seriously, especially the idea that genuine faith always demonstrates itself in concrete action. In high school Oden organized students in the United World Federalist movement, and in his college days gravitated to quasi-socialist philosophy as he worked ardently for the Students for Democratic Action at the University of Oklahoma. When Oden decided to attend Perkins School of Theology in Dallas, he based his choice on the hope that the church could effectively serve as a change agent in society, rather than on a strong personal commitment to the biblical message.

At Perkins, Joseph Matthews exposed Oden to secular and religious existentialist thought. Oden devoured the works of Sartre, Camus and Marcel. Rudolf Bultmann, however, best symbolizes the direction of Oden's thought. Bultmann's existentialist categories resurrected the Bible's relevance for Oden. Once again Oden could read the Bible, although through the interpretive lenses of what Oden was later to label "modernity."

As Oden left Perkins for graduate study at Yale under the guidance of H. Richard Niebuhr, a specific theological vocation crystallized within him. Oden's conception of this vocation, however, was itself shaped by his idealization of the new. As he was later to describe these early years, Oden as a young theologian believed his peers and students would judge his contribution to the academy and church by the criterion of innovativeness. The call to create and innovate superseded Oden's appreciation and appropriation of the church's own tradition and self-understanding. He continued to be avidly attracted to existentialism throughout the late fifties and early sixties, a fascination followed and complemented by an interest in post-Freudian psychology.

Novel experimentation, combined with a deep mistrust and disdain for the past, marked Oden's thought and work during this initial period. His interaction with Scripture and other theological texts was less a dialogue than a "filtering process" where he allowed sources to speak to him "only insofar as they could meet" his "conditions," "worldview" and "assumptions as a modern man."

I was determined not to accept any reports that could not be fitted into my modern worldview. . . . Furthermore, I was mentored (especially by Bultmann, Tillich, Heidegger and Rogers) to understand that what it meant to be a theologian was to struggle to create something new, to develop a new theology, to see things differently than any others had seen things before and thereby to offer my personal skill and subjective experience as a theologian to the emergent world.[11]

Some fruit spawned by the freewheeling sixties led Oden to question seriously his theological presuppositions and methodology. "By 1968 I could see the tremendous harm caused by sexual experimentation—even among my friends. I could also see their lives being torn up by family disintegration and mind-altering drugs. The wonderful world they thought they were creating was simply turning to dust, ashes, and pain—enormous pain."[12]

As Oden reexamined the direction his theological methodology had taken him, he understood he had come to a dead end. Where was he to turn? Modernity's well had run dry for Oden. Soon he would find himself drinking from unexpected sources.

Oden began teaching at Drew University in the early seventies and encountered there the Jewish philosopher and true renaissance man Will Herberg. Interestingly enough, it was Herberg who in no uncertain terms warned Oden that his overall understanding and theological perspective would remain grossly misshapen unless he supplemented his immersion in modern theological sources with a concentrated exposure to the world of the church fathers. Oden followed Herberg's advice and for the next five years devoted himself to an attentive study of patristic texts. During this time his understanding of how to do theology changed dramatically. As a result, Oden radically reshaped his theological agenda for the coming years.

His previous interpretive community had trained Oden to assume that theologians must be creative and novel in their work if they were to fulfill and validate their vocations in the church, seminary, university and broader intellectual community. The fathers challenged these fundamental assumptions. The more Oden read them, the more he realized how much of what he had assumed was new was as old as the apostolic tradition itself. The early Christian writers had intuited many ideas Oden had considered modern contributions.

As Oden studied patristic thought he increasingly realized that theology could be, indeed, must be done in the context of the worshiping community of the church, a fellowship that stretched across a vast expanse of years, cultures and languages. Yet Oden discerned themes and practices that remained constant in the church's life and reflection, a central "consensual" understanding of God's entrance into history in Jesus Christ. In the community of the church and its accumulated history and tradition Oden found a corrective to his tendency to idealize the "new" as inherently superior. The call to listen superseded the need to innovate.

> Then while reading Nemesius something clicked. I realized that I must listen intently, actively, without reservation. Listen in such a way that my whole life depended upon hearing. Listen in such a way that I could see telescopically beyond my modern myopia, to break through the walls of my modern prison, and actually hear voices from the past with different assumptions entirely about the world and time and human culture. Only then in my forties did I begin to become a theologian. Up to that time I had been teaching theology without having sufficiently met the patristic mentors who could teach me theology.[13]

Oden had experienced a "redirection," "a hermeneutical reversal" in which he "learned to listen to premodern texts." Oden came to understand that hermeneutics could not be severed from character, disposition and obedience, a patristic emphasis we will explore in future pages. Listening to a text and obedience to a text became for Oden "the most important single lesson I have learned hermeneutically. . . . Carl Rogers taught me to trust my experience. The ancient Christian writers taught me to trust that Scripture and tradition would transmute my experience."[14]

Oden's journey from modern theology to "paleo-orthodoxy" is remarkable. A number of other theologians and biblical scholars, many of them relatively young, are moving in the same direction. Why this swelling group of "young fogeys," as Oden calls them? Why have many become dissatisfied with modern ways of reading and interpreting Scripture? Only a closer look at how modern Christians read the Bible can answer these important questions.

T w o

The Modern Mind &
Biblical Interpretation

———————————

In a telling article in *The Reformed Journal*, William J. Abraham comments, "Any consensus in theology today begins with the rejection of the classical Christian tradition as this is generally known in Western Culture."[1]

Abraham particularly observes the strongly reductionistic flavor of much modern theology, a scientific reductionism he relates to the acceptance by modern theologians of the "canons of science" and "critical history" as normative criteria. Will the biblical narrative of God's saving work fit within reductionist boundaries? Not well, Abraham fears. Once theologians begin writing within the reductionist framework, they have little choice but to "reinterpret the tradition in terms that will speak, as they say, 'meaningfully' to the modern age."[2]

Abraham also describes and analyzes other characteristics of the modern worldview. A modern person is "one informed by the canons of rationality developed in the European Enlightenment." For some, Enlightenment rationality leads to a rejection of the possibility of special divine revelation and belief in miracles, largely because the possibility of divine intervention in history is no longer considered a valid option.

The unfortunate result is the isolation of the secularized person and theologian, "no longer shaped in any profound way by the institutions of Christianity but . . . cut loose and alone in a sea of individualism and autonomy."[3] In effect, Abraham argues, many modern theologians have endorsed secular values "as more Christian than those of the traditional believer and . . . seek to join the secular person in his or her quest for authenticity, community, peace, and justice." The result is theology that looks suspiciously like a reworking and expansion of the politics and ethics of the Enlightenment.[4]

Interestingly, Abraham's recommendations for regaining and maintaining theological health in the modern world focus on issues of character formation. That is, spiritually ill theologians produce sick theology. How can they get well?

For one thing, Abraham recommends a cultivation of the virtue of humility. Modern theologians have been tempted by their own hubris to think they can achieve more than is reasonably or humbly possible. A more humble and self-aware approach, Abraham advises, would cultivate "a sense of inadequacy in the face of the utter complexity and mystery of the divine order." Modern theology, however, has too often failed to acknowledge "the limitation of the human intellect in its attempts to unravel the mystery of God's action in the world." The modern theologian needs to be reminded that

> a true and truly Christian theology will surely be deeply rooted in revelation and tradition, in worship and prayer in the Christian community, in compassion and service in the world, in fear and trembling before the wonder of the Christian gospel, and in humble dependence on the grace and agency of the Holy Spirit. Yet precisely these notes are the ones missing from the prevailing canons of theological discourse.[5]

Revelation, worship and tradition are the "fundamental womb" in which theology is conceived, develops and flourishes. Yet ironically, too many seminaries have deserted these sources in a misguided attempt to communicate the gospel more effectively to their surrounding culture. As a sad result many seminary graduates feel compelled to construct their own theology out of whole cloth. Abraham acerbically describes the ludicrous expectation on many seminary campuses "that each theological student must, in the space of a semester or so and after a short period of study, develop his or her own creed and shortly thereafter be licensed to inflict this creed on the church at large."[6]

Tracy, Wilken, Oden and Abraham agree that the Enlightenment has significantly influenced how modern theologians go about their business and how modern Christians tend to read the Bible. Most, if not all, Western theologians—whether they be conservative or liberal—are children of the Enlightenment. Some, such as Tracy, welcome this family heritage, while Wilken, Oden and Abraham are much more guarded in their response to this development. If we are to understand how the church fathers read Scripture and to effectively enter their world, it is particularly important for us to examine carefully our own modern Enlightenment and post-Enlightenment background.

Positively, many Enlightenment thinkers, horrified and repulsed by years of religious warfare, championed religious toleration, freedom of conscience, the expansion of political liberty, democratic principles and philosophy, legal reform and humane punishment. Peter Gay rightly reminds us that Enlightenment leaders were in the forefront of expanding freedom on a number of important fronts: "freedom from arbitrary power, freedom of speech, freedom of trade, freedom to realize one's talents, freedom of aesthetic response . . ."[7]

Less positive was the drift among many of the Enlightenment's leading lights to question increasingly the coherence, significance and moral stance of Christian doctrine and authority. Stubborn adherence to theological and ecclesiastical tradition and perspective always ended, it seemed to many, with someone getting tried, tortured or killed.

This is not to say that the majority of Enlightenment thinkers immediately deserted belief in God. Voltaire argued that belief in God was a necessary support for a rational, moral life for all but the most advanced philosophers. "I want my attorney, my tailor, my servants, even my wife to believe in God, and I think that then I shall be robbed and cuckolded less often."[8] And yet the theology underpinning the religious belief advocated by Voltaire and others was a drastically pared down faith; fine theological distinctions and ecclesiastical dogmas would continue to be subjected to the grid of Enlightenment rationality and viewed with ever increasing suspicion.

Not only the behavior but the proliferation of Christian groups, each with their own doctrinal or cultural distinctives, seemed to undercut the plausibility of understanding Christian truth as a comprehensive, logically coherent whole. Voltaire gently pokes fun at such an idea.

> I know to be sure that the Church is infallible; but is it the Greek Church, or the Latin Church, or the Church of England, or that of Denmark and of Sweden, or that of the proud city of Neuchatel, or that of the primitives called Quakers, or that of the Anabaptists, or that of the Moravians? The Turkish Church has its points, too, but they say that the Chinese Church is much more ancient.[9]

Was it not more honest to admit that the horrors of the past one hundred years were the result of religious pride and a colossal loss of intellectual nerve, an unwillingness to embrace the possibilities human reason itself offered? Foggy thinking, it appeared, led directly to injustice. Voltaire had seen firsthand the horrific results of unbridled religious zeal. He warned, "Once your faith . . . persuades you to believe what your intelligence declares to be absurd, beware lest you likewise sacrifice your reason in the conduct of your life."[10]

Religious bloodletting and tyranny, however, were not the only factors raising doubt in the value of the church's heritage and authority. Key developments in science, mathematics and philosophy indicated that human reason was capable of astounding feats. The work of Bacon, Galileo, Descartes, Newton and Kepler opened up new vistas for the Western mind. Unrecognized and unexpected worlds appeared overnight and begged for exploration. For too long religious superstition and oppressive tradition had shackled reason and stifled its potential."[11]

For many, the principle of reason promised to free Europe from its religiously troubled past. Perhaps, on the basis of reason itself, humanity could delineate a way of thinking and living religiously that could avoid past mistakes and open up new horizons for the future. Freeing the mind from past superstitions and restraints could only facilitate this process. Possibilities seemed endless for the autonomous, reasoning individual.

The initial optimism that Enlightenment rationality and Christian faith were reconcilable, indeed allies, proved difficult to maintain. Some interpreters, such as Richard Tarnas, posit an inherent incongruence between the Enlightenment model of the universe as a mechanism with its own "mechanical forces, its material heavens, and its planetary Earth," and "traditional" Christian cosmology. How long would thinkers perceive the Earth and humanity as the center of God's purposes if the Sun and Earth were perceived "as merely two bodies among countless others moving through a boundless neutral void"?[12] Even a deeply committed Christian thinker such as Pascal appeared to shiver before the dimensions and implications of the new universe. "I am terrified by the eternal silence of these infinite spaces."[13]

With the increasing incongruity of the Enlightenment and Christian worldviews, would God long remain a necessary hypothesis in a world where human reason possessed the necessary keys to unlock life's deepest mysteries? As the years passed a palpable drift away from classical Christian orthodoxy rippled through Western culture.

For the first time in its long history European culture freed itself from its Christian parentage. While Enlightenment thinkers increasingly discounted the claims of revealed religion as reliable sources of truth and guidance, natural religion—founded upon universal principles and laws available to all people through the exercise of reason—promised to be a rich resource of insight for a new world breaking free from its past. "What was truly important had been written by the Creator in the great book of nature left open for all to read."[14]

Some attempted to retain Christianity as the most reliable interpreter of nature's religion. For many the Enlightenment's deep skepticism regarding the possibility of a supernaturally revealed interpretation in an authoritative text undercut the openness of the universe to God's intervention. Before long many Western thinkers bred on Enlightenment presuppositions would comprehend the world as a closed system of cause and effect, with little room left for God to operate. As Clark Pinnock observes, "The conception of a unified world, everywhere subject to the inexorable sequence of natural causes and effects, became the dominant mentality. The biblical history of salvation could only be regarded as myth."[15]

With astonishing speed, the progeny of early Enlightenment thinkers were soon to cast aside the necessity of a Christian framework for interpreting reality. Atheism became a widely accepted philosophical option for the first time in Western history. Ludwig Feuerbach interpreted God as the projection of humanity's deepest hopes and concerns. Karl Marx portrayed religious belief as a narcotic designed to sedate the proletariat from rebelling against the injustices of the moneyed upper classes. Freud linked religious belief to deep inner neuroses in the human psyche, a reflection of an infantile search for security and unwillingness to mature. And Nietzsche, a philosopher whose system wore too heavily on his own psyche, clearly perceived that in a godless world all values become relative and truth merely a linguistic and cultural convention.

Post-Enlightenment theology demonstrates repeatedly that it is tone-deaf to divine wavelengths beyond those resonating from general or natural revelation. As Pinnock puts it, the "extreme this-worldliness" of modern theology is "unnerving." Within its self-imposed perimeters the

> setting of human life shifts away from its context within God's purposes to an environment of meaninglessness, to nothing more ultimate than the ever-changing and relative arrangements of the human enterprise itself. Moderns now want to see themselves as creators of their own destinies, to live lives in no way undergirded by God or directed by any sacred rules but set within the realm of blind matter running its heedless course. What is real for such people are the profane, contingent, and blind causes that produced them and the artifacts and social institutions they have created for themselves. Life begins with birth and ends with death—there is literally no other meaning than the meaning they create for themselves.[16]

In retrospect, the philosophical and theological optimism of the Enlightenment shocks our sensibilities. Yes, certain Enlightenment principles have led to significant political reforms and technological advances. What is most striking and troubling in the Enlightenment perspective, though, is its naive confidence that reason operates autonomously, largely free from the effects of personal disposition, social context, cultural background and religious community. Not only does postmodern philosophy and hermeneutics challenge this assertion, but classical Christianity doubts its fundamental viability.

A primary dictum of the Western theological tradition, channeled through the conduit of Augustine and Anselm, had been that faith led to understanding. This was a faith in Christ grounded in personal self-awareness of sin and cognizant of the continual lure to self-deception, rooted in the intrinsic authority of Scripture and the divinely inspired revelation it communicated, and nurtured by the church's history of reflection on the meaning of God's word to humanity.

The Enlightenment perspective stood this approach on its head. Understanding would lead to a mature faith, rather than the reverse. Hence, those aspects of the Christian tradition that failed to meet the standards of human reason—liberated, autonomous reason—were regarded with suspicion and for many ultimately discarded. Is it surprising that the resurrection, incarnation, Trinity, miracles and other revelatory gifts soon became negotiables?

While one might hope that conservative Christians had escaped from the Enlightenment's crippling theological methodology, evangelical hermeneutics, particularly in the United States, has been particularly shaped by certain key Enlightenment presuppositions. Mark Noll, for example, has chronicled the attempt of conservative evangelical scholars to interpret the Bible by means of key Enlightenment categories.[17] Evangelical scholars assented to the Enlightenment's deep suspicion of tradition and proceeded to produce a traditionless hermeneutic. The "Bible alone" survived the Enlightenment assault against tradition, but only by becoming a timeless text filled with facts to be scientifically identified, analyzed and categorized.

To use Noll's words, "the 'Bible alone' (in both senses of the term—as the *supreme* religious authority but also as the *only* hereditary authority) survived the assault on tradition that characterized the era."[18] As Nathan Hatch observes, the Bible "very easily became . . . 'a book dropped from the skies for all sorts of men to use in their own way.'"[19]

Noll explains that conservative Christians widely expected that as they exercised their renewed reason under the guidance of the Holy Spirit they could both understand the Bible and restore the church to its New Testament purity. The church's history of exegesis, its tradition of reading the Bible since the founding of the initial Christian community in Jerusalem, now became an enemy to be avoided if one was to read the Bible correctly and safely. Alexander Campbell, a leading light in the Restorationist movement, set the tone for many others: "I have endeavored to read the Scriptures as though no one had read them before me."[20]

The Enlightenment's imprint left its mark as many evangelicals treated the Bible as a scientific text to be inductively studied through renewed reason alone. "The Scriptures admit of being studied and expounded upon the principles of the inductive method," James S. Lamar wrote in 1859 in his *Organon of Scripture; or, The Inductive Method of Biblical Interpretation*, "and . . . when thus interpreted they speak to us in a voice as certain and unmistakable as the language of nature heard in the experiments and observations of science."[21]

Noll contends that Lewis Sperry Chafer, one of the great founding lights of Dallas Theological Seminary, clearly based his own dispensational approach to the Bible and systematic theology on this seemingly scientific approach to reading Scripture well.

> Systematic Theology is the collecting, scientifically arranging, comparing, exhibiting, and defending of *all* facts from any and every source concerning God and His work. . . . The student of the Scriptures . . . will discover that God's great time-periods, characterized as they are by specific divine purposes, fall into a well-defined order. . . . God's program is as important to the theologian as the blueprint to the builder or the chart to the mariner. . . . Theology, as a science, has neglected this great field of revelation [typology]. . . . Contemplation of the doctrine of human conduct belongs properly to a science which purports to discover, classify, and exhibit the great doctrines of the Bible. . . . [T]he science of interpretation [is] usually designated *hermeneutics*. . . . [L]ogical procedure and scientific method [are the keys to hermeneutics].[22]

Chafer's interest in typology resonates well with many church fathers' interest in the same subject. How surprising, then, to see the common Enlightenment deprecation of tradition's possible contributions as a hermeneutical plank in Chafer's methodology. Indeed, Noll observes a self-confidence in Protestant fundamentalism "bordering on hubris, manifested by an extreme antitraditionalism that casually discounted the possibility of wisdom from earlier generations."[23] Noll notes that Chafer felt that his lack of formal theological training was actually an advantage, protecting him from past errors that might influence his own reading of the Bible. In Chafer's words, "The very fact that I did not study a prescribed course in theology made it possible for me to approach the subject with an unprejudiced mind and to be concerned only with what the Bible actually teaches."[24]

Noll contrasts Craig Blaising, a contemporary dispensationalist, who rightly critiques Chafer for his blithe disregard of historical context and its affect upon the biblical interpreter. Chafer, Blaising writes,

> possessed no methodological awareness of the historicity of interpre-

tation.... Furthermore, this hermeneutical deficiency was structured into the very meaning of dispensational thought and practice in its advocacy of clear, plain, normal, or literal interpretation.... We have, then, a generation of theologians who find identity in a self-conscious hermeneutic that lacks methodological awareness of the historical nature of interpretation.[25]

Blaising correctly contends that "all theological thought, including one's own theological thought, is historically conditioned by the tradition to which that theologian belongs as well as personal and cultural factors such as education or experience."[26] The question "which tradition?" must then replace the ephemeral hope of sidestepping tradition all together.

Escape from Tradition?

Recent developments indicate the Enlightenment attempt to sidestep all authority and tradition outside of the autonomous reasoning individual represents simply another intellectual and cultural tradition, "a tradition of disparaging the value of tradition."[27] While thinkers rooted in the Enlightenment's optimistic understanding of "history as progress" tend to keep their eyes forward, Roger Lundin is closer to the truth in arguing that "truth might reside in traditions that have been repressed, neglected, or forgotten and that stand in need of recuperation."[28]

Robert Wilken claims that the Enlightenment's exaggerated suspicion of tradition has led to the astonishing modern incapacity to "accept with gratitude what has come before it and what has been done on its behalf." He reminds us that human reason refuses to function within a vacuum. Rather, it is "found within rather than outside of things; it is not an abstract quality that exists independently in the human mind." If so, it is inherently and immensely reasonable to "allow one's hands to be guided by a master, and foolish to go it alone, as though one could learn to play the violin or sculpt a statue by studying a set of instructions."[29]

In many fields of creative work, immersion in tradition is the presupposition for excellence and originality. Think, for example, of music. On Saturday mornings I often listen to a jazz show on National Public Radio that features interviews with famous and not-so-famous jazz pianists, saxophonists, drummers, trumpeters, etc., and I am regularly struck at how they speak with such respect of teachers and masters, and how to a person they learned to play the piano by first playing in

someone else's style or learned to blow the trumpet by imitating Louis
Armstrong or someone else. Similarly, one is impressed with how often
a performer like folk singer Jean Redpath speaks about tradition as the
necessary condition for making and singing folk music. How often we
are admonished not to let the old traditions be forgotten. Why? Surely
not for historical or archaeological reasons, but because musicians, like
painters and writers and sculptors, know in their fingertips or vocal
cords or ears that imitation is the way to excellence and originality.[30]
The same can be said for the intellectual life and theological work. As
Thomas Oden puts it, watching the church fathers "play theology is like
watching Willie Mays play center field or Duke Ellington play 'Sophisti-
cated Lady.'"[31] If, as Wilken argues, the "way we learn to think is by
reading good thinkers and letting their thoughts form our thoughts," it is
best to submit oneself to learn from those writers who have demonstrated
their trustworthiness over time, those who have been tested by the years
and found to be reliable interpreters of God's redeeming act in Christ.
Wilken reminds us with Augustine that *authority* can designate trustworthiness rather than power, a trust established "through teaching with
truthfulness," residing "in a person who by actions as well as words invites
trust and confidence. . . . The student's trust is won not simply by words
but also by actions, by the kind of person the teacher is—in short, by
character."[32]

Wilken's perspective, one shaped by years of immersion in the writings
of the church fathers, offers a sound alternative to the exaggerated epistemological and theological individualism prevalent today. Christians,
Wilken insists, will find their identity only by recalling an unimagined
world, a world that pursued truth "with the mind in the heart"—a
community that insisted that how and what one thinks, who one is, and
how one lives are an inseparable whole—facilitating a holistic reading of
reality frequently reflected in the writings of the church fathers.

Postmodernism: Insights and Evasions

In reaction and response to the Enlightenment elevation of autonomous
reason, postmodern hermeneutics insists that it is impossible to separate
the interpretation of a text from the gender, culture, language and social
location of the interpreter. In various ways the postmodern perspective is
a helpful correction to the Enlightenment's exaggerated individualism in

which each individual, on the basis of reason alone, interprets not only the biblical text but the universe. Postmodern hermeneutics has helped us to see that our cultural, historical and social environment affects and conditions what we see and understand of another's text and world.

The danger of the postmodern corrective lies in its tendency to collapse ontology, epistemology and ethics into interpretation itself. As Richard Rorty states, "Hermeneutics . . . is what we get when we are no longer epistemological." Postmodern interpreters, then, are "interested not so much in what is out there in the world, or in what happened in history, as in what we can get out of nature and history for our own uses." Roger Lundin argues that many have lost faith in the power of language to mirror truth. Instead, we employ language as a "therapeutic" tool "to help us get what we desire."[33] The result is Lundin's "culture of interpretation" in which the isolated, expressive, autonomous self runs wild across a subjective landscape. Or, as Alasdair MacIntyre observes, "subjective perspectivism" triumphs because the postmodernist assumes the only alternative to the Enlightenment confidence in autonomous rationality is postmodern subjectivism.[34] Lundin describes this development:

> At a time when confidence in epistemology has eroded significantly, perspectivism appears to afford an opportunity for the isolated self—which has been at the center of Western science, philosophy, and art for more than three centuries—to sustain its faith in its own powers. Even though we may no longer believe in the ability of the self to achieve moral perfection or to acquire indubitable knowledge, we are still able, through our contemporary theories of interpretation, to sustain faith in that self's ability to find satisfaction through the exercise of its creative powers.[35]

Lundin highlights the questions of postmodern philosophers such as Stanley Fish who ask, "Can we any longer speak of absolute values or authorities outside of ourselves?" And what of tradition? Can the past reach us and teach us? Or are its riches forever hidden behind an impenetrable interpretive wall? If so, the result is what Nicholas Wolterstorff calls "interpretation-universalism," in which, as C. Stephen Evans writes, "reality cannot be known as it is in itself, but only as it appears to us humans. We only know things relative to our human conceptual systems, and such systems are irreducibly plural and contingent. . . . *It's all interpretation.*"[36]

Not only does interpretation devour conception, intention and communication, but texts actually serve as vehicles of manipulation, exploitation and oppression, and are attempts by authors to impose their understanding of reality upon us. Thus, the interpreter must handle texts with suspicion and caution. Only our own hermeneutical shield can protect us from the inevitable attempt of other authors to overpower us—a shield popularly known as the hermeneutics of suspicion. What's the hidden agenda? we ask. As C. Stephen Evans warns satirically, "Step aside, Foucault: *To find the truth you gotta read between the lines.*"[37]

Which author's perspective is correct? Victory goes to the author who possesses the greatest rhetorical skill and political power. Interpretation engulfs all reality and becomes the survival of the fittest, or perhaps the most clever. In Roger Lundin's words, "Instead of appealing to authority outside ourselves, we can only seek to marshal our rhetorical abilities to wage the political battles necessary to protect our own preferences and to prohibit expressions of preference that threaten or annoy us."[38]

In fact, as Stanley Fish argues, a society built on postmodern hermeneutical principles is in reality a society of pragmatists. Truth is transmuted into what works, personal and corporate preferences, private pleasures. "All preferences are principled," Fish contends.[39] Richard Rorty defines the just society as "one which has no purpose except freedom. It has no purpose except to make life easier for poets and revolutionaries while seeing to it that they make life harder for others only by words, and not deeds."[40] Freedom, it seems, is the only absolute the postmodern pragmatist can affirm, but it is difficult to discern how one would form a viable ethic on the basis of freedom alone. Virtues effectively developed and nourished only in a communal setting are destined to wither or be stillborn, dying a slow death perhaps, but nevertheless perishing in the individualistic pragmatism of postmodernism.

The Present State of Affairs

So where do we find ourselves in the late twentieth century? The autonomous inquirer of the Enlightenment has proven to be self-deceived and naive. Interpretation and the acquisition of knowledge do not occur in a vacuum. And yet the insights the postmodernists offer seem to lead to the cul-de-sac of pragmatism and perspectivism. Is there a way out? Or have we posited a false dichotomy between the affirmation of tradition and its complete rejection? MacIntyre might well fault us at this point for erring in our concept of tradition. Perhaps, "a genuine tradition is not marked by unreflective rigidity but is distinguished by its very ability to respond to legitimate challenges; in meeting such challenges, the tradition may expand or modify itself in previously unchallenged ways."[41]

It is my belief that the tradition embodied in the reflections of the church fathers on Scripture possesses the flexibility and responsiveness to meet the interpretive and ethical challenges the contemporary world poses. Of course, many will doubt the wisdom and viability of attempting to build a bridge between the world of the fathers and the contemporary world. Enlightenment modernists, still advocating the epistemological sufficiency of autonomous reason, will bristle at the need to look beyond their own rational capabilities. Postmodernists will chuckle at my naiveté, viewing my attempt to link with another's world as an exercise in futility and disguised exploitation. At best, they will argue, my interpretation of early Christian thought and culture will not harm others and may increase my own benefit and pleasure. The hermeneutical distance between our two worlds, though, will remain unbridgeable and I deceive myself to think otherwise.

Many conservative Protestant interpreters, though uncomfortable to find themselves slumbering with Enlightenment and postmodernist bedfellows, will fail to discern or acknowledge the necessity of studying the fathers. The deep-seated Protestant suspicion of tradition and its confidence in the ability of renewed reason alone to understand Scripture will lead many to shy away from investing time and energy in exploring patristic thought, believing it better to focus on the world of the Bible itself. The intervening centuries, some will assert, have largely been characterized by distortion and error, especially in the Roman Catholic and Orthodox worlds. To return to the fathers as a source of interpretation appears to necessitate a return to Rome or Constantinople. For some, radical reformers such as Menno Simons seem much closer to the truth in their call for a return to the pristine world of the early first-century Christian community.

Some early Christian writers struggled with similar issues. Tertullian, writing in the third century, strongly argued that the Christian faith would only develop safely within its own cultural, philosophical and biblical cocoon:

What has Jerusalem to do with Athens, the Church with the Academy, the Christian with the heretic? Our principles come from the Porch of Solomon, who had himself taught that the Lord is to be sought in simplicity of heart. I have no use for a Stoic or Platonic or dialectic Christianity.[42]

Bridges Under Construction

Is it genuinely possible for people living at the dawn of the second millenium to comprehend meaningfully the world of the church fathers? Many will have their doubts, but I believe the attempt should be made. Yet if we succeed in building a bridge to the fathers' world, what will we find when we arrive at their front steps? Will we discover and experience a hospitable environment? Will we be fed or choked by the food they offer us? Can a patristic writer's ideas be relevant and comprehensible to a contemporary person?

Conceptual and ethical bridgebuilding is never easy, whether we are attempting to understand the world of the church fathers or Scripture itself. How well, for example, can one expect a contemporary person raised in a sexually overheated society to understand the idea of chastity? As Tim Stafford observes, "Look at the magazine covers in the grocery-store check-out line, and you will be reminded of how crazy the biblical view sounds to modern people. The ordinary North American takes it as a given that people want things that are not theirs. . . . Of course a woman looks at Paul Newman and thinks how good he would be in bed. What is wrong with wanting it—so long as you don't commit a crime to get it?"[43]

Our modern myopia might convince us that the sexually repressed fathers surely could not understand or identify with twentieth-century sexual propensities, struggles and temptations. And yet once we enter their world we discover that the current inability to distinguish between lust and love was also part of their cultural and personal landscape. They also inhabited a sexually heated society. Augustine sounds terribly contemporary as he relates his infatuation with love itself and its accompanying pleasures:

I went to Carthage, where I found myself in the midst of a hissing cauldron of lust. I had not yet fallen in love, but I was in love with the idea of it, and this feeling that something was missing made me despise myself for not being more anxious to satisfy the need. I began looking around for some object for my love, since I badly wanted to love something.... To love and have my love returned was my heart's desire, and it would be all the sweeter if I could also enjoy the body of the one who loved me.[44]

Perhaps the Greek and Roman world provides more parallels and possibilities for mutual understanding than one would have thought at first glance. As we have seen, both the Roman and contemporary world are sexually fevered and confused. What of Western society's materialistic, self-centered and self-indulgent propensities? Was the world of the fathers any less so? Extravagance and self-indulgence mark both ages, both without the church and within. One thinks of the Roman emperor Vitellius, formerly the male prostitute of Tiberius, avid gambler, master of ceremonies for Nero's debut on the Roman stage and notorius glutton.[45] Suetonius describes a particularly costly night out:

The most notorious feast of the series was given him by his brother on his entry into Rome: 2,000 magnificent fish and 7,000 game birds are said to have been served. Yet even this hardly compares in luxuriousness with a single tremendously large dish which Vitellius dedicated to the goddess Minerva and named 'Shield of Minerva the Protectress.' The recipe called for pike-livers, pheasant-brains, peacock-brains, flamingo-tongues, and lamprey-milt; and the ingredients, collected in every corner of the empire from the Parthian frontier to the Spanish Strait (Straits of Gibraltar) were brought to Rome by warships.[46]

Vitellius survived his binges through the use of emetics, but one feels for his friends. We sympathize with Quintus Vibius Crispus, a frequent host for Vitellius's prolonged suppers, who "was once compelled by illness to absent himself for some days from the convivial board. But this, he commented privately to an associate, had saved his life. 'If I had not fallen ill,' he declared, 'I should have died.' "[47]

Sadly enough, we find church fathers such as Clement of Alexandria encountering this same propensity toward extravagance and self-indulgence in their own congregations:

Those who take delight in what they have hoarded up in their storehouses are foolish in their greed. . . . It is farcical and downright ridiculous for men to bring out urinals of silver and chamber-pots of transparent alabaster as if they were introducing their advisors, and for rich women in their silliness to have gold receptacles for excrements made, as though being wealthy they were unable to relieve themselves except in a grandiose style.[48]

The temptation to live in two worlds—the kingdom of this world and the kingdom of God—tugged as consistently on the fathers and their congregations as it does on the contemporary Western Christian. Therefore, perhaps we can use the image of two worlds to our advantage as we prepare to investigate the world of early Christian writers.

Through Other Lenses

Allow me to speak for a moment of my own culture, that of the United States of America. Most Americans have grown up speaking and reading only one language. Enlightenment ideals have deeply shaped American culture—philosophically, politically, socially and religiously. Most Americans have been raised in nuclear families. Some have had significant relationships with grandparents and aunts and uncles. Others have not. Too many Americans have suffered the pain of growing up with only one parent as a result of divorce. Economic opportunities abound for many Americans. Many Americans are accustomed to a high standard of living. We tend to view our money and possessions as our own private sphere. Prying eyes are not welcome here. Sexual issues occupy much of our thinking, perhaps exaggeratedly so. Increasingly, we have more and more leisure time. We are entertainment oriented and media driven. Violence both repels and attracts us. We know what we want and we want it now. Immediate self-gratification appears to be a top priority. We have a hard time waiting, whether it be at the grocery store check-out counter, the bus stop, the airline terminal or in church. While other characteristics of American culture might occur to other Americans, I have chosen to present a sampler of how Americans tend to view and live in the world around them.

How might growing up in the modern global village both facilitate and cripple my understanding of the gospel? What aspects of my family background, language, political philosophy, media exposure, gender, ecclesiastical heritage, national history, psychological make-up and other cultural and personal characteristics aid and obstruct my understanding of Scripture and its central message? What are the personal and cultural lenses through which I read the Bible? What aspects of Scripture do they bring into clear focus? What aspects do they blur or skew?

Learning to read the Bible through the eyes of Christians from a different time and place will readily reveal the distorting effect of our own cultural, historical, linguistic, philosophical and, yes, even theological lenses. This is not to assert that the fathers did not have their own warped perspectives and blind spots. It is to argue, however, that we will not arrive at perspective and clarity regarding our own strengths and weaknesses if we refuse to look beyond our own theological and hermeneutical noses. God has been active throughout the church's history and we rob ourselves of the Holy Spirit's gifts if we refuse to budge beyond the comfort zone of our own ideas.

Michael Casey offers wise advice at this juncture. He reminds us that "the Holy Spirit did not cease being active in the Church with the last page of the New Testament." Rather, throughout the centuries Scripture and God's Spirit "have so infused the lives of countless men and women that they themselves became living gospels." As these Christians—in this case the church fathers—lived and thought out the implications of the Bible, the latent wisdom of Scripture bubbled to the surface in their sermons, commentaries, treatises and prayers. This did not happen infallibly or inerrantly but in such a manner that Christians living in later ages can still drink profitably from the well of patristic exegesis.

> Such insights were not automatically guaranteed. It was only when generations of believers found in them accurate reflections of their own spiritual experience that these secondary texts began to have some measure of *auctoritas*. . . . Just as a good preacher can make the inspired word come alive for those who hear, so reading these classical Christian treatises can help translate the Bible from the past of history to the present of our own lives.[49]

As we have seen, many postmodern interpreters doubt the possibility of genuinely entering another's world. I disagree, but realize the task is a formidable one, requiring certain dispositions on the part of the voyager. Foremost among these is humility—a willingness to admit that our own self-estimation is often inflated and exaggerated. We must be convinced that the church fathers, people who often spoke differently and lived strangely—at least at first glance—actually have something they can teach us. Our ability to learn from them will largely be determined by our willingness to remain quiet and simply listen, perhaps listen more fervently than we have for a long time. In turn, our willingness to listen will be influenced by our expectations, hopes, prejudices and presuppositions. Some of us, especially those unfamiliar with the world of patristic thought, will have to trust the testimony of many who have come before us or have recently discovered the riches of patristic exegesis. The advice of Ambrose comes to mind:

> For there is but one true teacher, the only one who never learned what he taught everyone. But men have first to learn what they are to teach, and receive from him what they are to give to others. Now what ought we to learn before everything else, but to be silent that we may be able to speak? . . . It is seldom that anyone is silent, even when speaking does him no good.[50]

Listening will not come easily. We will struggle to overcome deep-set suspicions. Past prejudices will need silencing. Some of us will be tempted to react too quickly to perceived error. We will need to familiarize ourselves with new words, themes and concepts. And yet the effort will prove rewarding if we persevere. One of my goals in this book is to provide as broad an informational and conceptual grid as possible for understanding the thought of the fathers as they read the Bible.

My counsel is to surround your entrance into the world of the fathers with humility, self-awareness, a listening ear, prayer and a sense of humor. It is better to chuckle at the periodic patristic quirk than to allow our self-righteous anger to wall off their insights. We are all prone to error. We are all quick to spot the exegetical log in our brother or sister's eye. We are all apt to be blind to our own weaknesses in reading Scripture. We are all hermeneutically disabled in one area or another. How can we hope to understand the Bible if we needlessly cut ourselves off from our own community's reflection and history? We need one another and each other's insights, past and present, if we are to understand the Bible. The desert fathers were especially sensitive to the necessity of humility and community if one was to comprehend Scripture:

> They tell the story of another old man who persevered in fasting for seventy weeks, eating only once a week. He asked of God about [the meaning of] a certain passage in holy Scripture and God did not reveal it to him. He said to himself, "See how much labor I have undertaken and it has been of no profit to me. I will go, therefore, to my brother and ask him about it." He went outside and closed the door to go out and an angel of the Lord was sent to him, saying, "The seventy weeks

you fasted did not make you any closer to God. Now, because you have been humbled and are going off to your brother, I have been sent to explain the passage to you." He opened to him what he sought and then went away.[51]

We will occasionally find the fathers infuriating, dense and perplexing. At other times we will wonder, Why have I never seen this in the Bible before? Why was I never taught this? How could I have been so blind? In their best moments the fathers will lead us into a renewed sense of wonder, awe and reverence for God and the gospel. Through the fathers' influence, prayer and worship may well become more frequent companions to our exegetical study. And though greater familiarity with the fathers will periodically magnify their own weaknesses, our own blind spots will be much more clear to us because of the time we have spent with figures such as Augustine, Chrysostom, Athanasius, Jerome, Gregory of Nazianzus, Basil, Ambrose or Gregory the Great.

What are the blind spots in our culture or our own lives that need to be exposed to the light of ancient wisdom? Francis Young believes that the church fathers belonged to an important intellectual tradition and wrestled with many of the same issues theologians, philosophers, pastors, and laypeople face today. "To see these questions debated in a quite different intellectual [and historical setting]" is edifying, says Young, "for it enables us to step outside our own culturally-conditioned presuppositions and see the issues" in a clearer light.[52] The distance between the contemporary reader and the fathers, then, can genuinely become an advantage to be appreciated. Michael Casey describes the liberation made possible by this distance:

> One of the factors that I appreciate in reading ancient authors is that they come from a distant culture. This means they build on a distinctive infrastructure of beliefs and values. When they comment on a text or discourse on a value, they approach things from a different angle and so often have something original to say. This is not to assert that their cultural values were necessarily better than ours. It simply means that they were more aware of some aspects of truth than we are—just as we know more than them in some matters. When we have recourse to writers of antiquity, we have the opportunity to compensate for the blind spots inherent in our particular culture. They help us move toward a more integral wisdom by challenging many of our presuppo-

sitions. Because they are unaffected by our particular cultural bias, they can help liberate us from the invisible ideology inherent in our uncritical assumptions about the nature of reality.[53]

Simply put, reading the fathers can be surprisingly relevant for the contemporary Christian because the fathers tend to grasp facets of the gospel that modern sensibilities too often overlook. They hear music in Scripture to which we remain tone-deaf. They frequently emphasize truths that contemporary Christians dearly need to remember. As this chapter draws to a close, I first want to share a story from a modern exegete illustrating this principle, and second, to relate a specific instance of a patristic insight widely overlooked today.

Hermeneutical Proximity

New Testament scholar Dale C. Allison Jr., a leading authority on the Gospel of Matthew, comments that Matthew "did not trumpet all his intentions."[54] Although Matthew's agenda is clear in many instances, Allison observes that "he also left much, even of importance, unsaid." For example, Matthew includes the names of four women in his opening genealogy of Jesus' heritage, but never tells us why. What is he up to? Allison speculates that "Perhaps our evangelist expected too much of his readers. Or—and this is my own supposition—his first readers were better equipped than us." That is, Matthew's initial readers "had a knowledge we lack, a knowledge . . . of the tradition behind the Gospel, which tradition has ceased to be."

Not only does Matthew not inform the reader as to all his intentions, but he also fails "to instruct us about his literary methods." Matthew is writing within the context of common cultural and literary conventions that he takes for granted, as do his first readers. There is no need to explain something everyone understands. Hence the problem for contemporary readers. They will have to hunt for conventional information earlier folk already understood.

Allison sees Matthew's Gospel as "a chapter in a book." By this he means that "the ubiquitous scriptural citations and allusions—which are anything but detachable ornamentation—direct the reader to other books and so teach that Matthew is not a self-contained entity: much is missing." Matthew's Gospel, Allison understands, "stipulates that it be interpreted in the context of other texts. . . . [I]t is, in a fundamental sense, an incomplete utterance, a book full of holes." It is the reader who must supply what is missing, a reader possessing the knowledge Matthew presupposes, which comes from "a pre-existing collection of interacting texts, the Jewish Bible." Matthew's text, then, is a "mnemonic device, designed . . . to trigger intertextual exchanges which depend upon informed and imaginative reading."

The central problem facing contemporary readers is their lack of this intertextual background. Without it, how are they to know when a biblical writer is alluding to another text? Allison believes that biblical scholars fail to provide the scholia readers need to spot readily the texts' literary artistry and interconnections. "Time removes us from all texts and subtexts and so cripples our ability to detect tacit references—which is why, as history marches on, annotated editions of the classics, including the Bible, become longer and longer."

The central difficulty is the contemporary reader's "historically conditioned deafness to oblique allusions in the Bible." In fact, because of our deafness we can begin to doubt whether allusions are present at all. Are the musical notes genuinely present in the text or not? Before we conclude that we are simply imagining false melodies, however, Allison provides a helpful contemporary analogy.

Those who habitually listen to music over the radio can often identify a popular song after hearing just the smallest portion of it. There are in fact contests—I have heard them—which require people to name a musical piece after hearing only a slight excerpt from it, one lasting no more than a second or two, and consisting of no more than two or three notes or chords. The uninitiated will discern only noise. But to those with the requisite musical knowledge (gained, be it noted, not through arduous study but through effortless listening), the briefest extract can conjure up a world: a song, an album, a musical group. Was it maybe not similar with those Jews who first heard the Gospel of Matthew? Are we not sometimes forced to pick up a concordance in order to perceive connections which were once immediately grasped by trained ears with unconscious sureness?

At this juncture the *hermeneutical proximity* of the fathers to the biblical text is especially helpful. "For they were, in so many ways, closer to the first century Christians than we are—for they, unlike most of us, lived and moved and had their being in the Scriptures." In many ways, the

Scriptures—listened to for many years by patristic writers—were their popular music.

They still read aloud. They still had a small literary canon. They still had, because of their educational methods, magnificent memorization skills. And they still heard Scripture chanted. They were accordingly attuned to *hear* things we no longer *hear*, things which we can only *see* after picking up concordances or doing word searches on our computers. I have come to believe that if we find in Matthew or another NT book an allusion to the OT that the Fathers did not find, the burden of proof is on us; and if they detected an allusion which we—here I am thinking of modern commentaries—have not detected, investigation is in order.

How might Allison's viewpoint on the fathers encourage biblical scholars and readers to understand and interact with the Bible more effectively? Referring to Jesus' statement in the Beatitudes, "Blessed are the meek, for they shall inherit the earth," Allison admits, "No commentary known to me—this includes my own—refers to Moses in connection with Matt. 5:5." And yet, Allison observes, Chrysostom, Theodoret of Cyrrhus and Eusebius link Moses to Jesus' teaching. Theodoret cites Numbers 12:3, a text referring to Moses as "very meek, more than all men that were on the face of the earth." Eusebius comments that "whereas Jesus promised the meek inheritance of the earth, Moses promised Israel inheritance of the land." Allison suggests:

> Perhaps we should follow the interpretive lead of Theodoret and Eusebius and set Matt. 5:5 against the Moses traditions. Moses was, in meekness, the exemplar. He promised the Israelites inheritance of the land. And he himself did not enter the land. From this last fact, sufficiently unexpected to have engendered much rabbinic reflection, one might extract that the third beatitude pledges something Moses never gained. On such an interpretation, the members of the new covenant would be more blessed than the chief figure of the old: if, in the past, the meek one did not enter the land, now, that the kingdom of God has come, "the meek shall inherit the earth." One thinks of Matt. 11:11: the least in the kingdom of heaven is greater than all of those who came before.

Allison remains undecided about the Moses allusion in Matthew 5:5. He does believe, though, that such an allusion should be seriously considered, that it has fruitful homiletical possibilities, and that it clearly tells us what the fathers themselves heard when they listened to the passage. Again, the hermeneutical proximity of the fathers to Scripture has picked up tonal qualities of the text that would remain mute for modern readers if the scholar, pastor or layperson relied solely on recent exegesis. The fathers hear and see where we tend to be deaf and blind.

Exegesis and Spiritual Formation

The fathers affirmed a deep connection between the spiritual health of biblical interpreters and their ability to read the Bible well. For the fathers, the Scripture was to be studied, pondered and exegeted within the context of worship, reverence and holiness. The fathers considered the Bible a holy book that opened itself to those who themselves were progressing in holiness through the grace and power of the Spirit. The character of the exegete would determine in many ways what was seen or heard in the text itself. Character and exegesis were intimately related.

For example, in his well-known work, *On the Incarnation*, Athanasius adamantly insists that

the searching and right understanding of the Scriptures [demands] a good life and a pure soul. . . . One cannot possibly understand the teaching of the saints unless one has a pure mind and is trying to imitate their life. . . . Anyone who wants to look at sunlight naturally wipes his eye clear first, in order to make, at any rate, some approximation to the purity of that on which he looks; and a person wishing to see a city or country goes to the place in order to do so. Similarly, anyone who wishes to understand the mind of the sacred writers must first cleanse his own life, and approach the saints by copying their deeds. Thus united to them in the fellowship of life, he will both understand the things revealed to them by God and, thenceforth escaping the peril that threatens sinners in the judgment, will receive that which is laid up for the saints in the kingdom of heaven.[55]

Gregory of Nazianzus offers much the same advice in his theological orations. Studying and speaking well about God does not belong to everyone, not "before every audience, nor at all times, nor on all points; but on certain occasions, and before certain persons, and within certain limits." Gregory insists that theological study "is permitted only to those who have been examined, and are past masters in meditation, and who have been previously purified in soul and body, or at the very least are being purified."[56]

Neither Athanasius nor Gregory envisioned exegesis or theology as the academic activity of biblical scholars or theologians divorced from the life of the church or personal spiritual formation. Rather, the fathers believed, the best exegesis occurs within the community of the church. The Scriptures have been given to the church, are read, preached, heard and comprehended within the community of the church, and are safely interpreted only by those whose character is continually being formed by prayer, worship, meditation, self-examination, confession and other means by which Christ's grace is communicated to his body. That is to say, the fathers argue that any divorce between personal character, Christian community and the study of Scripture will be fatal for any attempt to understand the Bible. This holistic, communal approach is surely a methodology that warrants a close investigation in our highly individualistic, specialized, segmented world.

The fathers' insistence on spiritual health and integrity as we approach the Bible is advice we must heed. Sadly, our words and lives too often do not fit together. We are not one piece. The fathers' call to wholeness and integrity, to allow our lives to be shaped by the narrative of Scripture within the community of the church—so that we can understand and communicate that narrative in an ever more faithful manner—is a sine qua non for understanding how and why the fathers go about the business of exegesis. The dialectic between spiritual growth, character formation and understanding Scripture is a crucial patristic insight. We will examine this relationship in more detail in future chapters.

THREE

WHO ARE
THE FATHERS?

THE APPELLATION "CHURCH FATHER" RAISES A NUMBER OF
questions for modern persons: What is a church father? Who qualifies as
a father? How did these men receive this designation? What qualifications
had to be met to receive the title? Are certain fathers particularly important, in some ways in a class by themselves?

What of the "Mothers" of the Church?

And what of "church mothers"? Were there not significant women con-
tributing to the life and thought of the early church? Does not the title
"church father" discriminate against them, leaving modern readers with
the impression that the only significant figures in early Christianity were
male? Would not a title such as "early Christian writer" be more appropriate and overcome the danger of misunderstanding, prejudice and dis-
crimination? Is it fair or wise to retain such a loaded and potentially
harmful title as "church father" in a modern context?

Without doubt there were many significant women in the life of the early church, some of whom served as models and mentors for key church fathers.[1] We have the example of the Roman widow Marcella, one of the first female ascetics in Rome. Jerome praises both her devotion to Christ and her active, inquiring mind.

> And because my name was then especially esteemed in the study of the Scriptures, she never came without asking something about Scripture, nor did she immediately accept my explanation as satisfactory, but she proposed questions from the opposite viewpoint, not for the sake of being contentious, but so that by asking, she might learn solutions for points she perceived could be raised in objection. What virtue I found in her, what cleverness, what holiness, what purity.... I will say only this, that whatever in us was gathered by long study and by lengthy meditation was almost changed into nature; this she tasted, this she learned, this she possessed. Thus after my departure, if an argument arose about some evidence from Scripture, the question was pursued with her as the judge.[2]

Jerome's closest personal female friend was Paula, whose wealth made possible the construction of a number of monasteries in Bethlehem.[3] Paula died in A.D. 404. Jerome penned the following lines in his memorial letter to Paula's daughter Eustochium. He was especially touched by Paula's willingness to endure separation from her children for the sake of the gospel.

> Among the harsh fates of captivity, of being in the hands of enemies, none is more cruel than parents being separated from their children. She endured this with full confidence, though it is against the law of nature; yes, she sought it with a rejoicing spirit, and making little of the love of her children by her greater love for God.... I confess that no woman loved her children like this; before she departed, she disinherited herself of earthly things and bestowed all on them, so that she might find an inheritance in Heaven.[4]

Not only Paula's devotion catches Jerome's eye. In a letter written shortly after Paula's death, Jerome comments on Paula's sharp intellect.

> She had memorized the Scripture.... [S]he urged me that she, along with her daughter, might read through the Old and New Testaments. ... If at any passage I was at a loss and frankly confessed that I was ignorant, she by no means wanted to rest content with my reply, but by fresh questions would force me to say which of the many possible meanings seemed to me the most likely. And I will say something else

here that perhaps will seem unbelievable to malicious people: from the time of my youth, I have learned the Hebrew language to some extent, through much effort and sweat, and I study it indefatigably so that if I do not forsake it, it will not forsake me. When Paula wanted to learn it, she pursued the project to the point that she chanted the Psalms in Hebrew and her diction echoed no trace of the distinctive character of the Latin language.[5]

Melania the Elder was also renowned for her learning and intellect. Palladius comments that she "was very learned and a lover of literature. She turned night into day by going through every writing of the ancient commentators, three million lines of Origen, and two hundred fifty thousand lines of Gregory, Stephen, Pierius, Basil, and other excellent men." In fact, Palladius observes, Melania read each work "seven or eight times."[6]

Olympias, a deaconess in the church at Constantinople, was inspired by the example of Melania the Elder. She, like Melania, possessed a sizeable personal fortune that she readily dispersed on behalf of the Christian community. Palladius writes that Olympias willingly distributed her possessions "to the poor. She contended eagerly in no minor contests for the sake of the truth, taught many women, held solemn conversations with priests, honored the bishops, and was deemed worthy to be a confessor on behalf of truth."[7]

The relationship between Olympias and John Chrysostom, bishop at Constantinople, demonstrates the love and support not infrequently expressed between leading male and female leaders in the church. On June 20, A.D. 404, Bishop John left Constantinople under military escort, never to return. He was exiled to the backwater town of Cucusus, in the mountains of Armenia. From there he carried on an active correspondence with Olympias. She had also been exiled because of her support of John.

The intimacy and care Chrysostom and Olympia demonstrated in their relationship is often expressed in the letters they exchanged while in exile. Chrysostom shares openly with Olympias his recent health problems and encourages her to investigate a medicine he has lately found helpful for his own nausea. "Pay great attention to the restoration of your bodily health," Chrysostom counsels Olympias. "For a few days ago when I suffered from a tendency to vomiting, owing to the state of the atmosphere, I had recourse to the drug which was sent me . . . and I found that no more than three days' application of it cured my infirmity." Chrysostom gently scolds his "most reverend and divinely favored deaconess Olympias. . . . If you would take the requisite care of yourself, you would be in a more satisfactory condition."[8]

For her part, Olympias continued her material and spiritual support of John. It had been her practice to care for John's material needs in Constantinople and she continued to do so during the last years of his life in exile. The *Life of Olympias, Deaconess* describes Olympias as possessing "an appearance without pretense, character without affectation . . . a mind without vainglory, intelligence without conceit . . . character without limits, immeasurable self-control . . . the ornament of all the humble."[9]

Despite the frequent and often lavish praises women receive from the fathers, marked ambiguity flavors the patristic response to their female counterparts. Elizabeth Clark argues that the "most fitting word with which to describe the church fathers' attitude toward women is ambivalence." Women are portrayed by the fathers as both a

> good gift to men—and the curse of the world. . . . They were weak in both mind and character—and displayed dauntless courage, undertook prodigious feats of scholarship. Vain, deceitful, brimming with lust— they led men to Christ, fled sexual encounter, wavered not at the executioner's threats, adorned themselves with sackcloth and ashes.[10]

The fathers' own interpretive lenses, colored by the strongly patriarchal culture in which they lived, led them to read the Bible's statements about women selectively. In their exegesis they leaned toward passages that appeared to indicate a subordinate position for women, and largely overlooked the implications of texts such as Galatians 5:1 and 3:28 for relationships between the sexes.

The fathers' patriarchal culture was not the only factor coloring their perspective on women and the relationship between women and men in the church. Women occupied positions of leadership within "sects on the fringes of mainstream Christianity" such as heterodox gnostic groups.

> Various Gnostic sects probably let women baptize. Charismatic movements that appealed to the Holy Spirit's inspiration were also natural ones to allow women a larger role, for it could be argued that God did not discriminate sexually in distributing the *charismata*, the spiritual gifts. It is likely that the Catholic Church reacted to such sects, that were indeed a genuine danger to orthodox Christianity's survival and

power, by drawing firm lines of differentiation between the types of church office permitted to women in the sects and the types of church office permitted to women in the Catholic Church.[11]

Hence, the role of women in the early church was circumscribed within specific boundaries. Yet, as we have already seen, women could expand those boundaries significantly through renouncing traditional sexual and domestic roles for a life of Christian asceticism—behavior that fathers such as Jerome encouraged.[12] Indeed, close to one third of the letters we possess from Jerome are addressed to women and largely focus upon theological considerations and biblical exegesis.[13]

Jerome applauds Paula's decision to modify drastically her behavior as a Roman matron, though her surrounding society—including many Christians—responded to her lifestyle changes with great suspicion, slander and gossip. In *Epistle 45* Jerome complains sarcastically and angrily:

O craftiness of Satan that forever hunts down holy things! No other women in the city of Rome afforded gossip except Paula and Melania who, despising their wealth and deserting their love-pledges [i.e., their children], raised the Lord's cross, one might say, as a standard of the faith. Had they . . . selected perfumes, had they used their riches and widowhood as incitements to luxurious living and freedom, they would have been called proper ladies, holy women. Now they are willing to appear beautiful in sackcloth and ashes, and with fasting and lice to sink to the fires of Hell![14]

The pathway to freedom for women willing to pay the price, then, was to leave the normal routines of domestic life in a patriarchal culture for the rigors of an ascetic lifestyle marked by devotion to spiritual disciplines such as prayer, fasting and alms-giving. Within this context, however, having shed the more threatening and debilitating aspects of their sexuality, opportunities for learning and teaching did exist—though teaching men in an official ecclesiastical role remained off limits, as did the priesthood.

The *Apostolic Constitutions*, a late fourth-century document on church order reflecting church practice in the East, allows women to function officially within the church as widows and deaconesses, but not as priests or public teachers. Clark finds it significant that according to the Eastern tradition represented in the *Apostolic Constitutions*, deaconesses were ordained. This was not the practice of the Western church. The order of deaconesses, Clark observes, was short-lived in the West. From the early Middle Ages, "their role seems to have been subsumed under that of the nun."[15]

The life of Macrina, sister of Gregory of Nyssa and Basil the Great, is a remarkable example of theological acumen and practical spirituality. In fact, Macrina is often known as the "Fourth Cappadocian," in addition to Gregory of Nazianzus and her brothers Basil and Gregory of Nyssa.[16] Jaroslav Pelikan provides this description:

> Not only was she, according to Gregory's accounts, a Christian role model for both of them by her profound and ascetic spirituality, but at the death of their parents she became the educator of the entire family, and that in both Christianity and Classical culture. Through her philosophy and theology, Macrina was even the teacher of both of her brothers, who were bishops and theologians, "sister and teacher at the same time . . ." as Gregory called her in the opening sentence of the dialogue *On the Soul and the Resurrection*.[17]

Even as a young girl, Gregory tells us, Macrina studied the Scriptures, particularly the Song of Solomon and the Psalms.

> She went through each part of the Psalm at its special time, when getting up, when engaging in work, when resting, when she took her meals, when she arose from the table, when she went to bed or arose for prayers; always she had the Psalms with her like a good travelling companion, not forsaking them for a moment.[18]

Both the quality of Macrina's life and the brilliance of her intellect deeply impressed her two brothers. Indeed, it was the influence of Macrina that convinced Basil to repent of his intellectual pride over his rhetorical abilities. As Gregory puts it, Basil "despised all the worthy people and exalted himself in self-importance above the illustrious men of the province." It is Macrina who "drew him with such speed to the goal of philosophy that he renounced worldly renown."[19]

Even on her deathbed Macrina performed the role of the teacher for her brother Gregory.

> When she saw me come near the door, she raised herself on an elbow, not able to come towards me, for already the fever had consumed her strength. . . . She introduced topics on her mind and by asking questions, gave me a chance to talk. . . . She went through such arguments in detailed manner, speaking about natural phenomena, recounting the divine plan hidden in sad events, revealing things about the future life, as if she were possessed by the Holy Spirit. As a result my soul seemed to

lack little from being lifted outside human nature by her words, and with the guidance of her speech, to stand inside the heavenly sanctuaries.[20]

Basil, too, was later to recall the lasting effect of the teaching of both his mother Emmelia and his grandmother Macrina (the elder).

The teaching about God that I had received as a boy from my blessed mother and my grandmother Macrina, I have ever held with increasing conviction. On my coming to the mature years of reason, I did not shift my opinions from one to another, but carried out the principles handed on to me by my parents. Just as the seed when it grows is tiny at first and then grows bigger but always preserves its identity, not changed in kind though gradually perfected in growth, so I consider that the same doctrine has in my case grown through a development. What I hold now has not replaced what I held at the beginning.[21]

It is unfortunate that because of cultural, historical and misconstrued theological considerations and developments we do not have a significant body of writing from the gifted women who inhabited the early church.[22] Comments from Ammas (Mothers) such as Syncletice and Sarah do appear in the sayings of the desert fathers,[23] and poems from Christian Roman matrons such as Proba have been translated into English.[24] Jaroslav Pelikan incorporated many of the theological and exegetical insights of Macrina the Younger into his Gifford lectures on Christianity and classical culture.

For the most part, though, we lack a significant body of exegetical work from early Christian women. Thus, though I am tempted to title this book *Reading the Scripture with the Fathers and Mothers*, I fear such a title, while honoring early Christian women and soothing modern sensibilities, would not reflect past realities faithfully. We simply do not have a broad enough exegetical base to draw upon from early Christian female theologians and commentators. As we have noted, however, the lack of such literature is more a regretful commentary on the church's ambiguous response to the women in its midst than a lack of ability, intelligence, desire, gifting or insight in its female constituents.

What Is a Church Father?

We move now to the title "church father" itself. The idea of a father in the faith has a long history in biblical and ecclesiological usage. The apostle Paul speaks of himself as a father to the Corinthian church. "Even though you have ten thousand guardians in Christ, you do not have many fathers, for in Christ Jesus I became your father through the gospel" (1 Cor 4:15 NIV). At times the rabbis were called father, and the term also occurs in Pythagorean and Cynic circles. It generally designates a teacher who is instructing and guiding disciples to religious and philosophical truth.[25] Clement of Rome calls the apostles fathers as he exhorts the Corinthians to live "in harmony without bearing malice, in love and peace with constant gentleness, just as our fathers, of whom we spoke earlier, pleased him."[26] In the late second century Irenaeus stated simply, "He who has received the teaching from another's mouth is called the son of his instructor, and he is called his father."[27] Clement of Alexandria elaborated thus: "Words are the progeny of the soul. Hence we call those that instructed us fathers . . . and every one who is instructed is in respect of subjection the son of his instructor."[28]

The term took on a more technical meaning from the fourth century on, especially in the context of the theological controversies that filled the fourth and fifth centuries. While bishops—the teachers of the church—had been called fathers from the second century forward, bishops who faithfully preserved and protected the decisions of the Council of Nicaea (A.D. 325), Constantinople (381) and Chalcedon (451) received this designation as persons worthy of special regard for having preserved orthodox teaching during a time of great testing.

This more comprehensive meaning of "father" was "extended to ecclesiastical writers in so far as they were accepted as representatives of the tradition of the Church."[29] Augustine, for example, calls Jerome a father even though Jerome was not a bishop because Jerome had faithfully protected the traditional doctrine of original sin.[30] Interestingly, Vincent of Lerins critiqued Augustine's writings against the Pelagians because they were not sufficiently supported by the "fathers."[31] Vincent clearly believed the opinions of the fathers merit special consideration.

> If some new question should arise on which no such decision has been given, they should then have recourse to the opinions of the holy Fathers, of those, at least, who, each in his own time and place, remaining in the unity of communion and the faith, were accepted as approved masters; and whatsoever these may be found to have held, with one mind and one consent, this ought to be accounted the true and catholic doctrine of the Church, without any doubt or scruple.[32]

Key Characteristics

Boniface Ramsey has identified the four central criteria used for determining whether a given church figure merits the title "father."

1. *Antiquity.* "Father" and related terms such as "patristic," "patrology" and "patrologist" suggest, Ramsey believes, "a certain venerable quality associated with age."[33] Ramsey lists the period of the fathers as beginning around the year 96 with the writing of *First Clement* and concluding in the East with the death of John of Damascus in 750. The Western tradition sometimes lists alternate dates for the end of the patristic era, such as the deaths of Gregory the Great in 604, Isidore of Seville in 636 or the Venerable Bede in 735.[34] Other scholars terminate the age of the fathers with the "ecumenical councils of Ephesus (431) and Chalcedon (451)."[35]

2. *Holiness of life.* Both Ramsey and Johannes Quasten list holiness of life as the second characteristic of a father. At first glance, as Ramsey admits, one wonders how some of the fathers could qualify. "Tertullian displays a very unpleasant fanatical and even cruel streak, Jerome had a notoriously nasty and unforgiving temperament, Theophilus of Alexandria was an opportunist of the worst sort, and Cyril of Alexandria persecuted his enemies relentlessly."[36] Perhaps a different understanding of holiness, Ramsey argues, more in line with Psalm 149:6, would capture the spirit of the fathers: "May the praise of God be in their mouths and a double-edged sword in their hands" (NIV).

The fathers exhibited a tremendous zeal for God and the Scriptures. And, often like us, their zeal manifested itself in both their strengths and weaknesses. They have much to teach us about reverence, awe, self-sacrifice, self-awareness and self-deception, worship, respect, prayer, study and meditation. Their theological contributions remain foundational for Christians in the Roman Catholic, Orthodox, Anglican and many Protestant communions. Occasionally, though, their zeal in these areas spilled into the cracks in their own personalities. As Ramsey comments, "[S]uch a zeal is very frequently combined with less laudable aspects—unwillingness to compromise, self-righteousness, rigidity, manipulativeness, irascibility and the like."[37]

We would be wise to realize from the start that the fathers were intensely human. Most often they wore their hearts and thoughts on their sleeves. At times they were impatient, short-tempered and narrow. Some had a very hard time listening to perspectives other than those they endorsed. Yet their hearts were set on fire by the gospel. They lived and breathed the Scriptures. And many willingly laid down their lives for the sake of Christ. They are well worth studying. We would err if we allowed their weaknesses to blur or block the significant contributions their thoughts and lives can give to the church today.

3. *Orthodox doctrine.* Ramsey focuses on two aspects of this characteristic. To qualify as a father one must have left behind a teaching of some kind, however small, or at least a reputation. Second, and most importantly, the church must have recognized a father's teaching as resting within the bounds of Scripture and tradition.

Ramsey admits that this can be a fairly arbitrary standard. Some fathers fell into opinions that the church would later identify as heterodox. Subordinationism, the idea that the Son and Spirit are in some way inferior to the Father, creeps into some patristic teaching. Origen, one of the great biblical scholars in the church's history, is generally not recognized as a father because of his idea of *apokatastasis*—the teaching that God will ultimately reconcile all creation and created beings to himself, including Satan. How and why did Origen drift away from orthodox doctrine in his understanding of the extent and nature of reconciliation?

Origen firmly believed his ideas about *apokatastasis* were the natural implication of biblical texts such as Psalm 110:1 (Ps. 109:1 LXX): "The LORD says to my lord, 'Sit at my right hand until I make your enemies your footstool.'" "We think, indeed," Origen comments, "that the goodness of God, through His Christ, may recall all His creatures to one end, even His enemies being conquered and subdued."[38] Origen argued that God's Word was "stronger than all evils in the soul," and that the healing, reconciliation and renewal brought by the Word applied "to every man." The goodness of God and the power of the Word demanded "the destruction of all evil" in the final consummation with the ultimate reconciliation of all members of God's creation, whether in heaven or on earth.

Origen appears to err by allowing his rational inferences from certain aspects of the biblical revelation to blind him to other equally important facets of the scriptural narrative. If sin, evil and death are to be finally and completely destroyed, Origen asks, how can they remain in existence as God's enemies in the age to come when all creation is reconciled to God? Through a slow and imperceptible process, one lasting "countless and unmeasured ages," even the last enemy—death—will be reconciled to God.

[A]nd thus God will be 'all,' for there will no longer be any distinction of good and evil, seeing evil nowhere exists. . . . [T]hat condition of things will be re-established in which rational nature was placed, when it had no need to eat of the tree of the knowledge of good and evil. . . . [W]hen all feeling of wickedness has been removed, and the individual has been purified and cleansed, he who alone is the one good God becomes to him 'all,' and that *not in the case of a few individuals, or of a considerable number, but He Himself is 'all in all.'* [emphasis added] And when death shall no longer anywhere exist, nor the sting of death, nor any evil at all, then verily God will be 'all in all.'[39]

For evil, the demonic, Satan or hell to remain in existence, at least as Origen viewed matters, would prevent God from being "all in all." At this juncture, the church said "No." It judged Origen's deduction to be outside the bounds of orthodox thought and Origen lost the possibility of being considered a father in the strict sense of the term, though his thought continues to be studied and appreciated by many and will be a topic considered in some detail in this book.

Ramsey notes that many developments in church doctrine, especially in Roman Catholicism, are not found in the fathers, making the criterion of orthodox teaching difficult to apply fairly or ecumenically. For example, Roman Catholic emphases on Mary and the papacy developed more fully in medieval and modern times and have not been recognized by all Christian communions. "Roman Catholics would say that such teachings represent a natural development and are at least not contrary to the mind of the fathers, but most people in the Reformation tradition would say that they are rather a kind of deviation."[40] I would agree. Hence, the necessity of applying somewhat broader and more flexible theological boundaries in determining the theological orthodoxy of a father. We must surely include the insights of the Roman tradition, but in relationship with those of the Orthodox, Anglican and Protestant perspectives on patristic exegesis.

The fathers do affirm a broad set of theological propositions that have remained central to Christian orthodoxy across almost all denominational lines. Ramsey specifically lists belief in a triune God, the fully divine and fully human natures of Christ, the redemptive efficacy of Christ's death on the cross, the absolute authority and infallibility of Scripture, the fallen condition of humanity, the significance of baptism and Holy Communion, and the vital importance of prayer and a disciplined spiritual life. "Belief in these things, which the fathers unanimously proclaimed, even if they proclaimed them in different ways, continues to be the distinguishing mark of Christianity to this day."[41]

The fathers were serious theologians, but their primary vocation was as pastors within the church. Many were leading bishops. Their theology and exegesis possesses a marked pastoral emphasis and concern and is immensely practical. Reflections on the Trinity and Incarnation are interwoven with profound thoughts on prayer and worship. The fathers blend profundity and practicality in an inextricable fashion. As shepherds of the church they theologized, prayed and preached with the needs and concerns of the church at heart. Their identity and task as fathers was inseparable from the church itself. Pier Franco Beatrice describes their role:

> It was above all the task of the Fathers of the Church to elaborate those responses that, because of their authority, still remain binding points of reference for the ecclesiastical consciousness today. The Fathers of the Church are those personages, almost always bishops and thus endowed with particular pastoral responsibilities, who decisively influenced by their preaching and writings both the development of Christian doctrine and the formation of Christian custom.[42]

Because of the key role the fathers played in the formation of both doctrine and practice, their writings and lives can help us to understand who we ourselves are as Christians and why we believe and behave as we do in Christ's body. Some readers will readily resonate with the fathers' theology and exegesis because they are members of Christian communions closely affiliated with patristic foundations. Other readers will feel they are visiting a foreign country as they read the Bible with the fathers, at least in part because their Christian communities are less closely linked to the world of the early church. Openness and a willingness to listen remain key attributes for those who would hear the music the fathers sing. Michael Casey lists three reasons for studying the fathers, words of advice to remember in future pages:

First, the fathers are "more proximate beneficiaries of the apostolic tradition." To use my own phrase, the fathers lived and worked in *hermeneutical proximity* to the biblical writers, especially those of the New Testament.

Second, the fathers "help us to understand our own roots" in faith.

Third, most fathers wrote and lived as pastors. "They wrote to help people come to grips with the teaching of Christ. As far as I know, theology was not seen as a profession or occupation in the first millenium. It was seen more as a concomitant of pastoral care. . . . Texts written from such a perspective tend to be existential, experiential, and practical. Theory is not allowed to run loose."[43]

4. *Ecclesiastical approval.* This final characteristic designates that a father has been affirmed as such by the church itself. As we have seen, some significant early Christian writers such as Origen have not received this designation because the consensus of the church judged certain of their ideas to be outside the boundaries of orthodoxy.

Still, the patristic call to humility remains as we evaluate exegetes such as Origen. Creedal orthodoxy, as Henry Chadwick contends Origen himself understood, "suggests clear-cut and absolute lines of division. . . . Origen saw that the formal creedal propositions have to be stated in an unqualified and dogmatic form." Chadwick asks perceptively, though, "whether there are degrees of understanding, whether, if we all see through a glass, darkly, some may be able to see a little more clearly than others."[44]

In Origen's case, his speculative bent led him to search for "the reasons and the underlying pattern" beneath central creedal affirmations and sometimes led him into error, but Chadwick cautions all against the danger of theological overconfidence. Origen himself warned that in "advanced matters of theology absolute confidence is possible only for two classes of people, saints and idiots."[45] Humility, the willingness to listen again and again to the text of Scripture and to how others read, interpret and understand it, all the while remembering our fallen desire to escape from the truth addressing us, remains a fundamental prerequisite for understanding the fathers, their strengths and weaknesses, and ourselves.

Within the broader classification of "church fathers" we encounter the eight doctors of the church: Ambrose, Jerome, Augustine and Gregory the Great in the West; Basil the Great, Gregory of Nazianzus, Athanasius and John Chrysostom in the East. While Gregory the Great stretches the boundaries in meeting the criterion of antiquity, all eight satisfy the other three characteristics of the church fathers. In addition they meet two further qualifications: *eminens eruditio* (eminent among the fathers for the depth of their learning) and *expressa ecclesiae declaratio* (set apart by the express declaration of the church).[46] In light of the special status of these eight, we will take a more detailed look at their lives and writings in the next two chapters, focusing first on the four great doctors of Eastern Christianity.

Four

The Four Doctors
of the East

Athanasius, Gregory of Nazianzus,
Basil the Great & John Chrysostom

IN THE FOUR DOCTORS OF THE EAST WE ENCOUNTER THE PREEMINENT teachers who exemplify the riches of Eastern patristic insight and exegesis. All four illustrate the fruitfulness of patristic biblical interpretation, although these fathers practiced their exegetical craft in response to different issues. Athanasius and Gregory of Nazianzus interpreted the Bible within the context of the Arian controversy. Their use of Scripture in resolving a tangled theological question demonstrates well their interpretive technique and the fruit it yields. As for Basil and John Chrysostom, both showed themselves to be gifted exegetes, but in a generally less heated and volatile setting. Here are two of the great pastors of the church, Basil serving as the head of a monastic community, John pastoring the church in Antioch and then in Constantinople. Both read and explained the Bible in light of their pastoral responsibilities and in doing so offer insights to pastors and parishioners, then and now.

Athanasius (295-373)

There were no neutral responses to Athanasius. His friends would have willingly given their lives for him. His enemies longed to see him and his memory erased from the earth. Some mocked him as the "black dwarf."

Within Athanasius burned a lively intelligence and a heart on fire for Gód, the God who had freely and miraculously entered human history to rescue humanity, becoming what we are to rescue us from what we had become. Robert Payne writes that

in the history of the early Church no one was ever so implacable, so urgent in his demands upon himself or so derisive of his enemies. There was something in him of the temper of the modern dogmatic revolutionary: nothing stopped him. The Emperor Julian called him "hardly a man, only a little manikin." Gregory Nazianzen said he was "angelic in appearance, and still more angelic in mind." In a sense both were speaking the truth.[1]

Perhaps only a rough-edged personality like Athanasius could fight the theological, ecclesiastical and political battles that were waged for almost his entire lifetime. Gregory of Nazianzus described Athanasius simultaneously as the "pillar of the church" and as possessing "all the attributes of the heathen." In some ways, Athanasius was a theological street fighter, courageous, cagy and cunning. He was not above running up to the Emperor Constantine as he rode through the street, grabbing the bridle of his horse and scolding him over his theological shortcomings.

Here was a man who wrote two significant works—*An Oration Against the Heathen* and *On the Incarnation*—before the age of twenty. By the age of thirty-three he was bishop of the church in Alexandria. It was not to be an easy job. Over the course of the next forty-five years Athanasius was exiled from his church in Alexandria five times, largely because of his staunch opposition to the ideas of the presbyter Arius. Arius argued that the Son of God was an exalted creature. Athanasius responded with a consistent defense of the proposition that true God had genuinely entered into union with human nature in Jesus Christ. The battle between the two and their adherents would wax and wane for years.

Hermeneutical sampler. The incarnation of the Son of God was the great mystery that Athanasius defended for all of his life. God the Son, true God with the Father and the Holy Spirit, had in great love willingly joined his divine nature to human nature in the wonder of the incarnation. Only such loving humiliation and ineffable grace could possibly save humanity and offer the opportunity of human reformation into the image of God.

Only God could save. And God could do so only by becoming what we are.

The idea of a genuine incarnation, of God invading our world by becoming what we are, is an idea that makes little rational sense. The God described by biblical writers is uncreated, indivisible, omnipotent, omniscient, transcendent, infinite and immeasurable. These are only a few of the attributes that set an indelible, unmistakable, unbridgeable gap between the divine and the human, the creator and the created. Or so it would seem. And yet the gospel, at least as Athanasius understood it, proclaimed loudly and clearly that in Christ the line between divinity and humanity had been crossed. Indeed, Athanasius argued, it must be crossed if human beings were to be saved from the horrific effects of sin.

How an incarnation could actually occur or make theological sense was another matter. How could the uncreated become created? How could the infinite become finite? Could the immeasurable be measured in the thimble of human nature? What possible sense could one make out of such incomprehensible, seemingly irrational assertions? Not much at all, the presbyter Arius would assert.

Arius, representing the central theological antagonism in Athanasius's life for close to fifty years, founded his Christology on certain philosophical, theological, and biblical presuppositions. Arius contended, for example, that the divine essence was an indivisible unity. If this was true, it was rationally incoherent to believe that God could be divided in any way. For example, one could not divide God into parts: one part as the Father, a second the Son and a third the Holy Spirit. God could not "beget a divine Son," at least if the word "beget" retained any semblance to its generally recognized meaning when applied to human procreation.

Once Arius had asserted God's indivisibility as effectively foreclosing the possibility of deeper complexity within the Godhead itself, he had to make theological sense out of the Son he clearly encountered in the pages of Scripture. What was he to do? He had already concluded that this Son could not be divine in the same sense as the Father, because divinity was not a substance that could be parcelled out like helpings of mashed potatoes. The divine essence was an indivisible reality. Hence, the Son in some way must have had a beginning. He could not be eternal in the same sense that the Father was eternal. As Arius was to express it, "There was a time when he was not."

Now if this is the case, even if the Son is an exalted creature, he is still a creature, however elevated he may be. If one were to draw a line in the sand dividing deity from creation, the Son in his essence must be placed on the creation side of the line.[2] The deductions that Arius then made from this startling conclusion are jarring. If the Son is a creature, he must be inferior to God. He must be limited in his knowledge of God. He must be liable to change and even to sin.

On the more positive side, Arius insisted that the Son is the most elevated and exalted of all God's creation. He was created before time itself—he "was born outside of time." The preeminence of the Son, Arius argued, could be recognized from the glorious titles given to him in the pages of Scripture. He was even called "the Son of God." However, Arius adamantly believed that the titles given to the Son were metaphorical at best, honors pointing to his wondrous status as God's highest creation but misinterpreted if taken literally. As Arius phrased it, the Son "is called God not truly but in name only."[3]

Consider the following sampler of texts that appeared to support the Arian position:

In the garden of Gethsemane Jesus experienced grief and fear (cf. Mt 26:38). Would a divine being experience and express these emotions and responses? What of the questions Jesus asked during his lifetime? At the feeding of the four thousand Jesus asks his disciples how many loaves they possess (Mt 15:34). At his crucifixion Jesus asks why his Father has forsaken him (Mt 27:46). Jesus seems to be ignorant of the time when all things will be "accomplished" (cf. Mk 13:4, 32). The Father's knowledge seems clearly to be greater than that of the Son. If so, how could Father and Son share the same divine essence? As the Arians expressed it:

> If the Son were, according to your interpretation, eternally existent with God, He would not have been ignorant of the Day, but have known it as Word; nor would he have been forsaken if he was co-existent . . . nor have prayed at all. . . . [B]eing the Word, he would have needed nothing.[4]

Was Arian exegesis convincing? Were Arius's philosophical and theological presuppositions valid? Athanasius was horrified by the implications of Arius's teaching. Whereas Arius began with certain philosophical presuppositions concerning God's indivisibility, Athanasius started his exploration of the Son by studying Scripture's answer to the question, "What must God do if humanity is to be saved from sin?" While Arius searched for coherence and logical consistency in his understanding of Christ, Athanasius's focus was soteriological. If God was to save humanity, what would have to take place? And what did biblical writers insist had indeed actually happened?

Athansius's response to Arius can be summed up in two central assertions:

1. *Only God can save.* If the Father has sent the Son to save humanity through his death and resurrection, God has come to save. A mere creature can save no one. While Arius worked hard to preserve an exalted status for the Son, picturing him as elevated above all other creatures, his understanding of Christ faltered at this strategic juncture. The Arian Christ, Athanasius insisted, could save no one. No creature possessed the ability or prerogative to save from sin. Salvation was the prerogative, privilege and potential act of God alone. "The maker must be greater than what he makes ... and the giver has to bestow what is in his possession."[5]

Alvyn Pettersen writes that even if Christ were "the most sublime of creatures," human beings would still find themselves "fought over" by two created beings, the "Logos and the Devil." Final victory could not be guaranteed to either.[6] Thus follows Athanasius's insistence that only God can rescue humanity and that God desires to do so. "What help then can creatures derive from a creature that itself needs salvation? ... A creature could never be saved by a creature any more than the creatures were created by a creature."[7]

The Son "alone is able ... to suffer for all and is competent to be an advocate on behalf of all before the Father."[8] Only the infinite God, whose abilities, powers, love and grace remain unlimited, can save humanity. According to Pettersen, "He can relate to and act for all. Not one of those liable to mortal corruption is beyond the purview of the Highest."[9]

Not only does God possess the necessary attributes to save, but God desires to do so, lovingly experiencing the incarnation on our behalf.

[A]s it was right for him to wish to be of help to man, he came as man and took to himself a body like theirs, of humble origin ... in order that [man] who [was] unwilling to know him by his providence and government of the universe, yet by the works done through his body might know the Logos of God who was in the body, and through him the Father. For as a good teacher, who cares for his pupils, always condescends to teach by simpler means those who cannot profit by more advanced things, so does the Logos of God.[10]

2. *Christ is worshiped in Christian churches,* including churches following the teaching of Arius. How could the church rightfully worship Christ if Christ was not God? Athanasius asked. Did the Arians not realize what they were doing in their worship services, at least if their theology was correct? To worship a creature was to commit terrible blasphemy. In fact, Athanasius would contend, Arius and his followers committed blasphemy on two counts: they worshiped a creature as God and called God incarnate a mere creature. Arius's desire for, as C. S. Lewis calls it, a " 'sensible,' synthetic" religion had led him into a rationalistic cul-de-sac.[11]

For a good many years it appeared that the position of Arius had won the day. Despite the affirmation at the Council of Nicea (325) that the Son was *homoousios* with the Father, that is, shared the identical divine essence with the Father, the church wavered toward the more comprehensible and deadly solution of Arius. It truly seemed for a time that it was Athanasius *contra mundum,* against the world. His steadfast example prompted this praise from C. S. Lewis:

> We are proud that our own country has more than once stood against the world. Athanasius did the same. He stood for the Trinitarian doctrine, "whole and undefiled," when it looked as if all the civilised world was slipping back from Christianity into the religion of Arius— into one of those "sensible" synthetic religions which are so strongly recommended to-day and which, then as now, included among their devotees many highly cultivated clergymen. It is his glory that he did not move with the times; it is his reward that he now remains when those times, as all times do, have moved away.[12]

The hermeneutical response of Athanasius. Athanasius's reading of Scripture is often inextricably linked to his battle against Arianism. His four *Discourses Against the Arians* provide us with many examples of how Athanasius read the Bible and applied its contents to a specific theological problem of great moment. In his introduction to texts from the Gospels dealing with the nature of the incarnation, Athanasius first lists the common Arian objections to the possibility of God genuinely becoming incarnate.

How could the Son be "the natural and true power of the Father" if in the hour of his passion in the garden of Gethsemane his soul was troubled and he asked to be rescued from this hour? How could he ask to be delivered from the cup of his suffering? Surely if the Son shared the same essence with the Father he would have possessed the power to overcome all such fears.[13]

How could Jesus increase "in wisdom and stature, and in favour with God and man" if he were consubstantial with the Father? If he possessed all wisdom and knowledge, as surely deity does, why would he ask the disciples how many loaves they possessed at the time of the miracle of the feeding of the five thousand? Why would Jesus cry out on the cross, "My God, my God, why have you forsaken me?" Why, in response to the question of the disciples concerning the signs of the end times, did Jesus say, "But about that day or hour no one knows, neither the angels in heaven, nor the Son, but only the Father"? (Mk 13:32) How could there possibly be this division of knowledge within the Godhead, the Father knowing all things and the Son only some things?

How could God become a human being? "How could the Immaterial bear a body?" Whereas Jesus' Jewish adversaries had asked, How can a human being be God? Arius asked, How could God become a human being? "How can He be Word or God who slept as man, and wept, and inquired?"[14]

Athanasius's response to these and other questions focused on the relationship between Christ's deity and humanity. He contended that the "scope and character" of Scripture contained a "double account of the Saviour." The Bible, that is, affirmed both the deity and humanity of Jesus. As the Son, he existed as "the Father's Word and Radiance and Wisdom"; in the incarnation the Son willingly and lovingly took on human flesh "of a Virgin, Mary Bearer of God, and was made man."[15]

Athanasius believed this double focus "is to be found throughout inspired Scripture," and lists passage after passage that affirms either Christ's deity or humanity. He realizes that the crux of the problem is the relationship between Christ as God and Christ as human and centers his attention here. On the one hand, the Son has become what we are "for our sakes." Because the Son has joined himself in a genuine union to our "flesh," Athanasius expects the astute Bible reader will note that the "properties of the flesh" are realistically predicated of the Son because they are truly his in light of the incarnation. "[T]he properties of the flesh are said to be his, since He was in it, such as to hunger, to thirst, to suffer, to weary, and the like, of which the flesh is capable."[16]

On the other hand, because the Son is both genuinely human and genuinely divine, students of Scripture should not be surprised to encounter texts that stress Christ's deity, "the works proper to the Word Himself, such as to raise the dead, to restore sight to the blind, and to cure the woman with an issue of blood," wondrous works accomplished through the flesh that the Word had assumed. In a remarkable, ineffable sharing of properties, "the Word bore the infirmities of the flesh as His own, for His was the flesh; and the flesh ministered to the works of the Godhead, because the Godhead was in it, for the body was God's."[17]

Here was Athanasius's response to the Arians' confusion over Christ's humanity and deity. The Word was "not external" to the humanity it had assumed. Rather, when the incarnate Son ministered, humanity and deity were both at work in an incomprehensible union.

> And thus when there was need to raise Peter's wife's mother, who was sick of a fever, He stretched forth His hand humanly, but He stopped the illness divinely. And in the case of the man blind from birth, human was the spittle which He gave forth from the flesh, but divinely did He open the eyes through the clay. And in the case of Lazarus, He gave forth a human voice, as man; but divinely, as God, did He raise Lazarus from the dead. These things were so done, were so manifested, because He had a body, *not in appearance, but in truth*; and it became the Lord, in putting on human flesh, to put it on whole with the affections proper to it; that, as we say that the body was His own, so also we may say that the affections of the body were proper to Him alone, though they did not touch Him according to His Godhead.[18]

In short, Athanasius concludes, the divine nature appropriates the human, hallowing Christ's human nature and that of all those who come to believe in him. In love the Son comes to us, becomes what we are apart from sin, and invites us to "transfer our origin into Himself." Christ acts both divinely and humanly through his incarnate body. When he acts in power, healing the sick and raising the dead, we perceive his deity in action. When he becomes tired, asks questions, manifests fear, we see the manifestation of his genuine humanity.

The Arians had erred by reading Scripture poorly, seen in their failure to distinguish between what was proper to the Son's deity and to the Son's humanity. In their case, the failure to understand the relationship between the two had led them to deny the deity of the Son. Or, as Athanasius puts it, "looking at what is human in the Saviour, they have judged Him a creature." Other heretics would make the opposite error and deny the genuineness of the Son's humanity. Both fail to grasp who Christ is because of a failure to read Scripture in line with what the gospel itself demands if salvation is to be accomplished.

For further investigation. Athanasius's exegesis is generally scattered throughout his theological works, and writings focused solely on biblical exegesis itself are relatively rare. The clearest example of a work devoted to exegesis available in English translation is *The Letter of St. Athanasius to Marcellinus on the Interpretation of the Psalms*. It can be found attached to the St. Vladimir's Press translation of *On the Incarnation*.[19] It is also available in The Classics of Western Spirituality series published by Paulist Press, where it is accompanied by Athanasius's *Life of Antony*.[20] Athanasius did write commentaries on the Psalms, Ecclesiastes and the Song of Songs, and Genesis, but we only have fragments of these commentaries and they have yet to be translated into English. Athanasius's extensive work, *Four Discourses Against the Arians,* is a wonderful place to explore how Athanasius read the Bible and applied its teaching to a specific, extremely difficult theological question.[21]

Some might find Athanasius's thirty-ninth Festal Letter for the year 367 to be of interest. In this letter Athanasius critiques apocryphal works created by people "who have perfected themselves in a lying and contemptible science." So that people might be able to distinguish between the canonical Scriptures and fabricated works, Athanasius sets before his reader "the books included in the Canon, and handed down, and accredited as Divine."[22] Athanasius lists the twenty-seven books of the New Testament—the first time they have been declared to be canonical.[23]

Gregory of Nazianzus (ca. 329-390)

At first glance Gregory of Nazianzus, like many of the fathers, seems less than a likely candidate for pastoral leadership, and even less so for the episcopate. To speak somewhat anachronistically, Gregory appears to have been the perfect introvert, strongly attracted to solitude, prayer and the contemplative life. Moreover, he hoped to avoid the responsibilities of leadership. Robert Payne paints a vivid picture of this unlikely father:

He was a small shrunken vivid man, bald-headed, with a long red beard and red eyebrows like Athanasius, wrinkled, nearly always in pain, haggard with vigils and fastings.... He feared no one. He had an unruly humor. He is the only man who is known to have dared to laugh at Basil. He was quick-tempered, sullen, unhappy in the company of most people, strangely remote from the world. Appointed to the Patriarchate of Constantinople against his will, he found it Arian and in a few swift months converted it to the orthodox faith. He was the first Christian poet, and wrote prose so angelically, and throughout his life gloried in the Greek poet Pindar, who celebrated athletes and spoke only of human glory. He loved God, and then the art of letters, and then men—in that order.[24]

Who was this strange man who proved himself to be a gifted poet, pastor, bishop and theologian? Gregory was born in Cappadocia to a fairly wealthy family who resided in Nazianzus, a town of little distinction in the Mediterranean world. His father, Gregory the elder, was for a number of years a member of the Hypsistarii, "a Hellenized Jewish sect that worshiped one God, observed the Sabbath, and kept the food laws but rejected circumcision."[25]

Gregory's family could afford to provide him with an excellent education, and from the age of thirteen onwards Gregory studied in the great educational centers of the Greco-Roman world—Caesarea in Cappadocia, Caesarea in Palestine, Alexandria, and for a number of years in Athens. Gregory particularly focused on rhetoric and the classical Greek authors, manifesting a love for the power and beauty of words that is evident in his letters, orations and poems.

I tossed to the winds all other things: those who want them can have wealth and high birth, fame and the power to govern other men, all those earthly pleasures which pass like a dream. But there is one thing I cling to—my power of words, that alone, and so I do not grudge the vicissitudes by land and sea that gave me this. May the power of words be mine, and may it belong to him who calls me friend. I cherish it deeply, and so I shall always, placing it first except for that which is the very first—I mean all holy things and the hopes which stretch beyond the tangible world.[26]

He longed for the freedom to study in peace, and groaned against the desire of others to see him placed in positions of pastoral leadership.

Payne describes him as "the perpetual student, the man who spends his whole life quietly studying, with no desire for action."[27]

Johannes Quasten pictures Gregory as the "humanist among the theologians of the fourth century," in that Gregory clearly preferred the contemplative and ascetic life to the active life of ecclesiastical leadership. Yet, Quasten argues, Gregory's "accommodating disposition and his sense of duty" conflicted with his desire for study and solitude, continually beckoning him "to the turbulent world and the controversies and conflicts of his time." Gregory's life, then, appears as a series "of flights from, and returns to, the world."[28]

In Gregory we clearly encounter the conflicted Christian introvert, longing to be left to his books and the life of the monastic, but continually beckoned by his church to a life of communal service. It is the tension between these two lives and two desires that frequently extrudes Gregory's wisdom and insight to the surface of his consciousness for the benefit of the very community Gregory wanted to avoid.

Consider, for example, Gregory's call to the priesthood in Nazianzus. Gregory had been living in monastic solitude with his close friend Basil when he was summoned by his father to return home. Both Gregory's father and the Christian community of Nazianzus were convinced that God had called Gregory to the ordained ministry. However, after his ordination he fled from Nazianzus back to his monastic life in Pontus. Within a short time he relented, accepted his ordination and returned to Nazianzus. Out of this turmoil emerged his "In Defence of His Flight to Pontus," an oration that ranks with John Chrysostom's "On the Priesthood" for its clear presentation of the responsibilities and pitfalls facing the Christian minister.[29]

The same pattern of following the call to leadership and service and retreating from that call was to resurface in Gregory's life, reflective of the inner turmoil within him concerning his evident giftedness and his longing for seclusion. This conflict, Frederick Norris comments, "plagued him all his life. . . . He had the theological and preaching gifts to be a bishop, but the details of public administration found no resonance in his person. He more than once fled into monastic retreat after periods of difficult community demands."[30]

Thankfully, Gregory agreed to serve as assistant to his father in Nazianzus, and later acceded to the request of the church in Constantinople and the Emperor Theodosius to serve as bishop. This move to Constantinople, though, came after a period of intense suffering and grief. Within a few short years Gregory had lost four close family members and his closest friend to death's clutches: his brother Caesarius, his sister Gorgonia, his father Gregory the elder, his mother Nonna, and Basil the Great. Gregory wrote to the rhetorician Eudoxius of the deep grief these deaths brought and of his anxiety over the seeming unravelling of the orthodox Christian world under the onslaught of Arianism.

> You ask me how my affairs are. Miserable. I have lost two brothers, the one of the spirit, Basil, and the one of the flesh, Caesarius. I shall cry out with David, "My father and mother have left me" [Ps 27 (26):10]. My body is in a sorry state; old age is over my head. Cares and business worry me, as do false friends and the shepherdless state of the Church. Good is destroyed, evil is naked; we are at sea by night without any light, Christ is asleep. What further must I endure? There is only one release from evil—death; and even that frightens me, to judge from what I here experience.[31]

Who would have guessed that the introvert Gregory would shortly become the shepherd and beacon he despaired of ever finding in his troubled age, indeed the bishop of the great see of Constantinople? While Gregory's episcopal service in Constantinople was short-lived, his voice and theological insight reinforced the Nicene position in a city that had widely fallen into Arian hands. Five key theological orations that Gregory preached during this period remain the foundation for trinitarian doctrine and thought in Eastern Orthodoxy and have also influenced trinitarian thinking and formulation in the West.

In 381 Gregory stepped down as bishop of Constantinople, declining to embroil himself in the controversy that had erupted concerning the canonical legality of his appointment as bishop. Apparently, opponents from Alexandria contended that Gregory's episcopate at Constantinople violated canonical law because he had already served as a bishop elsewhere. "Even though he had not served at Sasima and had been only an auxiliary at Nazianzus," Norris writes, "he did not find the dispute worth the effort."[32] With a closing rhetorical flourish in a farewell oration, Gregory expressed vividly his disappointment over life in Constantinople and his relief to be heading home.

No one told me I was to contend with consuls and prefects and the most illustrious generals, who hardly know how to relieve themselves of their abundance of possessions. No one told me I was expected to put the treasuries of the church to the service of gluttony, and the poor-boxes to the services of luxury. No one told me I must be equipped with superb horses and mounted on an ornamental chariot, and there would be a great hush during my solemn progresses, and everyone must make way for the Patriarch as though he were some kind of wild beast, with the people opening out in great avenues to let me pass, as I came like a banner from afar. If these things offended you, then I say they all belong to the past. Forgive me.[33]

Gregory returned to Nazianzus, ministered there for a short time and finally attained his lifelong wish, retiring to a life of solitude and prayer on his family estate at Arianzus. He died there in 390.

Hermeneutical sampler. Edward R. Hardy suggests that Gregory of Nazianzus "would be an inconspicuous figure in Church history, if known to us at all," had it not been for his two years of intense and significant ministry at Constantinople.[34] It was during Gregory's time in Constantinople that he preached a series of homilies attacking the rampant Arianism that had infected the majority of churches in the city. These sermons, later to be known as the *Theological Orations*, earned for Gregory the title "Theologos" or "Theologian." How can they help us understand how Gregory read the Bible and conducted his work as a pastor and theologian?

To answer this question, we need to say a word or two about Gregory's theological opponents. We have already discussed the tenets of Arianism in our discussion of Athanasius's life and work. Gregory, too, responded directly to the Arian view of Christ as an exalted creature. In some ways equally important, however, is Gregory's response in *The First Theological Oration* to the warped disposition and attitude of his Arian opponents as they contemplate God, study the Scriptures and proceed to make their theological deductions. Gregory contended his opponents' devotionally deficient stance before God hampered their ability to interpret the Bible well. A diseased spiritual life crippled their ability to comprehend and explicate divine truth. Theology, Gregory argued, is not a science that operates in a spiritual or devotional vacuum. Rather, who one is, the state of one's spiritual health and devotional well-being, distinctly influences one's ability to interpret Scripture correctly and communicate its truth faithfully.

Gregory's attention appeared to focus on a radical Arian group known as the Eunomians. This group exalted their supposed ability to plumb rationally the depths of the divine being itself. The Eunomians believed they could clearly comprehend the divine essence and distinguish the relationships between Father, Son and Holy Spirit through the use of reason alone. Anyone with an ounce of sense, they believed, would surely recognize that there was only one God, the Father. To predicate further personal distinctions within God's being was to speak incomprehensible gibberish. In fact, there was scant room in Eunomian thought for incomprehensibility or mystery of any sort.

The Eunomians were a cocky, self-assured bunch, ready to use rational syllogisms to poke holes in the ideas of their opponents, but all the while blind to the drastic implications of their own theological methodology. Gregory of Nyssa chided them as amateur theologians. If you asked them for the price of bread, Gregory complained, they would "tell you the Father is greater and the Son subject to him, and if you want to order a bath . . . [they] reply that the Son is made out of nothing."[35]

In the *First Theological Oration* Gregory concentrates his attention on how the Eunomians read Scripture and do theology, rather than on their specific errors. It does not surprise him that they are making crucial errors, because their attitude from the beginning is faulty. He stands against them, opposed to both their "system of teaching" and their "tone of mind." The Eunomians, Gregory proclaims, are people "who delight in profane babblings, and the oppositions of science falsely so called," enjoying "strifes about words, which tend to no profit."[36]

Gregory speaks a language to the Eunomians that they probably will find "strange" and "contrary," precisely because the wonder of the incarnation demands the language of mystery and paradox; it is this rationally incomprehensible core at the heart of the incarnation that the Eunomians have attempted to eliminate through the use of an irreverent and rationalistic methodology. In their study of God, Gregory insists, they have forgotten who they are dealing with and have reduced God's wonders and mysteries to the boundaries of their own rational capabilities.

Gregory warns that it is not the right or prerogative of every Tom, Dick and Harry to plumb the divine mysteries: "the subject is not so cheap and low." Neither are the mysteries of God's character and works to be paraded before any audience. Instead, there is an appropriate place, time and audience for studying and expounding divine truth. And there are always important boundaries to preserve.[37]

Spiritual health and hermeneutical acumen cannot be separated. Those who speak of God must be persons who have been examined by the believing community, those who "are past masters in meditation, and who have been previously purified in soul and body, or at the very least are being purified."[38] How can an impure eye study the pure, or weak eyes safely gaze upon the sun, Gregory asks?[39]

Not only does theological discernment and wisdom arise from a character being formed into Christ's image, but theological study is not a sport or contest, a game one approaches flippantly or lightly. Divine truth will open itself only to those for whom it is a genuine concern. It will remain closed to "they who make it a matter of pleasant gossip, like any other thing, after the races, or the theater, or a concert, or a dinner, or still lower employments. To such men as these, idle jests and petty contradictions about these subjects are part of their amusement."[40]

Jaroslav Pelikan observes that it was not only the Eunomians who needed to hear the words of Gregory. By Gregory's time, close to fifty years after the conversion of Constantine, "Christian theology had become sufficiently widespread in its acceptance by polite Byzantine society to be trendy." Pelikan notes Gregory's complaint that "some devotees of theology" were "like the promoters of wrestling-bouts in the theaters," people whose "idle chatter about the dogmas of the faith," in Gregory's words, made "every square in the city buzz with their arguments." The only remedy was a pure mind and heart and good, old-fashioned study.[41]

> For is it not absurd that while no one, however great his boorishness and lack of education, is allowed to be ignorant of the Roman law, and while there is no law in favor of sins of ignorance, the teachers of the mysteries of salvation should be ignorant of the *archai* of salvation, however simple and shallow their minds may be in regard to other subjects?[42]

The Eunomians had gone astray on a number of fronts. First, as we have seen, they failed to interpret Scripture or speak of God in a reverent manner. They demonstrated their irreverence by attempting to step across the boundaries finite human reason must acknowledge in its search for understanding concerning God and God's redemptive acts in history. By prying farther than human reason can reasonably explore, Gregory's

opponents were in danger of turning a great mystery into a "little moment." They were like "hot-tempered and hard-mouthed horses" who had
thrown off "our rider Reason" by exercising it in a fruitless fashion.[43]

Gregory urged that rather than heedlessly delving into mysteries better
worshiped than ineffectively and naively understood, wise and reverent
scholars and pastors should devote their attention to "matters within our
reach, and to such an extent as the mental power and grasp of our audience
may extend."[44] Gregory did not want to discourage all speech about God,
but only discourse that has deceived itself by reaching beyond its own
capabilities. Enough of this irreverent and self-deceived speech, Gregory
exhorted. Instead, "let us at least agree upon this, that we will utter
mysteries under our breath, and holy things in a holy manner."[45]

Second, Gregory reminded his audience that the knowledge of God is
a gift to be reverently received and sweetly guarded. The Eunomians, by
changing exegesis and theology into a kind of recreational sport practiced
within any context, paraded holy things before people who could not hope
to understand them. To use Jesus' terms, they threw pearls to swine.
Behind this critique was Gregory's deep awareness that theology is a type
of worship, a holy endeavor, one that blossoms in a context of prayer,
devotion and adoration, but withers when transformed into an academic,
speculative mind game.

How, then, should one study and speak of God? First, we must "look
to ourselves, and polish our theological self to beauty like a statue."[46] This
polishing of character occurs as the theologian diligently refuses to accept
any kind of dichotomy between word and life.

> Why have we tied our hands and armed our tongues? We do not praise
> either hospitality, or brotherly love, or conjugal affection, or virginity;
> nor do we admire liberality to the poor, or the chanting of psalms, or
> nightlong vigils, or tears. We do not keep under the body by fasting, or
> go forth to God by prayer.... [W]e do not make our life a preparation
> for death; nor do we make ourselves masters of our passions, mindful
> of our heavenly nobility; nor tame our anger when it swells and rages,
> nor our pride that brings to a fall, nor unreasonable grief, nor unchas-
> tened pleasure, nor meretricious laughter, nor undisciplined eyes, nor
> insatiable ears, nor excessive talk, nor absurd thoughts, nor aught of
> the occasions which the evil one gets against us from sources within
> ourselves.[47]

Gregory's words remain a sharp and timely rebuke to the continuing temptation to practice theology as though we could separate the exercise of our mind from the development of our character. Admittedly, this will be a fairly novel, even strange idea for modern exegetes, particularly for those trained to do their exegesis and theology within the context and confines of the academy. Modern academicians have been trained to view the biblical text as an object of study and analysis that differs little from other ancient texts. Indeed, many modern exegetes would advocate the necessity of distancing oneself from the biblical text if one is to make sense of it. In the academy, anyone can do exegesis, regardless of one's faith stance. If a person has cultivated the necessary exegetical skills, tools and knowledge (e.g., languages, knowledge of cultural and historical background), one can comprehend the biblical text and message, regardless of a response of faith. Exegesis and theological exploration have become technical skills often practiced in separation from the life of the Christian community and the history of that community's reading of Scripture over the centuries. In their search for a home within the academy, many biblical scholars and theologians have planted themselves in soil that cannot provide the nutrients Gregory sees as nonnegotiables for theological and exegetical fruitfulness.

Once Gregory had laid the ground rules for thinking and speaking of God well, stressing the necessary link between spiritual discipline, spiritual health and theological insight, he was prepared to comment on central christological issues. The background for Gregory's christological responses was the Arian controversy, the theological disagreement concerning the Son's divinity that continued to rage in Constantinople in the late fourth century. Gregory's responses to the Arians, at times quite similar to those of Athanasius, help us to understand how Gregory read and interpreted the Bible, and illustrate well how he applied the text of Scripture to a specific theological question. It is in the *Third and Fourth Theological Orations Concerning the Son* that Gregory's exegetical skill and theological insight are especially apparent.

As we have observed in our discussion of Athanasius, a principal Arian objection to the divinity of Christ was the multitude of biblical passages that speak clearly of Jesus' weaknesses: he hungers, thirsts, occasionally manifests what seems to be ignorance, experiences anxiety in the Garden of Gethsemane and so on. How, the Arian party asked, could the church recognize or identify a person who manifests such patently creaturely features as divine in the same sense or manner as the Father? Gregory, like Athanasius, was quite familiar with these Arian objections, and actually employed them to accentuate the wonder of the incarnation.

Gregory argued that every one of these characteristics of the incarnate Son can be explained "in the most reverent sense, and the stumbling block of the letter be cleansed away," if the Arian objections are "honest, and not willfully malicious." Gregory's solution, like that of Athanasius, was to contend that those passages stressing Christ's weaknesses pertain to the human nature the Son had assumed on our behalf: "What is lofty you are to apply to the Godhead, and to that nature in him which is superior to sufferings and incorporeal; but all that is lowly to the composite condition of him who for your sakes made himself of no reputation and was incarnate."[48]

Gregory delighted in setting side by side the wondrous paradoxes contained in the indescribable union of Christ's deity and humanity:

He was baptized as man—but he remitted sins as God. . . . He was tempted as man, but he conquered as God. . . . He hungered—but he fed thousands. . . . He was wearied, but he is the rest of them that are weary and heavy-laden. He was heavy with sleep, but he walked lightly over the sea. . . . He pays tribute, but it is out of a fish; yea, he is the king of those who demanded it. . . . He prays, but he hears prayer. He weeps, but he causes tears to cease. He asks where Lazarus was laid, for he was man; but he raises Lazarus, for he was God. He is sold, and very cheap, for it is only for thirty pieces of silver; but he redeems the world, and that at a great price, for the price was his blood. As a sheep he is led to the slaughter, but he is the shepherd of Israel, and now of the whole world also. . . . He is bruised and wounded, but he heals every disease and every infirmity. He is lifted up and nailed to the tree, but by the tree of life he restores us. He dies, but he gives life, and by his death he destroys death.[49]

Many of the Arian objections can be met, Gregory believed, by recognizing a fundamental hermeneutical principle: in the incarnation the Son has willingly assumed the human condition in order to redeem and renew human nature. The Son has willingly and lovingly made our condition his own. Hence, when Jesus cries out on the cross, "My God, my God, why have you forsaken me?" he was not forsaken by the Father in terms of his deity, as though deity were forsaking deity, splitting God into parts as it were. Such a hypothetical division was a fundamental Arian objection to the possibility of Jesus' divinity. Rather, Gregory argued,

> [Christ] was in his own person representing us. For we were the forsaken and despised before, but now, by the sufferings of Him who could not suffer, we were taken up and saved. Similarly, he makes his own our folly and our transgressions; and says what follows in the psalm, for it is very evident that the Twenty-first Psalm [Ps 22 LXX] refers to Christ.[50]

Here, then, is a fundamental hermeneutical principle followed by Gregory and the fathers as a whole. While certain names and attributes of Jesus are clearly characteristic of and applicable to his inherent deity, the Son cannot be adequately or reverently comprehended apart or in distinction from his genuine humanity. He has become what we are while remaining what he has always been, and it is this movement in love from the infinite to the finite, the uncreated to the created, the divine to the embrace of the human, that provides the exegetical key for many biblical texts that would otherwise remain inexplicable.

In his *Fifth Theological Oration*, Gregory discusses the deity of the Holy Spirit, a doctrine disputed by a group known as the Macedonians. This group specifically denied the deity of the Holy Spirit and refused to recognize the validity of the creed established at Nicaea in 325 and expanded at Constantinople in 381. Apparently the Macedonians doubted the deity of the Holy Spirit because, among other things, Scripture seemed to be largely silent on the subject. Surely such a significant truth would have been communicated in clearer terms.

Gregory proposes to release his opponents from their misapprehension by discussing "things and names, and especially of their use in Holy Scripture."[51] More particularly, Gregory posits as a fundamental hermeneutical principle the idea of progressive revelation. That is, Gregory teaches that the Scripture presents with increasing clarity the purposes of God as God acts to rescue humanity from sin and its effects. First, Scripture describes God's providential acts in choosing and leading Israel through the transition from idols to the law. The next step leads from the law to the gospel. Finally, in what Gregory calls "the gospel of a third earthquake," there is a transition from this earth "to that which cannot be shaken or moved."[52]

These changes or transitions do not occur suddenly or haphazardly. Instead, God presents his purposes and plans in such a manner that humanity is persuaded to change and grow in line with God's desires. Therefore, "like a tutor or physician, he partly removes and partly condones ancestral habits, conceding some little of what tended to pleasure, just as medical men do with their patients, that their medicine may be taken, being artfully blended with what is nice."[53] Through these gradual changes, accommodations and transitions both Jew and Gentile will perceive and accede to the will of God, moving from a state of immaturity to maturity.

In the case of theology itself, Gregory reverses the process. Instead of change through subtraction or the weening process of God's providence, we attain doctrinal clarity through God building progressively on the revelatory foundation stones of the past.

> For the matter stands thus: The Old Testament proclaimed the Father openly, and the Son more obscurely. The New manifested the Son, and suggested the deity of the Spirit. Now the Spirit himself dwells among us, and supplies us with a clearer demonstration of himself. For it was not safe, when the Godhead of the Father was not yet acknowledged, plainly to proclaim the Son; nor when that of the Son was not yet received, to burden us further (if I may use so bold an expression) with the Holy Ghost.[54]

Rather, through gradual revelatory additions the deity of the Spirit became increasingly clear, and hence, the wonder of the triune God himself. Jesus' teaching, particularly in John 14—16, skillfully adapted itself to the capacity of the disciples to understand the work and person of the Spirit. The entire revelatory process, both of understanding the Spirit and experiencing the infilling of his presence, was carefully gauged to correspond to the capacity of the disciples to understand and embrace the truth.

> [H]e gradually came to dwell in the disciples, measuring himself out to them according to their capacity to receive him, at the beginning of the gospel, after the Passion, after the ascension, making perfect their powers, being breathed upon them, and appearing in fiery tongues. And indeed it is by little and little that he is declared by Jesus, as you will learn for yourself if you will read more carefully.[55]

Like "lights breaking upon us, gradually," the fuller revelation of the Spirit illustrates "the order of theology, which it is better for us to keep, neither

proclaiming things too suddenly nor yet keeping them hidden to the end."
To speak too quickly would be "unscientific," while to refuse to speak
when God had revealed deeper truth would be to act the part of an atheist.
Jesus had taught that there were still truths his disciples could not yet
bear. For a time these things were hidden from them. Still, Jesus also
predicted that he would send the Spirit and in coming the Spirit would
teach them "all things."

For Gregory, "all things" includes the surprising, wondrous revelation
that the Spirit is also divine, sharing the same divine essence with the
Father and Son. Again, this revelation was kept secret by God until a
"seasonable" time, when the capability of the disciples had been enlarged
to receive the deity of the Spirit without "incredulity because of its
marvelous character."

> This, then, is my position with regard to these things, and I hope it
> may be always my position, and that of whoever is dear to me: to
> worship God the Father, God the Son, and God the Holy Ghost, three
> persons, one Godhead, undivided in honor and glory and substance and
> kingdom.... For if He is not to be worshiped, how can he deify me by
> baptism? But if he is to be worshiped, surely he is an object of adoration,
> and, if an object of adoration, he must be God; the one is linked to the
> other, a truly golden and saving chain. And indeed from the Spirit
> comes our new birth, and from the new birth our new creation, and
> from the new creation our deeper knowledge of the dignity of Him
> from whom it is derived.[56]

Once Gregory has constructed this hermeneutical and theological underpinning, he proceeds to list and comment on a series of passages indicating
the deity of the Spirit. He finally concludes by describing the distinctions
between Father, Son and Spirit with a number of analogies, all of which
ultimately break down under the weight of the ineffable burden they are
called to bear. Gregory concludes it is best to leave the illustrations behind
as only "images and shadows," holding instead "to the more reverent
conception, and resting upon few words, using the guidance of the Holy
Ghost."[57]

Underlying Gregory's trinitarian analysis is the firm conviction that
isolated texts of Scripture should be read in light of the overarching
biblical narrative; because the Holy Spirit has inspired all the biblical
authors, it is perfectly legitimate to allow one text to shed light on another.

Rather than producing a forced harmony, the comparison of texts acknowledges the Spirit's overriding authorship of the entire Bible. Because the New Testament Scriptures are in continuity with those of the Old Testament, Gregory feels free to interpret the Old in light of the New. To fail to do so is to practice a wooden literalism that fails to observe the Bible's deeper unity in the Spirit. Frederick Norris explains:

> The Theologian [i.e., Gregory] worries that a kind of literalism may support Jewish rejection of Jesus as the Messiah; a love of the letter may serve as a 'cloak of irreligion' that blinds even Christians to the truth in Holy Writ about the Holy Spirit. Nazianzen accepts that the text written has an inner meaning which appears only when the Bible is read with great care.[58]

The inner meaning of the Bible reveals itself to those who read it in light of the gospel. "Holy Writ has its own *skopos*, its own intent," writes Norris. "And that intent is made known to the Church in worship."[59] How does this principle reveal itself in Gregory's exegesis?

Gregory's exegetical response to specific theological issues provides the answer. He has left us little prolonged exegesis upon specific biblical passages. Norris, perhaps the greatest Nazianzus scholar writing today, observes that Gregory's writings "always represent the thought of a constructive theologian who teaches and preaches within a context shaped both by polemical adversaries and by confessional friends."[60]

Chief among these issues, as we have seen, was the trinitarian controversy, itself a "debate about the interpretation" of Scripture "within the context of worshipping communities." Gregory and the other two great Cappadocian theologians, Basil the Great and Gregory of Nyssa, spent most of their lives defending theologically and exegetically the church's worship from those who would undercut it through a devaluation of the Son and the Spirit. Terms formulated at Nicea and Constantinople such as *homoousios*, *physis* and *ousia* were "shorthand contextualization of a large amount of exegesis."

> The Theologian argued that his positions were the true ones because they made more sense of more Scripture than did the views of the later Arians. . . . The great theological issues that the Cappadocians debated with their opponents can be followed rather closely by paying attention to how they interpreted Scripture and what principles they applied from within their community of faith.[61]

For example, Gregory's understanding of the importance of context and the semantic range of biblical phrases and words remains valuable for modern exegetes. Gregory's Arian opponents, exegetes who believed that Jesus was an exalted creature but not God incarnate, used a number of biblical passages to buttress their position. Among them were 1 Corinthians 15:25, Acts 3:21 and Psalm 110:1. All three passages seemed to indicate that Christ would reign "until" all his enemies had been defeated and the kingdom of God "restored to the Father." Surely, "until" indicated an end of some kind, a change of status related to the ultimate superiority of the Father. Norris clearly explains Gregory's exegetical methodology and reaction to the Arian position.

Gregory's response was twofold. First, he asked if other Scriptures might help to answer how these three texts should be interpreted. Luke 1:33 indicates that "he will reign over the house of Jacob forever; his kingdom will never end" (NIV). If the Spirit has revealed that Christ's reign will never end, he will not contradict himself through the mouth of Paul. What, then, does Paul mean?

Gregory answers this question by asking whether his Arian opponents are narrowly defining what "until" can mean in 1 Corinthians 15:25. Did its use in Scripture inevitably mean an ending of some sort, that is, an ending based on certain issues or events reaching their culmination or conclusion? Again, Gregory compares Scripture with Scripture. If "until" always means up to a given point but no further, what are we to make of Matthew 28:20, a text that speaks of Christ being with his disciples "until" the end of the age. As Norris rightly asks, did this mean Christ would not be with them after this time? Would their communion end? As Gregory clearly understands, "until" can "designate what happens up to a point and not deny anything about what occurs after that point."[62]

If "until" possesses this semantic flexibility Gregory can make sense out of a text such as 1 Corinthians 15:25: "For he must reign until he has put all his enemies under his feet." Arian exegetes insisted that Paul was teaching Christ's reign would end after his enemies had been overcome, indicating his inferior status to the Father. Gregory, in light of the broader meaning of "until," recognized that Paul said no more than that "when all those inferior to him have submitted to his rule, he no longer needs to produce submission in them. Only in that sense will his rule end."[63]

Norris notes that Gregory understood that "the meaning of a word in

Scripture can also be enhanced by knowing what options exist for the meaning of that word in everyday language as well as in the Bible."[64] The example Norris supplies from Gregory's work concerns the Eunomian controversy we have already discussed.

The Eunomians' denial of the equality of the Father and the Son was based on texts such as John 5:19. Here Jesus teaches that "the Son can do nothing on his own, but only what he sees the Father doing." The Eunomians interpreted Jesus' inability to act on his own as a sign of his inequality with and submission to the Father.

Gregory knew, however, that to "understand what 'can do nothing' means, the interpreter must ask what 'cannot' means."[65] Gregory responded with a detailed study of what "cannot" means and does not mean, an analysis largely based on how "cannot" functions in everyday language. Norris has identified at least five aspects of Gregory's exegesis of "cannot."[66]

1. It can "refer to an ability at a particular time in relation to a specific object. Young children are not accomplished athletes, but they may grow to be such. A little puppy with closed eyes certainly cannot fight, but later he may both see and attack."

2. "Cannot" can refer to "something that is usually true but is not true from a particular perspective." For example, Jesus speaks of a city "on a hill that cannot be hidden." Does he mean that it could never be hidden? No. "If one stands with a higher hill in the line of sight, the city cannot be seen."

3. "Cannot" can refer to "something unthinkable" or not sensible. "At the celebration of a wedding feast, the friends of the bridegroom 'cannot' fast while everyone around them is celebrating."

4. "Cannot" may "designate a lack of will as when Jesus 'could not' do miracles because of the people's lack of faith. Jesus did no mighty works in his home town, but that did not mean that he had no power to do them."

5. "Cannot" can refer to things that are simply "impossible," such as "God not existing or being evil, or something non-existent existing, or two plus two equaling ten, not four."

Having established a wide range of possible meanings for "cannot," Gregory then had to ask what definition best fits John 5:19, where Jesus says he "can do nothing" on his own. As Gregory compared Scripture with Scripture, he reached an inevitable conclusion, described by Norris:

> Because John 6:57, 16:15 and 17:10 make it clear that the Son has his being from God before the existence of time and without the involve-

ment of some extraneous cause, John 5:19 must be read as using 'cannot' in the fifth sense, that of something impossible. Surely Wisdom does not need to be taught. The Father does not model acts for the Son because the Son is ignorant and has to learn them. In context John 5:19 emphasizes that the Son has the same authority as the Father.[67]

In addition, Norris elucidates another helpful rule Gregory observed in exegeting the Bible. John 6:38 speaks of Jesus coming, not to do his own will, but that of his Father. Some Arians had interpreted this verse to mean that Jesus possessed a will "different from that of his Father. They see it as yet another indication that the two are separate and thus that the Son is indeed subordinate."[68]

Gregory countered this Arian exegesis with the hermeneutical principle that "not every negative statement can be turned into a positive one." Can Paul's statement that God saves us "not for righteousness we have done" (Tit 3:5) also be changed into a positive statement? If so, we end up with Paul saying "that God saved us because of 'righteousness we have done,'" turning the original on its head by attemping to change Paul's negative statement into a positive one. As Norris explains, "Understood in terms of this principle, John 5:19 means precisely that the divine Son does not have a divine will of his own; His divine will is one with that of the Father."[69]

For further investigation. We can organize the works of Gregory available in English translation into three categories: letters, orations and poems. In the late nineteenth century Charles Gordon Browne and James Edward Swallow translated twenty-four orations, including the five great theological orations Gregory delivered in Constantinople; their translation, dated and dusty, is available in the Nicene and Post-Nicene Fathers series published by Eerdmans and Hendrickson.[70] Browne and Swallow also translated a large collection of Gregory's letters. In 1954 Edward R. Hardy translated the five theological orations on the Father, Son and Holy Spirit for the Library of Christian Classics series published by Westminster Press.[71] Since Gregory did not write any biblical commentaries, how he read, interpreted and applied the Scriptures can perhaps best be gleaned by a close examination of the orations. Four of Gregory's funeral orations have been translated by Martin McGuire and are available from The Catholic University of America Press,[72] as is Denis Meehan's translation of three of Gregory's poems. They are filled with rich allusions to Scripture.[73]

Basil the Great (330-379)

The Roman province of Cappadocia was known for its horses, its heresies and the temperment of its inhabitants. Robert Payne provides this description:

> Men who lived in more favored regions liked to tell how a viper bit a Cappadocian, and the viper died. They were a sturdy people, and under the Romans had the reputation of being good chair-bearers and bad fighters, too provincial to care what happened in other countries, and their accents were uncouth, hard on the ears of the Greeks, so that Libanius, who had many Cappadocian pupils in his great school in Antioch, said: "I am teaching pigeons to be cooing doves."[74]

Basil, like Gregory of Nazianzus, was born into a wealthy Christian Cappadocian family, and his character reflects the firm resoluteness of his Cappadocian compatriots. His father, the elder Basil, was a successful lawyer and ardent believer. Basil's mother Emmelia shared the same faith as her husband and was the daughter of a martyr. Both were diligent in passing on their Christian faith to their many children.

The number of positive and impressive influences on the growing Basil are impressive. His paternal grandmother was Macrina, later to be known as "Macrina the elder," a disciple of Gregory the Wonderworker and the recognized matron of the family. One of Basil's brothers was Gregory of Nyssa. Later Christian tradition would recognize Basil, Gregory of Nyssa and Gregory of Nazianzus, Basil's close friend, as the three great Cappadocian fathers.

Perhaps the most impressive person in Basil's large family was Macrina "the younger," the oldest child in the family and a faithful guide in the faith to both Basil and Gregory. She was quick to discern the strengths and weaknesses in Basil's character and not afraid to chastise the pride Basil would battle for most of his life. In his *Life of St. Macrina* Gregory of Nyssa insists that it was Macrina who led Basil to a life of Christian asceticism.

> [T]he great Basil, brother of [Macrina], returned from school where he had been trained in rhetoric for a long time. She indeed detected that he was enormously puffed up with pride over his rhetorical

abilities; he despised all the worthy people and exalted himself in self-importance above the illustrious men of the province. Yet she drew him with such speed to the goal of philosophy that he renounced worldly renown. He expressed contempt at being an object of marvel on account of his rhetoric. He deserted to this laborious life of manual labor to prepare himself by complete poverty and unfettered life directed toward virtue. But his life and later pursuits, by which he became famous everywhere under the sun and obscured the glory of all those illustrious for their virtue, would require a thick book and much time.[75]

Basil, like Gregory of Nazianzus, had the good fortune to study in a number of important cities, spending the longest time in Athens, where he studied for six years. There he established his lifelong friendship with Gregory of Nazianzus and also immersed himself in the art of rhetoric, acquiring knowledge and skills that would serve him well as the leader of a monastic community, pastor, bishop and theologian.

Upon his return to Pontus from Athens, Basil accepted a position as a professor of rhetoric at the University of Caesarea. His academic career was to be short-lived, however. After a year of teaching Basil experienced a deep spiritual renewal and left the university to pursue a deeper relationship with the God who had been revealed to him in Christ. In a letter describing this time Basil recounts being awakened "as if aroused from a deep sleep." He describes his earlier devotion to rhetoric as "vain labor in which I was engaged, occupying myself in acquiring a knowledge made foolish by God." Touched by Christ, Basil "prayed that guidance be given me for my introduction to the doctrines of religion."[76]

Immediately Basil began to change his lifestyle and priorities, eagerly searching the Scriptures to determine how disciples of Christ should conduct their lives. As a man oriented to action, he was quick to take concrete steps to embody what he was learning. Christ's message to Basil allowed for no compromise.

> Accordingly, having read the Gospel and having seen clearly there that the greatest means for perfection is the selling of one's possessions, the sharing with needy brethren, the complete renouncing of solicitude for this life, and the refusing of the soul to be led astray by any affection for things of earth, I prayed to find some one of the brethren who had chosen this way of life, so as to pass with him over life's brief and troubled waters.[77]

Basil left to visit the monastic communities already established in Syria,

Palestine, Egypt and Mesopotamia. He was deeply impressed by what he found.

> I admired their continence in living, and their endurance in toil. I was amazed at their persistency in prayer, and at their triumphing over sleep. Subdued by no natural necessity, ever keeping their soul's purpose high and free in hunger and thirst, in cold and nakedness, they never yielded to the body; they were never willing to waste attention on it. Always, as though living in a flesh that was not theirs, they showed in very deed what it is to sojourn for a while in this life, and what to have one's citizenship and home in heaven. All this moved my admiration. I called these men's lives blessed, in that they did indeed show that "they bear about in their body the dying of Jesus." And I prayed that I too, as far as in me lay, might imitate them.[78]

This passage might well sound foreign to modern ears. Basil's rhetorical exaggerations may confuse us and his interpretation of discipleship may appear wild, radical, impractical and foolish. Yet for Basil discipleship could never be domesticated. Life was a short pilgrimage, a trip through a battlefield strewn with visible and invisible trapwires. One could navigate it safely and fruitfully only by a firm no to compromise and earthly safety and an unqualified yes to Christ. The stakes were too great to act otherwise.

Yes, Basil would make many modern Christians uncomfortable, particularly those raised in an affluent environment where every need for food, shelter and clothing is well met. The modern martyrs and prisoners of the faith would more readily recognize his voice. Without doubt Basil would consider the affluent Western lifestyle at best a spiritual smokescreen that, like the lifestyle of many of his own wealthy contemporaries, could blind one to the need for utter dependence upon God and sensitivity to the needs of the surrounding poor. Later, while serving as an auxiliary bishop in Caesarea, Basil would witness firsthand the horrors of famine and the even greater horror of wealthy Christians turning a blind eye to the needs of the poor.

> The pain of starvation, from which the hungry die, is a horrible suffering. Of all human calamities, famine is the principal one, and the most miserable of deaths is no doubt that by starvation. In other kinds of death, either the sword puts a quick end to life, or the roaring fire burns out the sap of life in some instances, or the teeth of beasts,

mangling the vital limbs, would not prolong the torture. Hunger, however, is a slow torture which prolongs the pain; it is an infirmity well established and hidden in its place, a death always present and never coming to an end. It dries up the natural liquids, diminishes the body heat, contracts the size, and little by little drains off the strength. The flesh clings to the bones like a cobweb. The skin has no color. . . . Now, what punishment should not be inflicted upon the one who passes by such a body? What cruelty can surpass that? How can we not count him among the fiercest of fierce beasts and consider him as a sacrilegious person and a murderer? The person who can cure such an infirmity and because of avarice refuses his medicine, can with reason be condemned as a murderer.[79]

Frederick Norris observes that Basil's administrative skills and heart for justice helped to prevent even greater suffering during the famine: "By selling some of his own inheritance, dissuading many merchants who had sought to make a profit from the opportunity, and getting funds from the wealthy, he helped avert a serious disaster in Cappadocia."[80]

Basil gave short shrift to those who would undercut or downplay the rigorous life of the Christian disciple. Still, in his letters, we occasionally glimpse a person who can be open and honest about his own shortcomings and can even picture his frequent infirmities in a self-deprecating light. In a letter to Meletius, the court physician, Basil describes the illnesses that often interrupted the effectiveness of his ministry: "[C]ontinuous and violent fevers so wasted my body that there has seemed to be something thinner even than I—myself thinner than myself. . . . I am so weak that I do not at all in this respect fall short of a spider's web."[81]

Not only was Basil's health suffering, but winter had trapped him: "[E]very road is impassable to me, and every gust of the wind brings more danger than mighty waves do to sailors. Accordingly, I must hide myself in my bedroom and await the spring, if only we may be able to last until then."[82]

The closing line of the letter is particularly illuminating: "Only pray that our life may be ordered to the advantage of our soul." Here is the genuine Basil; without doubt he is suffering, but he does not find this surprising. The present moment is not the time for self-indulgence or soft living. Only Christians who have trained themselves to accept willingly what God offers them for the growth of their souls and the extension of his kingdom will genuinely discern the heart of the gospel and how it is to be lived in this present sojourn toward our true home.

This is a tough message from a tough man. Basil demanded much from those closest to him and from himself. He could be highhanded, occasionally needing the loving rebuke of a close friend such as Gregory of Nazianzus. In a tart letter Gregory calls Basil to account for losing a healthy sense of self-perspective.

> How hotly and like a colt you skip in your letters! It does not surprise me that you must display the glory you have recently acquired, to make yourself more august. But then, if you continue to show such ostentation and such vast ambition, discoursing to me condescendingly, like a great Metropolitan talking to someone of small moment, well, I too can oppose pride with pride. And this, of course, is in everyone's power, and is perhaps the most reasonable course to pursue.[83]

Basil's struggles with pride, though, are the hairline fractures in an indomitable will, a reservoir of determination and endurance sorely needed in the theological, ecclesiastical and cultural maelstrom of the late fourth century. In all likelihood only one such as Basil, a man with great strengths and self-evident weaknesses, could have withstood a theological perspective that had lost its compass and was in danger of spinning the church further into the morass of Arianism for decades to come.

Basil's achievements are remarkable: the establishment of significant monastic communities in Cappadocia; the development of a detailed monastic code for regulating community life, a monastic rule later to influence Benedict in the West; strong ecclesiastical leadership in an age of turmoil, disunity and confusion; finely tuned theological acumen and courage in defending the full deity of the Son and the Holy Spirit and in developing the implications of trinitarian doctrine. Basil accomplished this all within a life of fifty years.

Hermeneutical sampler. The clearest example we possess in English translation of Basil's exegesis and homiletical style is his *Hexaemeron*, a series of nine sermons he delivered on the six days of creation. He preached them during the Lenten season at both morning and evening services, but the exact date of the sermons is difficult to determine.[84]

Gregory of Nazianzus, Basil's close friend, deeply admired Basil's *Hexaemeron* for its clear portrayal of the wonder of creation and its Creator. "Whenever I handle his *Hexaemeron* and take its words on my lips, I am brought into the presence of the Creator, and understand the works of creation, and admire the Creator more than before, using my teacher as my only means of sight."[85]

One striking feature of Basil's exegesis is the emphatic rejection of allegory in his interpretation of the creation account. Of course, by rejecting allegory Basil casts doubt on the value of much of Origen's exegetical work. This is particularly surprising in light of Basil's admiration for Origen. What was Basil thinking? Earlier and with the help of Gregory of Nazianzus he had gathered a large collection of Origen's work into what he and Gregory called the "Philokalia." And yet when Basil begins to exegete and preach the opening chapters of Genesis, he casts allegory aside as a viable interpretive tool. Why?

In his ninth homily on the *Hexaemeron*, Basil penned what Jaroslav Pelikan describes as "one of the most vigorous criticisms of allegorical exegesis to come from any orthodox Christian theologian in the fourth (or any other) century."[86]

> I know the laws of allegory, though less by myself than from the works of others. There are those truly, who do not admit the common sense of the Scriptures, for whom water is not water, but some other nature, who see in a plant, in a fish, what their fancy wishes, who change the nature of reptiles and of wild beasts to suit their allegories, like the interpreters of dreams who explain visions in sleep to make them serve their own ends. For me grass is grass; plant, fish, wild beast, domestic animal, I take all in the literal sense.[87]

In an earlier sermon Basil had already critiqued those who attempted to interpret the separation of waters in Genesis 1:6 in an allegorical fashion. The allegorists had "launched out into metaphor" and seen in the waters only

> a figure to denote spiritual and incorporeal powers. In the higher regions, above the firmament, dwell the better; in the lower regions, earth and matter are the dwelling of the malignant. . . . So, say they, God is praised by the waters that are above the heaven, that is to say, by the good powers, the purity of whose soul makes them worthy to sing the praises of God. And the waters which are under the heaven represent the wicked spirits, who from their natural height have fallen into the abyss of evil.[88]

Basil diplomatically acknowledges this "theory as ingenious without being able to acknowledge the truth of it." As in the ninth sermon, he compares this kind of allegorization to a dream or "old women's tales." Instead, Basil insists "that by water water is meant."

Basil especially criticized the allegorist's lack of hermeneutical control and linked the desire to allegorize to a fundamental dissatisfaction with the Bible's plain meaning. God has clearly told us, Basil argued, what we need to know for spiritual growth, edification and sound theological knowledge. The desire to move beyond God's revealed clarity to a hidden meaning is a sign of spiritual malaise.

> Shall I not rather exalt Him who, not wishing to fill our minds with these vanities, has regulated all the economy of Scripture in view of the edification and the making perfect of our souls? It is this which those seem to me not to have understood, who, giving themselves up to the distorted meaning of allegory, have undertaken to give a majesty of their own invention to Scripture. It is to believe themselves wiser than the Holy Spirit, and to bring forth their own ideas under a pretext of exegesis.[89]

Groups such as the Manichees, Marcionites and Valentinians, Basil reminded his readers, employed allegory in their own interpretive distortions. While Genesis states that "darkness was upon the face of the deep," a darkness Basil describes as "meant in reality—air not illumined, the shadow produced by the interposition of a body, or finally a place for some reason deprived of light," the Manichee, Marcionite and Gnostic were quick to imagine a deeper meaning. "For them 'darkness' is an evil power, or rather the personification of evil, having his origin in himself in opposition to, or perpetual struggle with, the goodness of God."[90]

The much safer hermeneutical path, Basil insisted, is to remain silent "about these metaphors and allegories, and, simply following without vain curiosity the words of Holy Scripture, let us take from darkness the idea which it gives us."[91]

Basil linked the authority of the Genesis text to the movement of the Holy Spirit in Moses,[92] insisting that the words of the text are inspired: "there is not one idle syllable."[93] Thus, because the text itself is holy, derived from the work of the Holy Spirit, interpreters of the text must approach it with a reverent disposition. Whatever is said about the ideas of the text must match the exalted nature of its divine source.

How earnestly the soul should prepare itself to receive such high lessons! How pure it should be from carnal affections, how unclouded by worldly disquietudes, how active and ardent in its researches, how eager to find in its surroundings an idea of God which may be worthy of Him.[94]

In an interesting prelude to his third sermon in the series, Basil reinforces his earlier words about the condition of one's heart and its relation to the comprehension of spiritual truth. As he begins his sermon he notices that a number of local artisans have delayed their work in order to hear him speak. Basil praises them, commenting that the "time which you lend to God is not lost: he will return it to you with large interest." And even if the business hopes of his audience are not fulfilled, "the teachings of the Holy Spirit are none the less a rich treasure for the ages to come." To understand Scripture's words, though, Basil's listeners must let go of their worldly concerns: "Deliver your heart, then, from the care of this life and give close heed to my words. Of what avail will it be to you if you are here in the body, and your heart is anxious about your earthly treasure?"[95]

The Scripture will reveal its depth to "industrious hearers," people prepared to "examine what they have just heard." Hearing is not enough. What is heard must be chewed and digested if it is to bring lasting benefit. Here the role of memory is decisive. "May their memory retain it for the profit of their soul; may they by careful meditation inwardly digest and benefit by what I say."[96] In his fourth homily, Basil challenges his audience further: "Shall we, whom the Lord, the great worker of marvels, calls to the contemplation of His own works, tire of looking at them, or be slow to hear the words of the Holy Spirit?"[97] Basil insists that "it is absolutely necessary that all lovers of great and grand shows should bring a mind well prepared to study them."[98] There is no greater spectacle than God's creation, and the "well prepared auditor" will be ready to have her understanding raised from the visible wonders of God's creation "to the invisible Being."

Basil has effectively laid a three-stage foundation for his exegesis: First, he has insisted that Scripture comes from the Holy Spirit. It is divinely inspired. There are no unimportant aspects to the text. Second, Basil reiterates that a holy text must be approached reverently, with a well prepared mind and a heart receptive to the address of the text itself. Third, Basil rejects allegory as an appropriate hermeneutical strategy. The literal sense of the text will provide more than enough material for contemplation, insight and application.

Basil quite clearly delights in the opening chapters of Genesis. Think, he urges his listeners, of the implications of the opening of Genesis, "In the beginning . . ." If there is a beginning, Basil contends, time itself has a beginning. The heavens and the earth are not eternal but are created by a reasonable being who then elaborates and develops his creation. Perhaps most importantly, created existence is not "conceived by chance and without reason." Rather, the created world has a purposeful end. It is a kind of "school where reasonable souls exercise themselves, the training ground where they learn to know God."[99]

In the created world, God's school, we should not be surprised to find important lessons in the most unexpected places. Basil takes delight in comparing aspects of creation to God's redemptive work and new creation, sometimes more or less successfully. The ocean, for example, is declared by God to be a good thing. How might this good thing point to an even greater good creation of God? With a hermeneutical stretch Basil finds the church reflected in the ocean's rhythms.

> If the Ocean is good and worthy of praise before God, how much more beautiful is the assembly of a Church like this, where the voices of men, of children, and of women, arise in our prayers to God mingling and re-sounding like the waves which beat upon the shore. This Church also enjoys a profound calm, and malicious spirits cannot trouble it with the breath of heresy.[100]

Basil stretches the imagination of his audience perhaps too far for modern sensibilities. Yet Basil cannot help but discern connections between God's creation and all God's creative and redemptive activities. "I want creation to penetrate you with so much admiration that everywhere, wherever you may be, the least plant may bring to you the clear remembrance of the Creator."[101]

If so, God's creation of green plants should lead us to think of human nature, a connection Basil spots in the Scripture's prophetic literature. Had not Isaiah said much the same thing when he wrote that "all flesh is grass"? The short life span of a grass shoot is a warning to the wise listener:

> Truly the rapid flow of life, the short gratification and pleasure that an instant of happiness gives to a man, all wonderfully suit the comparison of the prophet. Today he is vigorous in body, fattened by luxury, and in the prime of life, with complexion fair, strong and powerful and of

irresistible energy; tomorrow and he will be an object of pity, withered by age or exhausted by sickness.[102]

What of the varied mixture of grains created by God? Since for Basil "you find nothing in nature contrary to the divine command," surely the "bastard grains that mix themselves with the harvest" are an image of a greater truth: "of those who alter the doctrine of the Lord and, not being rightly instructed in the word . . . mix themselves with the sound body of the Church."[103]

Why would God create the different aspects of the moon as the month waxes and wanes? Basil responds:

It presents a striking example of our nature. Nothing is stable in humanity. . . . Thus, the sight of the moon, making us think of the rapid vicissitudes of human things, ought to teach us not to pride ourselves on the good things of this life, and not to glory in our power, not to be carried away by uncertain riches. . . . If you cannot behold without sadness the moon losing its splendour by gradual and imperceptible decrease, how much more distressed should you be at the sight of a soul, who, after having possessed virtue, loses its beauty by neglect, and does not remain constant to its affections, but is agitated and constantly changes because its purposes are unstable.[104]

Perhaps to some readers Basil's applications seem quaint or far-fetched. He has already insisted, however, that there is a divine plan and pattern in creation directing the attentive observer to God. Basil prays that God might well help his audience to see in the moon and sun "a still higher idea of their Creator." When compared with God the sun and moon "are but a fly and ant." Indeed, the "whole universe cannot give us a right idea of the greatness of God." It contains and God employs, though, "signs, weak and slight in themselves, often by the help of the smallest insects and of the least plants [to] raise ourselves to Him."[105]

From grass and moon Basil moves to animal life to make the same types of applications. Some fish, he notes, feed on mud. Others eat the herbs and grass they find in water. Finally, some fish eat other fish! A larger fish will eat a smaller and in turn be devoured by one yet larger. Such a strange economy. And yet is human life any different?

[D]o we act otherwise when we oppress our inferiors? What difference is there between the last fish and the man who, impelled by devouring greed, swallows the weak in the folds of his insatiable avarice? That fellow possessed the goods of the poor; you caught him and made him a part of your abundance. You have shown yourself more unjust, and more miserly than the miser. Look to it lest you end like the fish, by hook, by weel, or by net.[106]

Despite lacking the powers that humans have to plan, reason and will accordingly, fish still demonstrate the ability to live within the boundaries and wisdom that God has given them. They know, for example, to run from danger and to hide when larger predators appear. How well do their human neighbors follow their example?

If beings deprived of reason are capable of thinking and of providing for their own preservation; if a fish knows what it ought to seek and what to shun, what shall we say, who are honoured with reason, instructed by law, encouraged by the promises, made wise by the Spirit, and are nevertheless less reasonable about our own affairs than the fish, [trapped as we are by our] brutal indulgence [and] idleness, the mother of all vices.[107]

Yes, even the unreasonable animals can illustrate the virtues and vices of humanity. What animal of the ocean, Basil asks, can match the rancor of the camel? "The camel conceals its resentment for a long time after it has been struck, until it finds an opportunity, and then repays the wrong." Are humans any different? "Listen, you whose heart does not pardon, you who practise vengeance as a virtue; see what you resemble when you keep your anger for so long against your neighbour like a spark, hidden in the ashes, and only waiting for fuel to set your heart ablaze!"[108]

Basil genuinely rejoices in the fruitfulness of Scripture as it provides him with a menagerie of virtues and vices by way of analogy rather than allegory. As he puts it, if the Scripture states, "Let the waters bring forth fowl that may fly above the earth," the discerning reader will "inquire into the meaning of these words." In this further inquiry the "great wonder of the Creator appears."[109]

A perfect illustration of Basil's methodology is the analogy he draws between the life cycle of the caterpillar-butterfly and Paul's teaching on the resurrection body. For most Greeks, the idea of a resurrected body made little sense philosophically, religiously or physically. How, many wondered, could a body that had decayed be raised from the dead? How could this type of change actually take place? The mechanics of resurrection seemed an impossibility. Basil responded by encouraging his listeners to observe more closely the many creatures, such as the caterpillar, who demonstrate this kind of metamorphosis in their life cycle. The lesser surely can illustrate the greater.[110]

Finally, the creation narrative culminates in the creation of humanity. Basil warned his listeners that their own creation might well be the most difficult to understand and appreciate.

> In truth the most difficult of sciences is to know one's self. Not only our eye, from which nothing outside us escapes, cannot see itself; but our mind, so piercing to discover the sins of others, is slow to recognise its own faults. Thus my speech, after eagerly investigating what is external to myself, is slow and hesitating in exploring my own nature. Yet the beholding of heaven and earth does not make us know God better than the attentive study of our being does.[111]

Basil quickly moves away from humanity and its tendency toward self-deception, though, to an analysis of the God who has created. Why does Genesis 1:26 ("Let us make humankind") use the second person plural? Basil is unequivocal in his insistence that here we have a reference to the Son, the second person of the Trinity.

Many modern scholars would question Basil's deduction, viewing instead the plural as one of majesty. However, Basil defends his exegesis on two counts: first, by noting the existence of the second person plural pronoun; second, by referencing the many times New Testament writers refer to Jesus or the Son as the image of the Father, the image of God.

> To Whom does He say, "in our image," if not to Him who is "the brightness of His glory and the express image of His person," "the image of the invisible God"? It is then to His living image, to Him Who has said "I and my Father are one," "He that has seen me has seen the Father," that God says "Let us make humankind in our image."[112]

Basil here illustrates a fundamental patristic hermeneutical principle. The old must be read and interpreted in light of the new. The narrative of Scripture is a continuum progressing to a culmination in Christ. As the texts of the old covenant are watered by the revelation the new covenant brings, they themselves blossom even more fully.

For further investigation. Examples of Basil's exegesis are peppered throughout his letters. Four volumes of Basil's letters have been translated by Roy J. Deferrari in the Loeb Classical Library. The Loeb series will be of special interest to students with knowledge of Greek, as the Greek text of Basil's letters is included with Deferrari's English translation.[113] Basil's letters are also available in the Nicene and Post-Nicene Fathers (NPNF), published by both Eerdmans and Hendrickson.[114] The NPNF edition is particularly helpful since it includes an index to biblical texts interpreted or referenced by Basil. The Catholic University of America Press also offers a translation of Basil's letters, although only one volume remains in print. Perhaps Basil's best known dogmatic work is his treatise on the Holy Spirit, available in both the NPNF and in an accessible, modern translation by David Anderson.[115] I have found Basil's *Hexaemeron* to be a delightful and insightful work, perhaps the clearest example of Basil's exegetical and hermeneutical methodology. It is available in English translation in the NPNF.

John Chrysostom (347-407)

With John Chrysostom, readers concerned over the allegorizing tendencies of some patristic exegetes will immediately feel more at home. John cut his exegetical teeth in Antioch. Biblical scholars and theologians trained at Antioch were extremely wary of allegory, though still interested in the "spiritual" meaning of biblical texts. As we will observe in some detail in chapter seven, Antiochene biblical interpreters such as Theodore of Mopsuestia launched scathing attacks against the dangers of allegorical interpretation and championed greater caution and modesty on the part of exegetes. John, a close friend of Theodore, also was extremely wary of the perils and pitfalls of allegorization. Fortunately, modern readers have ample opportunities to encounter John's exegesis, since many of his sermons are available in English translation.

John, nicknamed "golden-mouth" (Chrysostom) one hundred and fifty years after his death in exile, grew up like Augustine in a spiritually divided household.[116] His father Secundus was a Roman official and bore the title *Magister Militum Orientis*, probably indicating he was a high ranking officer in the Roman army stationed in the eastern Mediterranean.[117] Anthusa, Chrysostom's mother, was a strong Christian and only twenty when Secundus died; John was still an infant. From that point on she devoted herself to John, providing him with an excellent education, including training in rhetoric under the pagan rhetorician Libanius. For a time John toyed with the idea of becoming a lawyer, but became convinced that God had called him to the monastic life. Anthusa, though, was less than enthusiastic about John's decision.

My child, I was not for long permitted to enjoy your father's virtues, for so it pleased God. His death followed very soon after my travail over you, and left you an orphan and me a widow before my time, with all the burdens of widowhood, which only those who have borne them can properly understand. . . . Please do not think I am telling you this now as a reproach to you. But in return for all this I ask for just one favour: not to inflict on me a second bereavement and rouse again my sleeping grief. Be patient till my death. . . . When you have committed me to the ground and united me with your father's bones, then set out on your long travels and sail whatever sea you please.[118]

Despite Anthusa's request, the lure of monastic life in the mountains proved too strong for John. John was never one to do anything half-heartedly. For two years John lived a harsh ascetic life in the mountains above Antioch. Here he apparently took too literally the command to "be watchful." Robert Payne describes his life during this time:

He retired to a cave, denied himself sleep, read the Bible continually and spent two years without lying down, apparently in the belief that a Christian must stand in order to obey the injunction: "Be ye watchful." The result was inevitable. His stomach shriveled up, and his kidneys were damaged by cold. His digestion permanently impaired, unable to doctor himself, he came down the mountain, walked to Antioch and appeared before Archbishop Meletius, who immediately sent him to a doctor.[119]

John's descent to Antioch was the beginning of a series of significant changes that would ultimately lead to his appointment as bishop of Constantinople, one of the great sees, or ecclesiastical centers, of the church. Before John's move to Constantinople he served as deacon and then as presbyter in the church at Antioch, and in the latter role preached for a number of years, demonstrating an amazing ability to bring Scripture to life, both in its theological richness and practical implications. Johannes Quasten believes many of these sermons were delivered at Antioch between 386 and 397; they illustrate well the difference between Antiochene and Alexandrian exegesis. Quasten summarizes John's hermeneutical and homiletical skill in this way:

Always anxious to ascertain the literal sense and opposed to allegory, he combines great facility in discerning the spiritual meaning of the Scriptural text with an equal ability for immediate, practical application to the guidance of those committed to his care. The depth of his thought and the soundness of his masterful exposition are unique and attract even modern readers. He is equally at home in the books of the Old and the New Testament and has the skill to use even the former for the conditions of the present and the problems of daily life.[120]

Two of John's favorite metaphors for the Christian priest and bishop were that of the athletic trainer and the physician.[121] In John's well-known and well-loved work, *On the Priesthood*, he compares the Christian pastor to a physician, one who has "discovered a multiplicity of drugs and various designs of instruments and appropriate forms of diet for the sick." John notes, however, that occasionally a healthy climate or deep sleep makes intervention by a physician unnecessary. Not so with physicians of the word. The preacher must carefully diagnose the ills and needs of his congregation, faithfully applying the only efficacious remedy, "teaching by word of mouth."[122]

That is the best instrument, the best diet, and the best climate. It takes the place of medicine and cautery and surgery. When we need to cauterize or cut, we must use this. Without it all else is useless. By it we rouse the soul's lethargy or reduce its inflammation, we remove excrescences and supply defects, and, in short, do everything which contributes to its health. . . . We must take great care, therefore, that the word of Christ may dwell in us richly. For our preparation is not against a single kind of attack. . . . Unless the man who means to win understands every aspect of the art, the devil knows how to introduce his agents at a single neglected spot and so to plunder the flock. But he is baffled when he sees that the shepherd has mastered his whole repertoire and thoroughly understands his tricks.[123]

Chrysostom proceeds to praise particularly the epistles of Paul, both as shields against false doctrine and as reservoirs of wisdom for sound living. Indeed, in light of John's ability to interpret Paul well, other fathers saw the two as soul mates. In commenting on Chrysostom's exegesis, Isidore of Pelusium writes that John's wisdom is particularly evident in his exposition of Paul's letter to the Romans. "I think (and it cannot be said that I write to flatter any one) that if the divine Paul wished to expound in the Attic tongue his own writings he would not have spoken otherwise than this famous master; so remarkable is the latter's exposition for its contents, its beauty of form, and propriety of expression."[124]

For Chrysostom, solid doctrine and sound living remained an inseparable whole. What we know must deeply affect how we live. If not, the truth of the gospel is short-circuited and the watching world perceives a skewed picture of the gospel's reality. Chrysostom views Paul, above all others, as the expert at fusing knowledge and life.

> For his writings fortify the churches all over the world like a wall of steel. Even now he stands among us like some noble champion, bringing into captivity every thought to the obedience of Christ and casting down imaginations and every high thing that is exalted against the knowledge of God. All this he does by means of those wonderful Epistles he has left us, so full of divine wisdom. His writings are not only useful to us for the refutation of false doctrine and the establishment of the true, but they help us very greatly, too, in living a good life.... Such is the quality and such the strength of the medicines left us by this man who was inexpert at speaking! Those who use them constantly know their worth.[125]

John drives home the importance of studying the Scriptures in his ninth homily on Paul's letter to the Colossians:

> Listen carefully to me, I entreat you.... [P]rocure books that will be medicines for the soul.... At least get a copy of the New Testament, the Apostle's epistles, the Acts, the Gospels, for your constant teachers. If you encounter grief, dive into them as into a chest of medicines; take from them comfort for your trouble, whether it be loss, or death, or bereavement over the loss of relations. Don't simply dive into them. Swim in them. Keep them constantly in your mind. The cause of all evils is the failure to know the Scriptures well.[126]

Chrysostom's own immersion in Scripture was to serve him well at the end of his life. A tangled web of personal, political and religious factors combined to result in John's expulsion from Constantinople on the order of the Emperor Arcadius in 404. The next three years, leading to his death in 407, were spent in extremely harsh and isolated living conditions in the small town of Cucusus, high in the mountains of Armenia. Here, as John's earthly pilgrimage moved toward its conclusion, years of reflection, exegesis and preaching bore fruit in John's own life.

Hermeneutical sampler. During these last years John wrote a final work titled *On the Providence of God*, an extended biblical, theological and devotional exploration of suffering in the life of the faithful Christian.[127] This treatise illustrates vividly how John read the Bible and applied its teaching to his own suffering.

John addresses the work to his congregation in Constantinople, "those troubled by the lawless deeds of recent days, that is, the pursuit and hoodwinking of the laity and many priests."[128] Chrysostom worries that his flock in Constantinople will be swept off their feet by his own trials and sufferings. To avoid this spiritual disaster, John proceeds to analyze in great detail how God's providential care encompasses even the very worst scenarios life has to offer. His methodology is to prepare "the medicine of the word [that] nourishes more than bread, restores more effectively than a drug and cauterizes more powerfully than fire without causing any pain. . . . Sharper than iron, it painlessly cuts away the infected areas without causing any expenditure of money or deepening one's poverty."[129]

Space allows for only a brief consideration of how Chrysostom used the Bible to illustrate his central considerations. John repeatedly asserted that though one may suffer as a human being and as a Christian, the only lasting harm results from sin itself. Think, he reminds his readers, of the many biblical characters who suffered unjustly, unexpectedly and inexplicably.

Abel is murdered by his brother. Jacob lives in hunger as an exile. Joseph suffers as a slave and prisoner, the victim of terrible slander. Moses endures the continual rebellion and rejection of Israel. The devil attacks Job with his myriad devices. The exile of Israel in Babylon exposes Shadrach, Meshach, Abednego, and Daniel to countless dangers. Elijah lives in dire poverty as a fugitive and wanderer. David suffers at the hand of Saul and later is attacked by his own son. Herod beheads John the Baptist.[130]

And yet, Chrysostom asks, were any of these biblical characters forever harmed by their sufferings? Intense suffering marks the life of each, but they all escape enduring harm. The martyrs of the church illustrate the same truth. "In what way," John asks, "were the martyrs harmed, whose souls were broken by the most severe tortures? Didn't they all shine most brightly at the very moment they were abused, at the time others set traps for them, when they nobly stood firm while suffering the worst agonies?"[131] Chrysostom consistently argues that the gospel of Christ has effectively sucked the poison out of the Christian's suffering. The realities God has introduced into the world through Christ have conquered harm as a continuing, unjust, unrighteous reality, a permanent source of lasting damage to the Christian. Suffering overcomes harm, John contends, through the cross of Christ.

Whether we are lastingly harmed by the sufferings we encounter in this life, then, depends upon our proper response to them in light of both *what* Christ has accomplished on our behalf and *how* he conducted and completed his work. Has the Christian's perspective, his disposition before the events of this life, been deeply shaped by Christ's cross? In his homilies on the Pastoral Epistles John writes, "For it rests with us either to profit, or to be injured, by affliction. It depends not on the nature of the affliction, but upon the disposition of our own minds."[132]

John did not underestimate or flippantly disregard the reality of human pain and suffering. He knew full well that suffering entailed genuine pain and sorrow and never tried to disguise or downplay that fact. In his letters to Olympias, a close friend also condemned to exile, he writes of his own suffering in Cucusus:

> For the winter, which has become more than commonly severe, brought on a storm of internal disorder even more distressing, and during the last two months I have been no better than one dead, no worse. . . . I spent all my time closely confined to my bed, and in spite of endless contrivances I could not shake off the pernicious effects of the cold; but although I kept a fire burning, and endured a most unpleasant amount of smoke, and remained cooped up in one chamber, covered with any quantity of wraps, and not daring to set a foot outside the threshold I underwent extreme sufferings, perpetual vomiting following headache, loss of appetite, and constant sleeplessness.[133]

Not only is John fully cognizant of the genuiness and validity of his own sufferings, but he is diligent to counsel Olympias to take care of her own health because of the oppressive nature of sickness and its tendency to sap away spiritual strength.

> So I beg you dear lady, and entreat you as a very great favour to pay great attention to the restoration of your bodily health. For dejection causes sickness; and when the body is exhausted and enfeebled, and remains in a neglected condition, deprived of the assistance of physicians, and of a wholesome climate, and an abundant supply of the necessities of life, consider how great an aggravation or distress this causes.[134]

Chrysostom's correspondence with Olympias demonstrates well his awareness of the frailty of the human condition and his sensitivity to the intimate relationship between physical and spiritual well-being.[135] We see the same insight in his counsel to those who are grieving. On the one hand, John does not hesitate to speak of the valuable lessons that can be learned from death and the attitude of faith a Christian should exercise when death occurs.

You were born a human being, and mortal; why then do you grieve that what is natural has come to pass? Do you grieve when you are nourished by eating? Do you seek to live without this? Act in the same way in the case of death, and being mortal don't seek for immortality. This has been appointed once for all. Therefore, don't grieve, nor play the mourner, but submit to laws laid on all alike.[136]

On the other hand, John is deeply aware of the pain that the separation of death produces for those left behind and recognizes this sorrow as a fitting and natural human response. In his homilies on 1 Corinthians, for example, John aptly balances both sides of the question in his discussion of Job's grief over the loss of his children. Job was "a father and a loving father; and it was appropriate that . . . the compassion of his nature should be shown." Self-control with no demonstration of genuine compassion and grief over the loss of his children could too easily be interpreted as "mere insensibility. Therefore he indicates both his natural affection and the exactness of his piety, and in his grief he was not overthrown."[137] Chrysostom rightly argues that even in our grief our minds are to recall the truths of the gospel, but also acknowledges that tears are more than appropriate, both for those who have suffered loss and for those who rightly identify with their grief.

John emphasizes the importance of identifying with those in sorrow in his homilies on Romans. "For there is nothing that ties love so firmly as sharing both joy and pain with one another. Do not then, because you are far from difficulties yourself, remain aloof from sympathizing too."[138] John reinforces this thought in his homilies on the Acts of the Apostles. "Let us have a soul apt to sympathize, let us have a heart that knows how to feel with others in their sorrows: no unmerciful temper, no inhumanity. Though you can offer no relief, yet still weep, groan, grieve over what has happened."[139]

As John mulls over the Scriptures, he draws the important distinction between suffering and harmful suffering. All Christians can expect to suffer. In fact, Christianity and suffering go hand in hand. But as a person absorbs the realities of the gospel any lasting, harmful effects of suffering are gracefully erased. The growth of the soul results.

This is our life, that is, the natural consequence of an apostolic way of life is to suffer countless evils. . . . [S]o the apostolic life is purposely designed to suffer abuse, to suffer evils, to never have a respite, to never have a cessation of hostilities. And for however many are vigilant, they are not only not harmed by these events, but instead profit from them.[140]

Harmful suffering only occurs in the lives of those who consider indifferent matters as true evils, or who willfully transgress God's moral order. That is to say, for Chrysostom, sin and genuine harm are intrinsically connected. A key example of this dynamic is Herod Antipas, the ruler responsible for the unjust execution of John the Baptist. Even though John the Baptist is beheaded, it is Herod who reaps the bitter harvest of sin. Chrysostom invites his readers to imagine the nature of Herod's sufferings as he was reproved for his sins by the prisoner John. Immediately after John's execution Herod's conscience is troubled "to such an extent that he believed John had been raised from the dead and was performing miracles."[141] In the final outcome Herod is reproved for all eternity, while John is crowned for his faithfulness. "Therefore, do not say: 'Why was John allowed to die?' For what occurred was not a death, but a crown, not an end, but the beginning of a greater life."[142]

As John pondered the Bible, he increasingly understood that in light of the cross evil and sin could never be the last word for the one who had embraced Christ. Instead, it is how one perceives the cross that makes all the difference. Think, John exhorts his readers, of the thief crucified with Jesus who believes in Christ during the last moments of his life. Both the thief and the crowd surrounding the cross see the same events taking place. And yet it is only the crowd who stumbles over the cross. The thief witnesses the very same event and yet responds in an entirely different manner. "Indeed, the thief on the cross condemns these kinds of people; for he saw Christ crucified and not only did not stumble in his faith, but in the event of the crucifixion received a greater reason to think like a Christian."[143]

What were the significant elements that framed the thief's discerning response to the cross? First, John responds, the thief was willing to move beyond human speculations. That is, the thief was willing to bridle the temptation to comprehend the ineffable. Second, the thief's incipient faith enabled him to move beyond the immediate situation. Broader considerations, including hope for the future, determined his present response to the apparent defeat and death of the Son. As John puts it, "[H]e was lifted up by the wings of faith, and meditated on the things of the future."[144] His attentive and submissive disposition before God's mysterious actions enabled him to perceive the situation correctly. The crowd, by way of comparison, are "senseless and negligent" and miss the wonder and benefit of the cross. Their observations are based on appearances. They remain unable to see beneath the surface to the deeper meaning of events. The event of the cross only opens itself to persons able to perceive God's act in that desolate place. One's spiritually attentive eyes and ears make all the difference.

Thus, the Scriptures become the interpretive grid John employs to understand his own situation in exile. He exhorts his flock in Constantinople and no doubt himself to learn "to think and live like a Christian." If they do so, the harm in the untoward events that have crossed John's path will be sidestepped and the greatest benefits will occur. John unfailingly insists that it is our human response—a response governed by a disposition formed by the Holy Spirit as individuals accept the truths of the gospel and incorporate them into their lives—that is the central determinant in the question of good and evil. In contrast, those who are "worldly, difficult to lead, self-willed, and utterly carnal," will continually misread God's providence because they lack the eyes to see him at work, a vision that only comes to those who are actively exercising faith by allowing their perspective to be shaped by the gospel and acting accordingly. The wise interpretation of Scripture and of life, in John's thinking, are inseparable.

For further investigation. Of all the church fathers other than Augustine, John's exegesis is the most intelligible, accessible and available to modern readers. As Johannes Quasten notes, "Among the Greek fathers none has left so extensive a literary legacy as Chrysostom."[145] We now possess in English translation 90 homilies on the Gospel of Matthew, 55 sermons on Acts, 32 homilies on Romans, 44 sermons on 1 and 2 Corinthians, 24 homilies on Ephesians, 15 on Philippians, 12 on Colossians, 18 on 1 Timothy, 34 on Hebrews, and a commentary on Galatians. Unfortunately, almost all of these works were translated in the nineteenth century and need at least to be reworked for a modern reader's eye and ear. All are available in the Nicene and Post-Nicene Fathers series published by Eerdmans and Hendrickson. The Fathers of the Church series has devoted two volumes to eighty-eight of Chrysostom's homilies on John. The archaic language of older translations has been modernized in the passages included in the Ancient Christian Commentary on Scripture series, edited by Thomas Oden and published by InterVarsity Press.

F I V E

THE FOUR DOCTORS
OF THE WEST

Ambrose, Jerome,
Augustine & Gregory the Great

THE FOUR LATIN DOCTORS REPRESENT AN EXEGETICAL TRADITION
noted for its variety and richness. Latin exegetes such as Jerome and Ambrose
mirror the Alexandrian tradition's reliance upon allegory in making sense of
biblical texts. Jerome, whom Gerald Bray describes as "undoubtedly the
greatest biblical scholar that the Latin church ever produced," was initially
attracted to the allegorical method of Origen, although later he severely
criticized it.[1] Ambrose was Augustine's first instructor in the Scriptures and
taught the allegorical interpretive methodology to Augustine. Augustine, in
turn, interpreted Scripture in both a literal and allegorical fashion. Gregory
the Great, one of the great pastors in the church's history, is similar to
Ambrose in his love for discerning a deeper allegorical meaning in the text of
Scripture. While all four of the Latin doctors used the allegorical method of
interpretation at least to some degree, their exegetical tradition is not easy to
categorize, as we will see in this chapter.

Ambrose (337/339-397)

Ambrose was born into a Roman family already graced with a distinguished Christian and Roman lineage. He was, as Robert Payne writes, "Born to the purple . . . continued to live in the purple throughout his life, and long before his death he was regarded as a saint, so wearing the purple for eternity."[2] Quite possibly the virgin martyr Sotheris, a victim of the Diocletian persecution, was a relative. Ambrose's father died when Ambrose was still quite young, and Ambrose grew up in Rome with his mother, two brothers and a sister. Information concerning Ambrose's childhood and adolescence is relatively sparse. The Roman government appointed Ambrose at the age of thirty-six as governor of the northern Italian province of Aemilia-Liguria. His responsibilities included maintaining the peace in the city of Milan. Charles Kannengiesser comments on Ambrose's Roman heritage:

> While formally enrolled as a catechumen, he remained true to his Christian family heritage but did not become involved in any theological dispute. His training prepared him for public service. His taste inclined him to prefer the Greek authors, old poets, and classical historians, as well as more recent authors. Of course, he knew Virgil and Cicero by heart. A son of wealthy landowners, eager to assimilate the humanistic traditions patronized by the Neoplatonic philosophers of his time, Ambrose is seen as one of the last Romans gifted with complete acquaintance with Greek culture.[3]

This cultural and linguistic background proved quite handy when Ambrose's career path suddenly changed, and he found himself chosen to replace the Arian bishop Auxentius as bishop of Milan. Ambrose's exposure to Greek philosophers such as Philo and Plotinus, together with his knowledge of Greek fathers such as Basil, would clearly influence how Ambrose interpreted the Bible. But why the sudden career change from Roman governor to bishop?

Auxentius had died, and the man who would replace him mattered greatly to both the Arian party (people who denied Jesus' divinity but affirmed him as an exalted creature) and to those who contended that Jesus was fully divine. The theological debate in Milan had heated to the extent that public order was endangered. In his role as provincial governor Ambrose intervened. Although Ambrose was strongly opposed to the Arian position and remained so for his entire life, both Arians and non-Arians were united in calling him to replace Auxentius as bishop. Possibly this unanimous affirmation of Ambrose can be traced to his reputation for fairness and impartiality in his role within the Roman government.[4] Standing only five feet four inches tall, Ambrose was physically unimpressive. The strength of his personality and faith, however, was soon to exert itself.

Ambrose resisted the call to Christian ministry, feeling better suited for a monastic life of solitude and prayer. After all, Ambrose had little formal training for Christian leadership and had yet to be baptized. The Christian community in Milan disagreed. Within one week he was baptized and consecrated as bishop. There was much to learn. Ambrose was later to reflect that he became an exegete by becoming, "despite himself," a bishop.[5]

Bertrand de Margerie observes, though, that Ambrose's background, at least in a generic sense, had prepared him well for the Christian ministry of the exegete, including "his knowledge of Greek—rare at that time—his habit (gained in school) of learning by heart, his exegetical aptitude resulting from the practice of reading and interpreting the literal and allegorical sense of a poetic text (Homer and Virgil) and above all its moral meaning."[6]

Under the guidance of Simplicianus, a presbyter in the church at Milan who would later succeed Ambrose as bishop, Ambrose began an intense study of the Scriptures, a discipline he would practice and model for the rest of his life. Augustine mentions this same Simplicianus in his *Confessions*, describing him as the spiritual father of Ambrose. Ambrose, Augustine comments, loved Simplicianus "like a father, for it was through him that he had received your grace."[7]

In turn, it was the preaching of Ambrose that touched Augustine in the midst of his own deep spiritual struggle. With great fondness Augustine described Ambrose as "known throughout the world as a man whom there were few to equal in goodness." Augustine was convinced that it was God who had led him to Ambrose, "so that I might knowingly be led by him to you." Ambrose welcomed Augustine "like a father and, as bishop, told me how glad he was that I had come."[8] Interestingly, it was not Ambrose's ideas that first attracted Augustine, but his character. "My heart warmed to him, not at first as a teacher of the truth, which I had quite despaired of finding in your Church, but simply as a man who showed me kindness."[9]

Ambrose's character, though, would not have been enough to convince Augustine to become a Christian. Rather, Ambrose read the Bible in such a way that the Scriptures became accessible to Augustine. For years Augustine had been repelled by the Bible's narrative, largely because portions of Scripture, especially in the Old Testament, seemed to him to present an unworthy picture of God. Ambrose helped Augustine to read the Bible in a new way, arguing that any biblical text possessed three senses—the literal, moral, and anagogical or mystical. The possibility that the Bible might have a deeper meaning encased or layered within its literal sense dissipated Augustine's despair over ever making sense of it.

> I began to believe that the Catholic faith, which I had thought impossible to defend against the objections of the Manichees, might fairly be maintained, especially since I had heard one passage after another in the Old Testament figuratively explained. These passages had been death to me when I took them literally, but once I had heard them explained in their spiritual meaning I began to blame myself for my despair, at least in so far as it had led me to suppose that it was quite impossible to counter people who hated and derided the law and the prophets. . . . I was glad too that at last I had been shown how to interpret the ancient Scriptures of the law and the prophets in a different light from that which had previously made them seem absurd, when I used to criticize your saints for holding beliefs which they had never really held at all. I was pleased to hear that in his sermons to the people Ambrose often repeated the text: *The written law inflicts death, whereas the spiritual law brings life.*[10]

It is important to note that the comments of Ambrose and Augustine concerning the "literal" meaning of a biblical text were made in response to Christian interpreters who disregarded common literary devices such as metaphor and insisted on interpreting the Old Testament in an extremely wooden, often corporeal sense. Too many in Ambrose's own congregation considered exegesis a "spontaneous, immediate, and unconsidered" exercise. Various "errors and absurdities" were the result. Ambrose did not ignore the literal sense of the text, "but in many cases called the spiritual sense what we would consider to be the figurative literal sense."[11]

In chapter six we will explore in greater detail Ambrose's hermeneutical methodology, a way of reading the Bible rooted in Hellenistic philosophy and practiced by many Christian theologians, particularly in the city of Alexandria in Egypt. Other church fathers seriously questioned the viability and usefulness of Alexandrian exegesis and this debate will warrant our close scrutiny. For the moment, though, a few examples of Ambrose's exegetical method and its results will have to suffice.

Hermeneutical sampler. Ambrose's many letters to emperors, bishops and priests are a treasure trove of resources for examining how he read Scripture and how he felt it should be preached. In Ambrose's letter to the bishop Constantius (before Lent A.D. 379) he describes Scripture as a "sea . . . which has within it profound meanings and the mysterious depths of the Prophets. Into this sea many rivers have entered. Delightful and clear are these streams; these fountains are cool, springing up into life everlasting."[12]

The image of water unlocks a stream of connections in Ambrose's mind as to the value of Scripture, both the importance of wrapping one's mind and heart around it and the choice of words used to preach its meaning effectively. If one drinks the water of Scripture, Ambrose teaches, one will become a cloud, shedding refreshing dew on the dry earth. Thus, Ambrose guides Constantius, "[F]ill the center of your mind so as to have your plot of land moistened and watered by fountains from the family estate. Accordingly, he who reads much and also understands is filled; he who has been filled sheds water upon others."[13]

This water will only nourish Constantius's audience if it is presented to them "in a clear and lucid manner." Hence, the importance of protecting the sermon with "its own weapons." Not one word should "go forth without meaning." Why? Speech "is a bandage which ties up the wounds of souls." Many who come to church will be "vexed by a serious sore." They will only hear if "the oil of speech" softens their hardened hearts. "[A]pply a poultice," Ambrose exhorts Constantius, "put on a bandage of salutary advice."[14]

The salutary advice Ambrose so eagerly wants to deliver to his flock often centers on the moral sense of Scripture. In a letter to the priest Horontianus (spring A.D. 387) Ambrose develops both the moral and mystical sense of the creation of the world in six days. Why did God create the world in six days and not immediately, "since a moment suffices for Him to do what He wishes"? God took six days because God is a God of order and creation itself demands order. "[T]hings which are made require an order and order generally requires both time and number."

Ambrose then quickly springs to the moral wisdom the text contains. God's creation of the world in six days gives us a pattern for our own work. "He observed a number of days and seasons. We, too, need time to do something well, so as not to hurry our plans and works, or fail to keep a proper order."[15] Finally, since God rested on the seventh day, Ambrose explores the possible links the number seven might have on a mystical or allegorical level.

Ambrose's interest in discerning a mystical or allegorical meaning in the biblical text is surely the aspect of his hermeneutics that many modern interpreters will find most troubling. The lack of hermeneutical control in allegorical interpretation seems to lay the biblical text wide open for subjective whimsy. When Ezekiel speaks of the outer gate of the sanctuary, for example, is he referring to the Virgin Mary as Ambrose argues?

> What is that gate of the sanctuary, that outer gate facing the East and remaining closed: 'And no man,' it says, 'shall pass through it except the God of Israel'? Is not Mary the gate through whom the Redeemer entered this world? . . . Holy Mary is the gate of which it is written: 'The Lord will pass through it, and it will be shut,' after birth, for as a virgin she conceived and gave birth.[16]

Many modern scholars might demur from Ambrose's judgment. Yet Ambrose would insist it was perfectly legitimate to read Scripture through the lens of its overarching narrative. After all, Jesus himself had taught that the law and the prophets spoke of him (cf. Lk 24:25-27). But, we may ask, how did they speak of him? Ambrose, like many fathers in the Alexandrian tradition, believed that behind the literal shell of a biblical text lay enclosed a deeper meaning, a message to be discerned through the Holy Spirit and in line with the central biblical narrative centered on God's work in Christ. Why, Ambrose would ask, should we find it surprising to find Ezekiel speaking in a veiled way of Mary if he is speaking prophetically through the Spirit?

The problem allegorical interpretation poses, among others, is how one is to discern and interpret this deeper meaning without being enveloped in hermeneutical subjectivism. Ambrose trusted that the biblical narrative itself supplied a brake on interpretive fancy. Consider his exegesis of the creation accounts and birth narratives of Genesis 2 and 4. Eve is created from Adam's rib and in turn becomes the mother of Cain and Abel. Ambrose reads these texts in light of Christ's incarnation and redemptive work, and also sees them as relevant for understanding the nature of Christ's body, the church. Why did Eve have children after the Fall? How was Eve's childbearing related to Christ's redemptive work? Ambrose consciously reads the Genesis account in the light of Paul:

> God preferred the existence of more than one whom He would be able to save rather than having just one man who was free from error. Inasmuch as He is the Author of both man and woman, He came into this world to

redeem sinners. Finally, He did not permit Cain . . . to perish before he brought forth sons. . . . [Eve, who] was the one destined to bring forth redemption . . . was deceived. . . . Yet [she, we are told] 'will be saved by childbearing' [1 Tim. 2:13-15], in which she generated Christ.[17]
Paul's teaching in Ephesians 5:32 also seems to be in Ambrose's thinking: "This is a profound mystery, but I am talking about Christ and the church" (NIV). Ambrose reads this passage of Paul in the light of Genesis 2:24. He understands Paul as seeing "Christ in Adam and the Church in Eve. The Church had therefore, in a way, sinned in Eve. However, Eve, (who represents the Church) was saved by generating Christ through Mary."[18]

This type of christological/ecclesiological interpretation occurs frequently among the fathers, precisely because they read the entire biblical narrative in light of its fulfillment in Christ.

For further investigation. A number of Ambrose's works are available in English translation, although the translations vary in quality. Perhaps the best way to start exploring Ambrose is by immersing oneself in Ambrose's *Letters*, volume 26 of The Fathers of the Church series by The Catholic University of America. Ambrose's colorful personality ripples through his correspondence. His letters introduce central characters, theological issues and, most importantly, how Ambrose reads the Bible. Volume 10 of the Nicene and Post-Nicene Fathers is devoted to select works and letters of Ambrose.[19] The English translations in the NPNF tend to be staid and fairly bumpy, but readers motivated to explore Ambrose further will find significant pastoral and theological treatises. Ambrose's ethical perspective is well represented in a fine modern translation of *The Duties of the Clergy* by Jan L. Womer in the Sources of Early Christian Thought series published by Fortress Press.[20] In the same series Ambrose's spirituality is illustrated in his treatise "Concerning Virgins," introduced and translated by Charles Kannengiesser.[21]

Ambrose's biblical exegesis is most clearly expressed in his commentary on Luke, the major commentary we have from his pen. Unfortunately, it has yet to be translated into English. The Ancient Christian Commentary on Scripture will present selections from this previously untranslated material.

Jerome (347-419/420)
Early Christians took their exegesis, theology and spirituality with great seriousness, and none more so than Jerome. In Jerome we find the

strengths and weaknesses of early Christianity embodied in dramatic form. Throughout his life he struggled to control an innate irascibility and extreme sensitivity. He was quick to take offense and to lash out fiercely at opposing positions and persons. He, like many of us, too closely identified his understanding of Scripture and theology with his own self-identity. To attack Jerome's opinion was to attack Jerome.

Robert Payne pictures Jerome as "tender and violent, gentle and rude, viciously proud and childishly humble, a man of deep hates and morbid passions whose brain was nevertheless permanently clear. He was a tissue of contradictions, and he seems to have been perfectly aware of it himself."[22] An example of his cruel side is his mean-spirited attack upon the priest Onasus. Jerome pokes fun at his name, misshapen nose and speech impediment. After penning a hurtful limerick concerning Onasus's appearance, Jerome comments cruelly, "Oh, cover your nose and shut your mouth: that is the best thing for you."[23]

This same Jerome could be remarkably gentle, particularly with children. In a letter written to a friend he offers advice for helping his daughter to learn the alphabet:

Have letters made for her, of box-wood or ivory, and let them be called by their names. Let her play with them, and let the play be part of her instruction. It is not only needful that she should place the letters in their right order, and put them to memory by singing their names, but sometimes she should mix the letters up, putting the last in the middle and the middle first: in this way you will know whether she has learned them by sight as well as by hearing. . . . Give her some little present, something acceptable to her tender age, as soon as she has learned to join letters and syllables together. . . . Do not scold her if she is slow. Arouse her ambition by praise. Let her desire victory; let her be pained by defeat. Above all, never let her hate her studies, otherwise the bitterness learned in childhood may last until she is of mature years. . . . No really learned man would blush to serve a child. . . . We should not despise the little ones, for without them great things cannot come to pass.[24]

Jerome's life is a wondrous example of God's grace working through human ambiguities. He struggled with his jagged personality all his life. He hurt many people willfully and unnecessarily. Yet tremendous intellectual gifts and spiritual insights percolated through his manifest weaknesses. In modern terms, Jerome displayed a finely tuned mind, a warm but troubled heart, and poor people skills!

Jerome is generally reckoned to be the finest scholar among the fathers. Between 360 and 367, when Jerome was in his early to late teens, he underwent a rigorous course of studies in Rome. Jerome studied the classics, in particular Virgil and Cicero. Later he would learn Greek and Hebrew, becoming truly, as he liked to put it, "trilinguis, Hebraeus, Graecus, Latinus."[25] Indeed, Jerome was the only church father who knew Hebrew well.[26] Jerome's linguistic skills and knack at translation manifested themselves later in his many translation projects, including his well-known translation of the Hebrew scriptures and sections of the Greek New Testament into Latin, later to be known as the Vulgate. Jean Gribomont praises Jerome's skill and the lasting influence of his translation:

> Jerome manifests a much surer taste than in the affectation of his letters or the animation of his polemics. On the one hand, the greatness of the inspired author can be felt through Jerome's translation, while on the other, fifteen centuries of prayer and reading have conferred on the text a certain patina like unto a venerable paleochristian basilica; it has enjoyed an authority over the arts and languages throughout the West. The very fact that the text has lived through so many ages is not one of the least elements of its beauty. The agility of the pen, though always mindful to the fidelity due to obscure oracles, nevertheless assured that the majesty of the subject did not dampen the liveliness and spontaneity of the text.[27]

How can a modern Christian best connect with the thought of Jerome? Because of the roughness of Jerome's personality, one must look beyond his occasional ill temper, mean-spiritedness and self-absorption to the insights erupting from a heart on fire for God. Jerome struggled, for example, with learning how to live between two worlds, the kingdom of this world and the kingdom of God—a struggle shared by many Christians living in the late twentieth century. What should the modern Christian's response be to the surrounding culture? Rejection? Embrace? Neutrality? How can one be in the world and yet not of the world? What should one read? What should one avoid for the sake of spiritual health? Can modern film harm or help us? Which films? Can one be a well-educated Christian while simultaneously living in a Christian ghetto, unfamiliar with literary, social, educational, political and entertainment trends? The list of questions seems to extend itself immeasurably.

In a famous letter written to Eustochium, the daughter of his close friend Paula, we find Jerome struggling with similar issues, but within his own cultural context. His love-hate relationship with secular writers such as Cicero and Virgil is quite evident. On the one hand, Jerome tells Eustochium that many years ago he had left family and friends "to be a soldier of Christ" in Jerusalem.[28] On the other hand, he admits,

> I could not do without the library which I had collected for myself at Rome by great care and effort. And so, poor wretch that I was, I used to fast and then read Cicero. After frequent night vigils, after shedding tears which the remembrance of past sins brought forth from my inmost heart, I would take in my hands a volume of Plautus. When I came to myself and began to read a prophet again, I rebelled at the uncouth style and—because with my blinded eyes I could not look upon the light—I thought this fault not of my eyes but of the sun.[29]

In the midst of this struggle Jerome fell ill and in his feverish state dreamed that he was standing before the judgment seat of Christ. Christ asked him his status. Jerome replied that he was a Christian. "And He who sat upon the judgment seat said: 'Thou liest. Thou art a Ciceronian, not a Christian. *Where thy treasure is, there is thy heart also.*' I was struck dumb on the spot."[30] Jerome begged for and received mercy, provided that he never read again "books of pagan literature."

Scholars are divided as to whether Jerome was able to fulfill this promise. Allusions to pagan authors fill his writing, perhaps creeping uninvited to the surface of a mind soaked in their thought. We might well argue that Jerome's writing is that much richer because of his conscious or unconscious willingness to interact with the best writers his culture had to offer. And what of our situation in the modern world? Relating our experience to that of Jerome can open up new avenues of insight into the call to discipleship in the late twentieth century.

Hermeneutical sampler. Jerome can also help us in other ways. His thoughts on the Scriptures are always thoughtful, reverent and at times fanciful. As Jerome reads the Bible in his world he helps us to discern its meaning in ours, both in our agreement with his exegesis and in our disagreement. For example, in light of modern questions about language, gender and theology, Jerome can help us—despite his own ambivalent attitudes toward women.

I never cease to be surprised at how often students at the college where I teach are unsure about the question of gender and God, particularly within God's own essence. When I ask them if God is male, many are clearly not sure. After all, do we not address God as Father? Do we not continually encounter the personal pronoun "he" in referring to God? Consider Jerome's response.

It is inconceivable that sex exists among God's agencies, since even the Holy Spirit, in accordance with the usages of the Hebrew tongue, is expressed in the feminine gender, *ruach*, in Greek in the neuter, *to pneuma*, in Latin in the masculine, *spiritus*. Hence we must understand that when there is discussion concerning the above and something is set down in the masculine or feminine, it is not so much an indication of sex as an expression of the idiom of the language; because God Himself, the invisible and incorruptible, is represented in almost all languages in the masculine gender, and since sex does not apply to Him.[31]

How about the grace of God? When Paul begins a letter with the salutation "grace and peace" what does he mean? Grace and peace, Jerome reminds Pope Damasus, sum up the heart of Christ's salvific work on the cross.

[G]race, which is not a payment due to merit, but has been granted as a gift; and peace, whereby we have been reconciled to God, having as propitiator the Lord Jesus, who forgave us our sins and expunged what was the handwriting of death against us, nailing it to the cross; and he made principalities and powers a show, triumphing over them on the tree.[32]

A closer look at two letters of Jerome to Pope Damasus will illustrate how Jerome functioned as a skilled biblical exegete. In these letters, more a biblical commentary on Isaiah's vision of God in Isaiah 6 than personal letters to Damasus, we have a good example of how Jerome moved easily between what he understood as the literal, moral and allegorical meanings of a text.

Jerome is well aware of the literal meaning of Isaiah's text. In discussing King Uzziah he supplies helpful background information, observes the mention of Uzziah in Kings and Chronicles, and duly notes Uzziah's strengths and weaknesses.

The literal meaning of the text immediately leads Jerome to consider its moral implications. The moral weaknesses of Uzziah and of the Egyptian pharaoh remind Jerome that while "sin reigns, we build cities for the Egyptians, we go about in dust and ashes, we seek chaff instead of grain and structures of mud instead of solid rock."[33] While Isaiah's moral integrity allows him to be lifted up to the vision of God, sinners (such as Jerome himself) see the Lord sitting in the valley of Josaphat, not on a hill, not on a mountain, but in a valley, the valley of judgment. . . . [W]hen I view Him with my mind's eye, reigning over thrones, dominions, angels, and all other virtues, I see his lofty throne. But when I consider how He deals with the human race and is said frequently to descend to earth for our salvation, I see His throne low and very near the earth.[34]

Jerome reads Isaiah's account in light of God's actions in Christ. He, like all the fathers, fully expects to hear the symphony of the gospel in Old Testament texts, though the movements of that symphony—clear in the New Testament—will only be discerned by the reverent and obedient ear of the skilled exegete.

Prayer is the beginning, middle and end of all fruitful exegesis. For example, as Jerome ponders the meaning of the seraphim who surround God's presence in Isaiah's vision, shielding God's presence from Isaiah's gaze, Jerome prays that the meaning of the vision might be made clear to him.

Since these questions raise no small cloud of dust and at the very outset interpose a difficulty of interpretation, let us pray the Lord together that to me also a coal may be sent from the altar, and that, when all the uncleanness of my sins has been swept away, I may be enabled first to contemplate the mysteries of God and then to tell what I have seen.[35]

The kinds of questions Jerome then asks of the vision are revealing and help us to understand how church fathers approached a biblical text. What does *seraphim* mean? Jerome refers the reader to his *Translation of Hebrew Words* and comments that it can be translated "fire" or "the beginning of speech." What fire is this? Jerome's mind begins to connect with other biblical passages mentioning fire. Jesus, he remembers, taught that he "came to bring fire to the earth, and how I wish it were already kindled!" (Lk 12:49) The disciples on the road to Emmaus encounter the risen Christ and he opens up the Old Testament scriptures to them. Jerome observes the disciples' response: "Were not our hearts burning within us while he was talking to us on the road, while he was opening the scriptures to us?" (Lk 24:32). What, then, does the holy fire of the seraphim symbolize? Jerome argues it is the Holy Scripture itself. "No one can doubt that it is in the holy books, by the reading of which all sins of men are washed away."[36]

It should not surprise us that Jerome contends the number of the seraphims' wings to be significant. For Jerome, as in rabbinic exegesis, the "words of Scripture are not simple, as some suppose; much is concealed in them."[37] Hence, if Isaiah mentions the number of wings the angels possess, that number must be significant. Jerome's exegesis becomes detective work as he links together a number of exegetical clues. If seraphim means fire and fire is closely linked with the fire of Scripture, should we be surprised that the combination of the two seraph's wings is the number twelve? There were, after all, twelve apostles, twelve stones on the altar that a human tool had never touched and twelve precious stones in the high priest's breast plate.[38] To which is Isaiah referring?

To answer this question Jerome ponders the seraphim's wings. With two they cover God's face, with two God's feet, and with two they fly.[39] The angels cover God's face to remind us that only God knows and understands God. "For who can know His beginning, which was in the eternity of things before He founded this [little] world." God's feet are covered to show us that God's purposes and future for his creation remain veiled.

> For who can know His bounds? What is to be after the consummation of the age, what after the human race has been judged; what life is to follow: whether there will again be another earth and other elements after the change or if another world and sun must be created.[40]

What of the remaining two wings? With these, Isaiah states, the angels flew. If the first four speak of veiling, Jerome argues, the last two wings speak of the revelation of God and God's purposes that can be presently known.

> *And with two they flew*: we know only the intermediate events which are revealed to us by the reading of the Scriptures: when the world was made, when man was fashioned, the time of the flood, when the law was given, how the entire expanse of the lands was populated from one man and how, at the end of the age, the Son of God took flesh for our salvation. But all the other things which we have mentioned these two seraphim have covered in veiling His face and His feet.[41]

Finally, as the two angels fly they cry out to one another, "Holy, holy, holy is the LORD of hosts; the whole earth is full of his glory" (Is 6:3). This exchange is more than appropriate, Jerome comments, for the Old and New Testament continue to speak to one another over the ages. "For whatever we read in the Old Testament, that we find also in the Gospel; and what was gathered in the Gospel, this is drawn forth from the authority of the Old Testament: nothing is discordant, nothing diverse."[42]

Of course, many modern exegetes would contest Jerome's assertion and his overall reading of Isaiah 6. It will appear to some as forced, contrived and fanciful. Here we see both the strengths and weaknesses of Jerome's approach. Because he is convinced that the overarching biblical narrative is one piece, inspired by the guidance of the Holy Spirit and continually pointing to God's culminating act in the incarnation and redemptive work of the Son, Jerome consistently looks for connections in the story, many of which are not immediately apparent. He, like other fathers, will force us to read the particular text in light of the whole gospel narrative within the context of the Christian community.

The danger of this approach, though, particularly for those fathers seeking an allegorical sense in the biblical text, is to discern a message in the text that only they can see. The danger of subjectivism is apparent. In future pages we will have to explore closely the question of whether the allegorical hermeneutic occasionally utilized by many fathers can be safely rescued for the modern interpreter and reader.

For further investigation. A thorough perusal of the many letters Jerome has left behind might be a good beginning for an exploration of Jerome's thought. Ancient Christian authors fully expected their letters to be published and available to the public. They were not above playing to the gallery. This presented problems, however, as Joseph W. Trigg explains:

> [There were] misunderstandings that arose from the semi-public char-
> acter of such correspondence in the ancient world. An accomplished
> letter-writer like Augustine or Jerome would retain copies of his cor-
> respondence for eventual publication, and he would expect the recipi-
> ent of his letters to share them. The letter-writer was thus writing for
> a larger public as well as the intended recipient. When he was a brilliant
> stylist writing to a controversial figure on a topic of broad interest, he
> could expect his letters to be copied and circulated widely. Such open
> letters could become lethal weapons. . . . Publicity was, therefore, a
> serious obstacle to any frank and friendly exchange of views.[43]

Jerome's letters reveal his views on a wide variety of theological topics and exegetical possibilities. By far the largest collection of Jerome's letters available in English is found in volume 6 of the Nicene and Post-Nicene Fathers (NPNF), Second Series, published by both Eerdmans and Hendrickson.[44] One hundred and fifty letters have been translated, but in an arcane, stilted style. Twenty-two letters are available in *The Letters of St. Jerome*, volume 1, published in the Ancient Christian Writers series (ACW) by Newman Press.[45] This translation tends to be more approachable, though still somewhat uneven.

Other works of Jerome in English are somewhat limited and are largely found in the Fathers of the Church series published by The Catholic University of America Press. Two volumes of Jerome's commentary on the Psalms and homilies on the Gospel of Mark are in print, as is one volume of dogmatic and polemical works. Joseph W. Trigg has translated extremely interesting sections of the correspondence between Jerome and Augustine on questions of biblical interpretation. This is the place to start for readers who are especially interested in how Jerome read the Bible. The translation is vibrant, lively and available in volume 9 of the Message of the Fathers of the Church, published by Michael Glazier.[46]

Augustine (354-430)

In Augustine we encounter a man who many consider the greatest of the fathers, a figure whose name, if not his thought, is well known to most modern Westerners. Augustine's personal pilgrimage to faith, recorded in an intensely personal form in his *Confessions,* mirrors for many modern Christians their own personal struggles: How can one live a sexually sane life in a sexually insane culture? How is love different from lust? How has sin affected the human personality? If God is infinitely powerful and infinitely loving, why is the world filled with such evil and suffering? Exactly what is evil? How did evil enter God's creation? Why am I so often unable to do the good I know to be good? Why do I consistently find myself loving the wrong things? How can I learn to love the good? How has sin affected my ability to love what is right and hate what is wrong? How can one make sense of the Bible? Why are the Scriptures so difficult to understand and interpret? How can one learn to read them well?

We can best understand Augustine's response to these and other questions by first reviewing key junctures in his own spiritual pilgrimage. His family background is similar to that of many households today. Augustine's father Patricius was more interested in his career than in his son and took little interest in Augustine's spiritual development. Patricius amply provided for Augustine's education, but was blind to his son's religious questions and concerns. Augustine mentions his father infrequently, and when he does speak of him one senses his ambivalence. Yes, his father provided well for his education, but fell short as the moral and spiritual guide Augustine so badly needed.

No one had anything but praise for my father who, despite his slender resources, was ready to provide his son with all that was needed to enable him to travel so far for the purpose of study. Many of our townsmen, far richer than my father, went to no such trouble for their children's sake. Yet this same father of mine took no trouble at all to see how I was growing in your sight or whether I was chaste or not. He cared only that I should have a fertile tongue, leaving my heart to bear none of your fruits, my God, though you are the only Master, true and good, of its husbandry.[47]

Augustine needed great help as he found himself trapped by the overwhelming lure of his senses and their appetites. He loved food, sex, friendship—indeed, love itself. Augustine increasingly perceived, though, that his search for love was wrongheaded; he loved, but he loved wrongly. His love overflowed its banks and rippled across a landscape it was never meant to traverse. Augustine's desires raged within him; love and lust merged in an unholy union.

I cared nothing but to love and be loved. But my love went beyond the affection of one mind for another, beyond the arc of the bright beam of friendship. Bodily desire, like a morass, and adolescent sex welling up within me exuded mists which clouded over and obscured my heart, so that I could not distinguish the clear light of true love from the murk of lust.[48]

The famous incident of the pears illustrates well Augustine's disordered love. Augustine describes a pear tree near his father's vineyard. It was loaded with fruit neither "attractive to look at nor to taste." Yet Augustine's "greedy love of doing wrong," together with a "lack of sense of justice or a distaste for what was right," moved him and his friends to pillage pears they did not desire or need. "We took away an enormous quantity of pears, not to eat them ourselves, but simply to throw them to the pigs. Perhaps we ate some of them, but our real pleasure consisted in doing something that was forbidden."[49] What was the source of this warped affection for injustice and evil?

Augustine was soon to make his way to Carthage, a metropolitan arena that would quickly feed and magnify his disordered loves. "Both love and lust boiled within me, and swept my youthful immaturity over the precipice of evil desires to leave me half drowned in a whirlpool of abominable sins."[50] In retrospect Augustine asked who other than God "can unravel that complex, twisted knottedness" of fallen human nature? "I went away from Thee, my God, in my youth I strayed too far from Thy sustaining power, and I became to myself a barren land."[51]

In Carthage Augustine's descent into sin accelerated. He found himself drifting away even further from his Christian roots. In this period Augustine seemed frustrated with himself, his Christian past and his inability to make sense out of the Bible. Soon he would find himself attracted to the Manichees, a group with strong gnostic tendencies, in large part because they seemed to offer a way of interpreting the Bible that made greater sense than that of the North African church. In order to make sense of Augustine's move toward Manichaeism, we must examine more closely how Christians in North Africa read and interpreted the Bible.

Hermeneutical sampler. Roland J. Teske, who recently translated Augustine's *Two Books on Genesis Against the Manichees*, argues convincingly that the young Augustine was frustrated with an anti-intellectual, superstitious and authoritarian biblical hermeneutic prevalent in the North African churches.[52] Peter Brown describes the extremely conservative nature of the North African churches and of the touchiness of the African bishops to anyone who would challenge their authority or their interpretation of Scripture:

> This was not a vague authority 'in faith and morals,' much less was it the highly-sophisticated right to persuade and protect the seeker after truth, that Augustine later would make of it; in the 370s, as previously, the bishops' authority stemmed directly from their possession of the 'Divine Law,' the Scriptures, and from their duty to preserve and expound them. The Bible . . . was treated as a quarry for rigorous legal rulings; and to be a true Christian meant, quite simply, to accept this 'Law' in its entirety, without asking awkward questions.[53]

Augustine had a number of questions about the Scriptures that he wanted answered but answers were not forthcoming. Why, for example, did North African Christians insist on using an old Latin version of the Bible, translated many years ago and filled with, as Peter Brown puts it, "slang and jargon." Augustine, trained in rhetoric and letters from an early age, found both the language and concepts of the Scriptures objectionable, at least as the North African church read and interpreted them.

He had been brought up to expect a book to be 'cultivated and polished': he had been carefully groomed to communicate with educated men in the only admissible way, in a Latin scrupulously modelled on the ancient authors. Slang and jargon were equally abhorrent to such a man; and the Latin Bible of Africa, translated some centuries before by humble, nameless writers, was full of both.[54]

Augustine's troubles with the Scriptures were more than the stylistic objections of the rhetorician. The Christians Augustine knew as a child and adolescent insisted on reading Scripture in an inflexible and literalistic manner, overlooking what seemed to him to be clearly identifiable figures of speech. Some argued that if humanity had been created in the image of God as Genesis 1:26 clearly stated, then God must be a material substance of some kind, perhaps even possessing the characteristics of the human body. Apparently most if not all North African Christians thought of God in such materialistic terms. Teske argues that Augustine's continuing difficulty in thinking of God as a spiritual substance is related to more than his own personal struggles with sin:

> What seems to have been the case is that the whole Western Church up until the time when Augustine came into contact with the Neoplatonic circle in the Church of Milan thought of God and the soul in materialistic terms. If whatever is real is bodily, as Tertullian and the prevalent Stoic materialism had held, then the fact that man is made in the image and likeness of God inevitably entails that God have the shape and form of the human body. And if the Church of Africa had no use for an intellectual understanding of the faith, if it rejoiced in the yoke of authority and terror of superstition and was largely content with the Old Latin Bible as its one book, it is easy to see why an educated young man like Augustine would be repelled by the Catholic Church into Manichaeism as a faith for the intellectuals.[55]

Against this materialistic hermeneutic Augustine's comments in the *Confessions* on his own struggles with Scripture make greater sense. He chaffed against the critique of the Manichees, the "fools" mentioned in Book 3 of the *Confessions*. They "asked me what was the origin of evil, whether God was confined to the limits of a bodily shape, whether he had hair and nails. . . . I did not know that God is a spirit, a being without bulk and without limbs defined in length and breadth."[56]

The Manichees seemed to offer an escape from the dead end of a wooden literalism. They were bright and intelligent, excellent in debate and skilled, as Peter Brown puts it, in winning over "the half-Christian students and intelligentsia of Carthage."

Their missionaries were 'exceedingly well-spoken and fashionable.' They enjoyed public debates, and could handle hecklers like accomplished Hyde Park orators. Their demolition of the traditional Christian Scriptures was intelligent and persistent. They claimed that, "putting aside the terror of authoritative commands to believe, they would lead all men who cared to hear them to God, and would free them from error, by a remarkably straightforward use of reason."[57] Augustine understood the Manichees to be "radical Christians" who could help him to understand the mysteries of the Bible and to offer a solution to the problem of evil, a theological and philosophical issue that Augustine was to ponder all of his life.

The Manichees, as Teske describes them, "explained the human predicament in terms of a metaphysical materialism cloaked in a highly imaginative myth." Manichees posited an eternal dualism between good and evil, light and darkness. Both realities had always existed in opposition to one another. Mani, the founder of the sect, taught that in the present "middle times" a conflict had occurred in which particles of light had been entrapped in matter, good within evil. As a result, human beings experienced themselves as "divided"; the human "soul" was "literally a particle of divinity imprisoned in the dark and evil body."

Moreover, as Teske explains, the Manichees taught that we are not the ones who commit evil. "Rather, we remain sinless, while the evil in which we are imprisoned bears the guilt for the wrong that is done."[58] Augustine admits this was a highly attractive idea. While in Rome he still associated with the Manichaean "elect." "I still thought that it is not we who sin but some other nature that sins within us. It flattered my pride to think that I incurred no guilt and, when I did wrong, not to confess it. . . . I preferred to excuse myself and blame this unknown thing which was in me but was not part of me."[59]

Redemption consisted in freeing these light particles to make their return to full brightness by way of the celestial ladder of the Milky Way. Strange stuff, but a fairly common gnostic theme with its own special variations. Manichees, then, spent most of their religious energy attempting to free light particles from their entrapment in matter. Mani himself claimed to have heard the cry of trapped light emerging from vegetables and plants as they were cut. Members of his sect were strict vegetarians and of course were concerned to take whatever steps were necessary to prevent more light from falling into matter. Hence, it should be no surprise that members of the sect were celibate and denigrated marriage.[60]

Pheme Perkins explains that in Manichaean mythology "demonic powers of the lower world had created the human body." The demons had followed a heavenly pattern as they designed the body, that of an "androgenous Adam/Eve." Redemption was possible because as "a result of the heavenly origins of their spirits, humans could become vehicles for the liberation of light" from its imprisonment in matter.[61] In Augustine's North Africa the suffering Christ was sometimes portrayed as representing "the suffering particles of light."[62] Or, in Peter Brown's description, the Manichee Christ personified "the principle of Wisdom *par excellence.*"

> This Christ enlightened men; He led them to a true knowledge of themselves; He had awoken Adam from his drunken slumber, to tell him [Augustine] precisely what Cicero would have told him in more classical terms: that is, that his soul was divine. "This name, Jesus, grace surrounds it." "He came, He separated us from the Error of the World; He brought us a mirror, we looked, we saw the Universe in it."[63]

For a number of years, particularly because the Manichees seemed to offer a solution to the intractable problem of evil and promised an answer to Augustine's continuing quest for the truth, Augustine counted himself as a disciple. The continuing prayers of Augustine's mother Monica, the death of a close friend and the ultimate incoherence of Mani's system nudged Augustine ever closer to Christ. During this time of deep questioning Augustine took the position of professor of rhetoric in Milan and met Ambrose, the bishop of the city.

Two central problems remained for the unconverted Augustine. First, there was the Bible itself. It appeared to contain much that to Augustine's mind was unworthy of God. It was Ambrose's figurative exegesis, especially of sections of the Old Testament, that convinced Augustine that Manichaean objections to Christianity were invalid and that Scripture could speak to the educated philosopher.

> First of all, it struck me that it was, after all, possible to vindicate his [Ambrose's] arguments. I began to believe that the Catholic faith, which I had thought impossible to defend against the objections of the Manichees, might fairly be maintained, especially since I had heard one passage after another in the Old Testament figuratively explained. These passages had been death to me when I took them literally, but

once I had heard them explained in their spiritual meaning I began to
blame myself for my despair, at least in so far as it had led me to suppose
that it was quite impossible to counter people who hated and derided
the law and the prophets.[64]

What was it about Ambrose's figurative exegesis that offered hope to
Augustine? For one thing, Ambrose made it clear that sections of the Old
Testament such as Genesis 1:26 were not to be interpreted in a wooden, literal
fashion, overlooking key figures of speech. If Genesis taught that humanity
was made in the image of God, this did not mean that God was a material
substance or possessed a physical body. Augustine's exposure to Western
Christian exegetes such as Ambrose opened his eyes to other possibilities.

I learned that your spiritual children, whom by your grace you have made
to be born again of our Catholic mother the Church, do not understand
the words *God made man in his own image* to mean that you are limited by
the shape of a human body, and although I could form not the vaguest
idea, even with the help of allegory, of how there could be substance that
was spiritual, nevertheless I was glad that all this time I had been howling
my complaints not against the Catholic faith but against something quite
imaginary. . . . I was on the way to conversion and I was glad, my God,
that the one Church, the Body of your only Son, in which the name of
Christ had been put upon me as a child, had no liking for childish
absurdities and there was nothing in the sound doctrine which she taught
to show that you, the Creator of all things, were confined within a measure
of space which, however high, however wide it might be, was strictly
determined by the form of a human body.[65]

Augustine's later exegesis of Genesis demonstrates the fruit that Ambrose's
teaching had borne. In *Two Books on Genesis Against the Manichees*, Augustine
demolishes the straw man the Manichees had created in their interpretation
of Genesis 1:26. The Manichees, Augustine contends, "taunt us for believing
that man was made to the image and likeness of God. They look at the shape
of our body and ask so infelicitously whether God has a nose and teeth and
a beard and also inner organs and the other things we need."[66]

Indeed, Augustine responds, both the Old and New Testaments use
bodily images in speaking of God, but those who have learned to read
Scripture "spiritually" have learned that these images relate "spiritual
powers," not "bodily members." The figures of speech in Genesis, which
"spiritual" believers will recognize, do not teach that "God is limited by a

bodily shape." Rather, "these words refer to the interior man, where reason and intellect reside." Because of these gifts, humanity "has power over the fish of the sea and the birds of heaven and all cattle and wild animals and all the earth and all reptiles which creep upon the earth."[67] Thus, although Augustine will use the term "spiritual" to refer to the type of allegorization prevalent in Alexandrian exegetes such as Origen, spiritual interpretation can also refer to the simple recognition of the figures of speech biblical writers often employ.

A second, perhaps even greater difficulty faced Augustine as he wavered in his willingness to convert to Christ. He knew himself. He knew what he was capable of doing. He acknowledged the deeply ingrained habit patterns he had formed over years of wild living. He knew how disordered his loves were. Would he fail if he converted to Christ? Would he genuinely be able to live a changed, holy, radically committed life? Did he possess the strength to make the changes Christ would demand of him?

Besides these cutting existential questions, other theological and philosophical issues remained. What of the origin and nature of evil? What of the human will? Would his own will ever be inclined to love the good? If so, how? As he contemplated these questions the teaching of Paul beckoned to him.

So I set about finding a way to gain the strength that was necessary for enjoying You. And I could not find it until I embraced the mediator between God and humanity, the man Christ Jesus, who is over all things, God blessed forever, who was calling to me and saying: I am the Way, the Truth, and the Life. . . . For I was not yet lowly enough to hold the lowly Jesus as my God, nor did I know what lesson his embracing of our weakness was to teach. For Your Word, the eternal Truth, towering above the highest parts of your creation, lifts up to Himself those that were cast down. He built for himself here below a lowly house of our clay, that by it He might bring down from themselves and bring up to Himself those who were to be made subject, healing the swollenness of their pride and fostering their love: so that their self-confidence might grow no further but rather diminish, seeing the deity at their feet, humbled by the assumption of their human nature: to the end that weary at last they might cast themselves down upon his humanity and rise again in its rising.[68]

The magnet of Christ's love was drawing Augustine ever closer, but the weight of his will's past decisions and continuing sexual struggles caused

Augustine to linger in doubt. Could he truly leave his false loves behind to grasp the object of his truest desire?

> I had almost made it . . . yet I did not quite make it. . . . Those trifles of all trifles, and vanities of vanities, my one-time mistress, held me back, plucking at my garment of flesh and murmuring softly: "Are you sending us away?" And "From this moment shall we not be with you, now or forever?" And "From this moment shall this or that not be allowed you, now or forever?"[69]

On the other hand, the possibility of a continent and holy life beckoned him, a life grounded in the grace of God and God's power at work within him. Continence personified beckoned to Augustine and asked him why he waited to embrace her in return.

> "Why do you try to stand in your own strength and fail? Cast yourself upon God and have no fear. He will not shrink away and let you fall. Cast yourself upon him without fear, for he will welcome you and cure you of your ills." I was overcome with shame, because I was still listening to the futile mutterings of my lower self and I was still hanging in suspense. And again Continence seemed to say, "Close your ears to the unclean whispers of your body, so that it may be mortified. It tells you of things that delight you, but not such things as the law of the Lord your God has to tell."[70]

Augustine's inner crisis had reached its climax. As he recalls, "a great storm broke within me, bringing with it a great deluge of tears." And then the famous voice from a nearby house reached Augustine's ears: "Take it and read, take it and read." In that small child's voice Augustine discerned the command of God.

> So I hurried back to the place where Alypius was sitting, for when I stood up to move away I had put down the book containing Paul's Epistles. I seized it and opened it, and in silence I read the first passage on which my eyes fell: *Not in revelling and drunkenness, not in lust and wantonness, not in quarrels and rivalries. Rather, arm yourselves with the Lord Jesus Christ; spend no more thought on nature and nature's appetites.* I had no wish to read more and no need to do so. For in an instant, as I came to the end of the sentence, it was as though the light of confidence flooded into my heart and all the darkness of doubt was dispelled.[71]

Augustine's Christian journey had begun, a journey that would end with the Vandals besieging the city walls of Hippo, where Augustine served as bishop for many years. As Augustine lay dying the names of three persons came continually to his lips: Monica, the mother who had been his faithful spiritual intercessor in his early, rebellious years; Adeodatus, the son his unnamed mistress had borne and who had died while still a young man; and the unnamed mistress herself.[72]

For further investigation. The works of Augustine fill the pages of over fifty volumes and a complete bibliography of Augustine's writings would far exceed the boundaries of this book. The principle work in which Augustine explains his hermeneutical methodology is *Christian Instruction (De doctrina Christiana)*, translated by John J. Gavigan in the Fathers of the Church series published by The Catholic University of America Press.[73] A new translation of this same work, *On Christian Teaching*, translated by R. P. H. Green, is available from Oxford University Press.[74]Augustine's exegesis of the beginning chapters of Genesis is especially illustrative of how he reads and interprets the Bible. Readers might begin with his *Two Books on Genesis Against the Manichees* or *On the Literal Interpretation of Genesis: An Unfinished Book*, both recently translated by Roland J. Teske in the Fathers of the Church series. John Hammond Taylor has translated Augustine's *The Literal Meaning of Genesis* in the Ancient Christian Writers series published by Paulist Press.[75] Two volumes of Augustine's sermons on the Psalms are also available in the Ancient Christian Writers series, translated by Dame Scholastica Hebgin and Dame Felicitas Corrigan.[76] The Fathers of the Church series has also published five volumes of Augustine's homilies on the Gospel of John and John's first epistle, all translated by John W. Rettig.[77] Augustine's sermons on the Gospel of John, the Psalms and the Sermon on the Mount are available in the Nicene and Post-Nicene Fathers series published by Eerdmans and Hendrickson. Unfortunately, the stilted translations will deter all but the most dedicated and inquisitive students. Finally, Joseph W. Trigg has translated the fascinating correspondence between Jerome and Augustine dealing largely with exegetical questions.[78]

Gregory the Great (540-604)

With Gregory the Great, we move roughly one hundred fifty years beyond the time of Augustine. Gregory's life appears providentially ordered for the pivotal role he played in the life of the Western church. Gregory's great-grandfather had been a pope (Felix II, 483-492), as had been another relative on his father's side (Anicetus I, 535-536). Outside of well-known worthies such as these, though, information about Gregory's life is fairly sparse and mostly comes from his own writings.[79] The large number of letters published in the Nicene and Post-Nicene Fathers series are filled with interesting details about Gregory, but only cover the time of his pontificate.[80] We do know that Gregory had a distinguished public life before becoming a monk; he had served as prefect of Rome. One is reminded of Ambrose's life in public service before he became the bishop of Milan.

Upon retirement from public life Gregory used his own personal funds to establish a number of monasteries, both in Rome and on the island of Sicily. The transition from prefect of Rome to monk and then abbot must have been a jarring one. As Robert Payne puts it, "He exchanged the purple toga for the coarse robe of a monk and began to live with extraordinary asceticism, eating only raw fruit and vegetables, praying most of the night, wearing a hairshirt, throwing himself into the manifold duties of an abbot."[81]

Gregory's monastic life was interrupted by the request of Pope Pelagius II that Gregory serve as episcopal representative in Constantinople. This appointment lasted for seven years and afforded Gregory the opportunity to familiarize himself with Eastern theology, spirituality and church life. During this sojourn in Constantinople Gregory began work on his well-known *Moral Discourses on Job* (*Magna moralia in Job*), a work of over two thousand pages of reflection available in the Oxford Library of the Fathers, a series published in the nineteenth century.[82]

When Gregory returned to Rome, he hoped to resume his monastic life at St. Andrews, one of the monasteries he had founded earlier. Pope Pelagius II, though, perished in a time of plague, and Gregory was the popular choice to be his replacement.[83] Gregory did not want the job. He doubted his spiritual readiness and qualifications to be the shepherd of the entire church. Then, too, the frenzied schedule of a pope would virtually eliminate Gregory's hopes for a life of solitude and prayer.

In a letter Gregory wrote to Theoctista, a sister of the Roman emperor, he expressed his sadness over his return to public ecclesiastical life and leadership. He had, Gregory laments, been "brought back to the world; in which I am involved in such great earthly cares as I do not at all remember having been subjected to even in a lay state of life."[84]

Hermeneutical sampler. Gregory's letter to Theoctista is not only interesting for the light it sheds on Gregory's reluctance to become pope. It also, almost in an offhand way, helps us to understand how Gregory read the Bible. As he explains to Theoctista his sadness over becoming pope, Gregory's mind is drawn to Genesis and especially to the account of Jacob's marriages to Leah and Rachel. Gregory's attraction to the devotional life corresponds to Rachel, "barren, but keen of sight and fair (Gen. xxix.), who, though in her quietude she is less fertile, yet sees the light more keenly." Leah, though, has been "coupled" to Gregory "in the night, to wit, the active life; fruitful, but tender-eyed; seeing less, but bringing forth more." Suddenly Gregory's mind is drawn to Mary and Martha. "I have longed to sit at the feet of the Lord with Mary, to take in the words of His mouth; and lo, I am compelled to serve with Martha in external affairs, to be careful and troubled about many things."[85]

In a later letter Gregory defends his exegesis by arguing that in the "understanding of sacred Scripture whatever is not opposed to a sound faith ought not to be rejected." Surely, Gregory believes, the principles he has derived from the Genesis text are Christian ones, a necklace of gold he has molded from the text. Other exegetes might create "rings," "bracelets" or "various ornaments." Gregory exults in this exegetical diversity, largely foreign to modern biblical interpreters. It is a sign of the richness of Scripture itself. "[S]o from the same knowledge of sacred Scripture different expositors, through innumerable ways of understanding it, compose as it were various ornaments, which nevertheless all serve for the adornment of the heavenly bride."[86]

Forty of Gregory's gospel homilies have been translated by David Hurst and published by Cistercian Publications.[87] In these sermons Gregory's homiletical and exegetical skill are richly intertwined. A few examples will demonstrate this.

Mark 4:23—"If anyone has ears to hear, let him hear" (NIV). Gregory immediately comments that since all listening to Jesus must have possessed physical ears, "he surely meant the ears of the heart." Gregory admonishes his listeners therefore to

Take care, then, that the word which you have received remains in the ears of your heart; take care that the seed does not fall beside the way, lest the evil spirit come and take away the word from your memory; take care that rocky ground does not receive the seed and send forth the fruit of good works without the roots of perseverance. What they hear is pleasing to many persons and they propose to themselves the beginning of good works; but as soon as adversities begin to weary them they abandon what they have begun. The rocky ground had not moisture; it did not bring forth to fulfillment in the fruit of perseverance.[88]

Luke 18:41—Jesus asked the blind beggar, "What do you want me to do for you?"

Was one who could restore light ignorant of what the blind man wanted? But he wants to be asked for what he already knows; we shall request and he will grant. But he counsels us to be untiring in our prayers, and yet he says: *For your Father knows what you need before you request it of him.* (Mt 6:8) And so he questions that we may ask him, he questions to rouse our hearts to prayer.[89]

Matthew 5:13—"You are the salt of the earth."

If we are salt, we should season the hearts of believers. You who are shepherds, consider that you are pasturing God's living beings. . . . We often see a block of salt put out for brute animals. . . . A priest must be careful about what he says to individuals, to counsel each one in such a way that anyone associated with the priest may be seasoned with the taste of eternal life as if by contact with salt. We are not the salt of the earth if we do not season the hearts of those who hear us. One who does not withhold his preaching gives this seasoning to his neighbor. But then we truly preach what is right to others, if our words are revealed in our actions, if we ourselves are pierced by divine love, and if we wash away with our tears the stains of human life which we daily acquire, since we cannot live without sin.[90]

Mark 16:1-7—(Post-resurrection account). Gregory's remarks on this passage remain especially relevant for all tempted to think past mistakes eliminate the possibility of future forgiveness or service to Christ and his church.

But go, say to his disciples and Peter that he is going on ahead of you into Galilee. We must ask why Peter is distinguished by his name from "the disciples." If the angel had not expressly named him who had denied his master, he would not have dared to come with the others. He was called by name so that he would not lose hope as a result of his denial. In this connection we must ask ourselves why almighty God allowed the one he had decided to put over the entire Church to be afraid of the voice of a serving maid, and to deny him. Surely we recognize that it was done by an act of divine goodness, so that he who was going to be shepherd of the Church might learn from his own fault how he ought to have mercy on others. Accordingly, God first made him known to himself, and then put him over others, that he might perceive from his own weakness how mercifully he ought to put up with the weaknesses of others.[91]

In these homilies we witness Gregory at his best, theologically astute and pastorally sensitive. His mind is soaked in Scripture, like the rest of the fathers. Gregory analyzes and exegetes almost any biblical character or theme (e.g., the apostle Peter, creation ex nihilo in Genesis or the nature of the resurrected body) from a deep scriptural awareness honed by the biblical mindset and exegetical tradition of the Christian community in which he had rooted himself. That is, to refer to Dale Allison's earlier metaphor, Gregory hears specific themes and tones in the biblical text because he has been listening attentively to the music the church has heard as it has read the Bible throughout its history.

Of course, the central question many modern interpreters pose is whether the exegetical music heard and produced by the church during the patristic period is a symphony or cacophony. Only with further investigation will we be able to provide an answer. Clearly, though, the fathers did not think it strange to forge the exegetical chains that are present so often in their reflections on Scripture. On the negative side, there is the continuing danger of exegesis linked to the scriptural text in the loosest of ways. On the positive side, a methodology such as Gregory's can open up possible layering in a text we might too quickly overlook. Robert Payne defends Gregory on these grounds:

[T]he method Gregory followed—a method that continued to be followed throughout the Middle Ages—has much to commend it. The Old Testament provided a fruitful source of metaphors. By quoting from the Old Testament, by attempting to discover the link between the old and the new, by seeing mysteries where everything was plain, by coloring the New Testament with the richer colors of the Old Testament, drama and depth were gained. Just as a modern poet like William Butler Yeats will describe his own time with amazing accuracy by conjuring up a vision of Byzantium, so the church fathers brought Christ closer to themselves when setting him against the background of the Old Testament. A phrase from the book of Job could be detached from its setting, impregnated with new meanings, and be all the richer, for the poetic process was at work and the final product possessed an authenticity of its own.[92]

A final example from Gregory demonstrates Payne's thesis, and also illustrates its possible dangers. Picture Gregory contemplating the instructions given to Moses for the curtains of the tabernacle. Yahweh tells Moses that the curtains must be woven out of fine linen. Their color is also important—scarlet and blue keep reappearing in the divine blueprint for the curtains. The covering for the tabernacle itself is to be made out of goats' hair. Without dismissing the literal meaning of the text, Gregory asks himself why the colors red and blue are important. What do they symbolize? The same question pertains to the text concerning goats' hair. Why the hair of goats? What deeper meaning might goat hair signify?

One problem Gregory faces is the paucity of other direct connections or chains in the biblical narrative to deeper meanings for blue, red, or for goats' hair. Thus, Gregory's desire to exegete symbolically these attributes of the tabernacle becomes highly subjective. What does the blue, red, and fine linen of the tabernacle represent? "[T]he life of holy men, delicate, but brilliant." And what of the goats' hair? Just as the goats' hair protects the more delicate blue and red curtains within the tabernacle, so within the church there are those who work in the world and those who do not. Frequently the one protects the other. Therefore, Gregory concludes, "Let not him who now gleams with spiritual brightness within Holy Church, murmur against his superior, who is employed in worldly business. . . . For if you glitter securely within, like scarlet, why do you blame the goats' hair with which you are protected?"[93]

Gregory has transmuted an Old Testament text into a trenchant devotional comment on ecclesiastical life. Would Moses have understood God's instruction in this manner? Obviously not. Can the tune Moses heard be later developed into the more complex thematic structure Gregory envisages? Here the fathers themselves disagreed, as exegetes trained in Alexandria more likely agreed with conclusions such as Gregory's, while those educated in Antioch raised more severe doubts about the safety of allegorizing a biblical text in such a radical manner.

For further investigation. As is the case with many of the fathers, perhaps the best way to acquaint oneself with Gregory is to browse through the large collection of his letters available in the Nicene and Post-Nicene Fathers series.[94] These letters do much more than show us how Gregory read the Bible. They reveal Gregory's pastoral heart and his fervent desire to see the church act in a just, honest and loving way with both friend and foe. Gregory, unlike a scholar such as Jerome, was first and foremost a pastor of souls, and his letters reveal his warm pastoral sensitivities. We can explore further the depth of his pastoral insight in his well-known *Pastoral Care (Regula Pastoralis)*, published in a modern translation by Paulist Press.[95] Thomas C. Oden provides a helpful handbook to this work in his *Care of Souls in the Classic Tradition*, published by Fortress Press.[96] This work clearly illustrates the contemporary relevance of patristic pastoral wisdom. Readers interested in investigating Gregory's exegetical skills further would do well to peruse Gregory's gospel homilies, translated by David Hurst and published by Cistercian Publications.[97]

Conclusion

The riches of the Latin tradition are not limited to the contributions of these four great Latin fathers. Indeed, Joseph W. Trigg argues that highly respected Latin lights such as Augustine stand on the shoulders of lesser known interpreters such as Ambrosiaster, who through Augustine "significantly influenced . . . the entire Latin exegetical and doctrinal tradition."[98] Readers interested in exploring the work of Ambrosiaster, much of which remains untranslated, can begin with Trigg's translation of Ambrosiaster's exegesis of Romans 7.[99]

Our discussion of the eight doctors of the church and their hermeneutical strategies illustrates well the areas of agreement and disagreement within the fathers themselves concerning how the Bible should be interpreted. Some, such as Ambrose and Gregory the Great, felt quite at home using allegory as a legitimate hermeneutical tool. Others, such as Basil and John Chrysostom, criticized the use of allegory and advocated a more literal approach. The hermeneutical disagreements between these key individuals correspond to those between two key interpretive centers in the ancient Christian world, Alexandria and Antioch. In the following two chapters we will take a more direct look at these differing perspectives, particularly as they are modeled by significant hermeneutical representatives such as Origen at Alexandria and Theodore of Mopsuestia at Antioch.

SIX

THE FATHERS
& SCRIPTURE

Exegesis at Alexandria

READING AND INTERPRETING SCRIPTURE WELL IS NO EASY MATTER. Our survey of the eight doctors of the church has shown that they themselves shared points of agreement and disagreement about how one should interpret the Bible. All agreed that the Bible is an inspired text. All agreed that personal disposition and spiritual health affect one's ability to read Scripture well. All agreed that once the exegete has determined the meaning of a biblical text and plumbed its possible applications, the text's inherent divine authority summons the biblical interpreter to obedience. All agreed that biblical interpretation is a Christian communal endeavor the exegete must practice within the context of Christ's body, the church. Most possessed a profound respect for the exegetical efforts of other interpreters in the church's history, even when they disagreed with their conclusions. Exegesis is never, the fathers argued, to be practiced in a historical, traditional or communal vacuum.

The Bible as a Multileveled Text
Despite these points of agreement, however, the fathers we have surveyed

occasonally disagreed. Controversy periodically erupted among them over a fairly specific question: How was one to identify and interpret the levels of meaning in a biblical text? For many modern readers this might seem a strange question. Most evangelical students of biblical hermeneutics, for example, would affirm that the grammatical-historical interpretation of a biblical text leads to only one valid meaning—that intended by the author. To add other layers of meaning is to create a hermeneutical labyrinth, a maze in which interpreters will soon find themselves hopelessly confused and lost.

The fathers, however, saw the grammatical-historical meaning of a text—what they would probably call its "literal" meaning—as only one of its possible senses. All the fathers expected to find layers of meaning within a biblical text. The question they posed to each other is in what way and to what degree this layering manifests itself.[1]

Typological interpretation, "whereby parts of the Hebrew Bible are read as a foreshadowing and prediction of the events of the Gospels," was practiced to a lesser or greater extent by virtually all the fathers.[2] Allegorical interpretation, defined by James L. Kugel and Rowan A. Greer as an interpretive approach in which "biblical persons and incidents become representative of abstract virtues or doctrines," was enthusiastically embraced by certain fathers and viewed with suspicion by others.[3] For some fathers, the distinction between typology and allegory was blurred at best.

Indeed, some modern scholars question whether the distinction between allegory and typology is one that early Christian writers observed. Manlio Simonetti comments that New Testament writers such as the apostle Paul interpreted key Old Testament texts in a "spiritual" sense, "in that a meaning other than the literal or immediate sense is perceived from the text."[4] Normally Paul labels his spiritual reading of Old Testament texts as a *typos* (type; cf. Rom. 5:14; 1 Cor. 10:6), but on at least one occasion he refers to the Hagar and Sarah narrative in Genesis as an *allegoroumena* (allegory). Quite possibly, as Simonetti argues, Paul considered *typos* to be synonymous with *allegoroumena*.[5]

A comparison of 1 Corinthians 10:1-6 with Galatians 4:24 seems to bear out Simonetti's conclusion. Paul writes to the Corinthians that the experiences of Israel in Egypt and the wilderness model deeper Christian realities. All Israel "passed through the sea, and all were baptized into Moses in the cloud and in the sea, and all ate the same spiritual food, and all drank the same spiritual drink. For they drank from the spiritual rock that followed them, *and the rock was Christ.*" (1 Cor 10:1-4). The larger Christian narrative turns out to be encased in key Old Testament texts.

In Galations 4:24 Paul refers to the sons of Hagar, a slave woman, and of Sarah, a free woman. Each son was born according to a different principle: Ishmael according to "the flesh," Isaac according to "the promise." Paul then explicitly allegorizes each woman: Hagar represents both Mount Sinai, "bearing children for slavery," and the "present Jerusalem," while Sarah "corresponds to the Jerusalem above; she is free, and she is our mother" (Gal 4:24-26).

Again, the fulfillment of the Old Testament story in Christ allows Paul to interpret the Old Testament narrative in the light of God's redemptive work in Christ. Only on this basis does the identification of the rock in the wilderness with Christ become explicable. One rock nourishes the old Israel in the wilderness. The second greater rock nourishes the new Israel in its present sojourn. Even more surprisingly, the rock in the wilderness turns out to be "spiritual" in nature and validly identified with the rock that has come in the fullness of time.

Whether we choose to distinguish between typology and allegory or see them as fluid in their meaning, as Paul apparently did, both are based on the fundamental premise that a biblical text possesses a deeper meaning in light of God's action in Christ. Or, as Simonetti writes, this deeper spiritual meaning in a text "was rooted in the firm conviction that the old Law was consistently directed towards the great Christ-event, and that, as a result, it would give up its true significance only to those who interpreted it in christological terms."[6]

Irenaeus, a father from the late second century, insisted on the unity between the Old and New Testaments, especially in light of the attempt by both Gnostics and Marcion to drive a wedge between the teaching of the Old Testament and that of the New. "If anyone, therefore, reads the Scriptures with attention, he will find in them an account of Christ, and a foreshadowing of the new calling." How so? It is Christ who is the treasure hidden in the field (Mt 13:44), for the field is "this world." Christ is "the treasure hid in the Scriptures."

Until Christ's appearance in this world, however, the Old Testament "types and parables" pointing to him remained unrecognized. "For every prophecy, before its fulfillment, is to men full of enigmas and ambiguities.

But when the time has arrived, and the prediction has come to pass, then the prophecies have a clear and certain exposition." Hence, Irenaeus argues, when the law is read to his Jewish contemporaries "it is like a fable; for they do not possess the explanation of all things pertaining to the advent of the Son of God."[7]

Some thirty years before Irenaeus penned these words Justin Martyr had said much the same thing in his debate with Trypho, a Jew. Justin and Trypho were debating the meaning of Isaiah 7:14. Was Isaiah predicting that a child would be born of a "virgin," Justin's interpretation, or a "young woman," the position advocated by Trypho? Justin, like Irenaeus and other early Christian exegetes, attributes Trypho's inability to perceive the christological significance of Isaiah's text to spiritual blindness.

If I undertook . . . to prove this by human doctrines or arguments, you should not bear with me. But if I frequently quote Scripture passages, and so many of them, referring to this point, and ask you to comprehend them, you are hard-hearted in the recognition of the mind and will of God.[8]

By way of contrast, Justin, Irenaeus and others claimed that when Christians read the Old Testament they readily discern its unity with the New. As Irenaeus explains,

[I]t is a treasure, hid indeed in a field, but brought to light by the cross of Christ, and explained, both enriching the understanding of men, and showing forth the wisdom of God, and declaring His dispensations with regard to man, and forming the kingdom of Christ beforehand. . . . For thus it was that the Lord discoursed with the disciples after His resurrection from the dead, proving to them from the Scriptures themselves "that Christ must suffer, and enter into His glory, and that remission of sins should be preached in His name throughout all the world" [Lk 24:26, 47]. And the disciple will be perfected, and rendered like the householder, "who brings forth from his treasure things new and old" [Mt 13:52].[9]

Irenaeus recalls the testimony of the apostles to support his belief that the same God reveals himself in both the old and new covenants, the old finding its fulfillment and deepest explanation in the new.

For all the apostles taught that there were indeed two testaments among the two peoples: but that it was one and the same God who appointed both for the advantage of those people . . . who were to believe in God. . . . [T]he first testament was not given without reason, or to no purpose, or in an accidental sort of manner; but . . . . exhibited a type of heavenly things, inasmuch as man was not yet able to see the things of God through means of immediate vision; and foreshadowed the images of those things which now actually exist in the Church, in order that our faith might be firmly established; and contained a prophecy of things to come, in order that man might learn that God has foreknowledge of all things.[10]

For some fathers, especially those trained in the school of Alexandria, it was more than appropriate to approach the New Testament with the expectation that it would speak on different levels. Origen, the greatest advocate of allegorical interpretation, explains the manifest and the hidden aspects of Scripture:

Then [we believe] that the Scriptures were composed by the Spirit of God and that they have not only a meaning that is manifest but also another that is hidden as far as most people are concerned. For what has been described are the forms of certain sacraments and the images of divine things. About this the universal Church is in accord, that the whole law is spiritual. What the law is full of, however, is not known to all but only to those to whom it is given by the grace of the Holy Spirit in a word of wisdom and knowledge.[11]

Origen was not the first scholar to advocate the allegorical interpretation of ancient texts. Simonetti mentions a number of ancient interpreters who employed allegory to make sense of Greek, Jewish and Christian texts. For example, some Greek interpreters understood Homer's *Iliad* and *Odyssey* as extended allegories. The wanderings of Ulysses represented "an allegory of the soul returning to its homeland." Particularly from the fifth century B.C. on, other Homeric tales were increasingly interpreted as pointing to deeper realities, often "as symbols of natural or other forces." Interpreters realized that if these stories were understood in their literal sense, the gods appear clearly immoral and much too similar to human beings in their weakness and foolishness.[12]

Here the defense of allegory resembles Origen's later justification for his own allegorical hermeneutic. Origen was to argue that the literal meaning of some biblical texts was incomprehensible or self-contradictory. Certain actions and characteristics of God, particularly in the Old Testament, seemed unworthy of God. How, for instance, was one to interpret God's commandment in the book of Joshua to slaughter the men, women and children of entire cities such as Jericho and Ai?

The Alexandrians simply could not believe that God would demand something like that, so they said that the people of Jericho represent our sins and that God wants us to eliminate them, right down to the tiniest one. Today this would sound like a forced interpretation, but in the third century, when exegetes faced either a barbarous literal interpretation or an allegorical one that preserved the beneficient view of God, the latter method saved the Bible for the Christians.[13]

Philo

Other Alexandrian interpreters such as the Jewish exegete, philosopher and theologian Philo relied heavily on allegorical exegesis in an attempt to make the Bible more accessible to a Hellenistic audience by emphasizing the close relationship between Greek philosophy and Jewish theology. In addition, Philo attempted to tame those "aspects of Scripture that seemed barbarous in an alien cultural context."[14] Or, as Simonetti puts it, Philo's allegorical exegesis

allowed him, on the one hand, to give satisfactory explanations of so many anthropomorphisms in the earlier books of the Old Testament, which, like the Greek myths, upset the sensibilities of educated pagans. On the other hand, by a process of interpretation which made plentiful use of philosophical concepts and terminology, especially Platonic and Stoic, he was able to introduce to the Greek mind a religious perceptive which had been quite foreign to it.[15]

Joseph Trigg cites Philo's allegorical exegesis of the Abraham, Sarah and Hagar narrative in Genesis to illustrate Philo's attempt to recognize Greek ideas in a Jewish document.

Abraham's wife, Sarah, symbolizes philosophy; her handmaiden, Hagar, the general studies that prepare for philosophy; and Abraham, the soul that learns by instruction. Sarah gives Abraham Hagar because philosophy cannot bear fruit until the soul is prepared for it.[16]

Simonetti identifies the interpretive key Philo uses to perceive and unlock biblical allegory:

For Philo, the Bible has far greater importance than this or that myth might have for a pagan, so that he does not entirely ignore the literal meaning of the passage before him. But the value he assigns to it is quite secondary; it is for the many, while the hidden meaning, attainable by the allegorical approach, is for the few who concern themselves with the realities of the Spirit. . . . The progression from the literal to the allegorical level is facilitated by certain indicators in the text which hold special significance for the shrewd exegete. This could involve details to which (for various reasons) the literal meaning is not pertinent: names of animals or particular items, above all the proper names of people or places. These are then interpreted etymologically, following a procedure given general application by the Stoics in their interpretation of the Greek gods. These are all procedures which we shall have to recall when dealing with Christian exegesis in Alexandria.[17]

Examples of Philo's allegorical interpretations include the following (note that in every allegorization Philo has broadened the Jewish perspective to encompass the wider Gentile world):

The temple in Jerusalem=The world

The parts of the temple=The different parts of the world

The four colors of the Jewish priest's vestments=The four elements of nature

Adam=Human intelligence

The creation of animals=Human passions

Eve=Human sensitivity

The union of Abraham and Sarah=The union of intelligence and virtue[18]

Predecessors to Origen

Origen was not the first early Christian exegete to employ allegory in interpreting the Bible, although exegetes from the Alexandrian school were the first to employ allegory extensively in interpreting the New Testament.

Earlier second-century Christian writers such as Justin Martyr and Irenaeus identified both a literal and typological/allegorical meaning in a number of biblical texts. Justin refers to Noah and the flood as representing a number of important christological themes:

For righteous Noah, along with the other mortals at the deluge, i.e., with his own wife, his three sons and their wives, being eight in number, were a symbol of the eighth day, wherein Christ appeared when He rose from the dead, for ever the first in power. For Christ, being the first-born of every creature, became again the chief of another race regenerated by Himself through water, and faith, and wood, containing the mystery of the cross; even as Noah was saved by wood when he rode over the waters with his household.[19]

Irenaeus read Scripture in a number of interesting ways, combining literal exegesis with two different types of allegory. Simonetti distinguishes them as "typological" and "vertical" allegory. Typological allegory presumes that an Old Testament text possesses a deeper meaning fulfilled in the actions and words of Christ. For Irenaeus, even the smallest details of a biblical text can bear new and exciting fruit when viewed in light of Christ's coming. Taking the example of the dietary regulations of Leviticus 11:2ff., Simonetti demonstrates how exegetes such as Irenaeus used this method:

> [T]o eat animals that part the hoof and chew the cud is taken as referring to Christians, pagans and Jews; the first are symbolised by animals which are clean, in that they chew the cud, i.e. meditate on the Law of God day and night, and part the hoof, i.e. have a stable faith in the Father and the Son; pagans are symbolised by animals which neither chew the cud nor part the hoof, because they lack both the characteristics of Christians; the Jews, finally, are represented by animals which chew the cud but which do not part the hoof, because they meditate on the Law of God, but do not believe in Christ.[20]

Vertical allegory presumes that "sacred, earthly realities" or structures such as the temple or tabernacle represent "heavenly realities."[21] Irenaeus illustrates vertical allegory in this way:

> Now the gifts, oblations, and all the sacrifices, did the people receive in a figure, as was shown to Moses in the mount, from one and the same God, whose name is now glorified in the Church among all nations. But it is congruous that those earthly things, indeed, which are spread all around us, should be types of the celestial, being [both], however, created by the same God.[22]

Irenaeus is acutely concerned to preserve the lasting value of the Hebrew Scriptures and the God presented in them from the attacks of Gnostic teachers. Many Gnostic exegetes pictured the Old Testament deity as a lower, second-class god responsible for the mistake of creation. According to Simonetti, "Their dualism and their disregard for the material world led them also to disdain the Old Testament as being the revelation of the

God of creation, the Demiurge, in contrast to the New Testament, the revelation of the supreme, good God."[23] Irenaeus's allegorization of key Old Testament passages, then, preserved the authority of the Old Testament from its detractors and more fully illustrated its connection to the New Covenant established by Christ.

Irenaeus also tends to allegorize passages that make little sense to him on a literal reading. How, he asks, can Isaac's blessing on Jacob make sense on a literal level? That is, did Jacob ever literally receive the blessings Isaac promised? If not, surely the promises made to Jacob signify a much greater blessing to take place in the future.

> If any one, then, does not accept these things as referring to the appointed kingdom, he must fall into much contradiction and contrariety, as is the case with the Jews, who are involved in absolute perplexity. For not only did not the nations in this life serve this Jacob; but even after he had received the blessing, he himself going forth [from his home], served his uncle Laban the Syrian for twenty years; and not only was he not made lord of his brother, but he did himself bow down before his brother Esau, upon his return from Mesopotamia to his father, and offered many gifts to him. Moreover, in what way did he inherit much corn and wine here, he who emigrated to Egypt because of the famine which possessed the land in which he was dwelling, and became subject to Pharaoh, who was then ruling over Egypt. The predicted blessing, therefore, belongs unquestionably to the times of the kingdom, when the righteous shall bear rule upon their rising from the dead; when also the creation, having been renovated and set free, shall fructify with an abundance of all kinds of food, from the dew of heaven, and from the fertility of the earth.[24]

It is questionable, though, whether Irenaeus was entirely successful in his attempt to overcome Gnostic interpretation of Scripture. He chose a hermeneutical approach—the allegorization of key texts to make a significant theological point—that the Gnostics themselves practiced. Who is to say that Irenaeus's allegories possessed greater inherent worth than those of his Gnostic opponents?

Manlio Simonetti argues that Irenaeus never clearly formulated a hermeneutical principle to regulate his own allegorizing. Irenaeus faulted his Gnostic opponents for exercising imaginations that "range beyond God, they having in their hearts surpassed the Master Himself, being indeed in idea elated and exalted above [Him], but in reality turning away from the one true God."[25] Yet Irenaeus, Simonetti believes, left himself open to the same critique.

Irenaeus's only defense, as far as Simonetti is concerned, was his dependence upon the principle of authority: "[T]he Catholic Church alone is the touchstone of truth in the interpretation of Scripture in that it is the storehouse of authentic apostolic tradition."[26]

Exegesis in Alexandria

Allegorical methodology and practice reached its zenith in Alexandria, with Origen as perhaps the best known representative of the Alexandrian approach to biblical hermeneutics. Before looking at specific examples of Origen's exegesis, however, a wider look at the Alexandrian school is in order.

Why the pronounced interest in allegory in Alexandria? Of central importance was the apologetic motive among Alexandrian exegetes. As we have already seen in the case of Philo and Irenaeus, both Jewish and Christian interpreters faced the question of how to communicate the gospel effectively in a deeply Hellenized world. Philo employed allegory to reach Hellenized Jews and convince them of the relevance of the Old Testament. For Christian interpreters in Alexandria, the first task was to reach the Greek mind and heart with the gospel, then to combat the Gnosticism that ran rampant through many quarters of the city.

Gnostic interpretation of the Scriptures was a genuine threat to both Jewish and Christian perspectives. Gnostic teachers largely denigrated the Old Testament as the work of an inferior deity. A key Gnostic conviction was that creation was a vast mistake, the work of an inferior, misguided god. Matter by definition was evil. Indeed, the spiritual life's goal was freedom from the contaminating effect of embodied existence through the attainment of *gnosis* or knowledge. Sacred writings such as the Old Testament that praised the goodness of creation were either to be avoided as delusionary or interpreted as actually pointing to a radically different reality than the literal meaning of the text represented.

The New Testament also was radically reinterpreted by Gnostic teachers, often through an exaggerated allegorical approach, to reinforce Gnostic theology and cosmology. Allegory was attractive to Gnostic teachers because it provided them with an exegetical tool that enabled them to retain New Testament documents in their quest for a Christian Gnosticism, while equipping them to interpret those documents in accordance with Gnostic cosmology.

Therefore, the Christian exegete in Alexandria needed to respond convincingly to the Gnostic threat by demonstrating the unity between the God and Scriptures of the Old Testament and the God and Scriptures of the New. Furthermore, this demonstration must be plausible to the Greek mind. How were Greeks, many trained from birth to seek levels of meaning in literary texts and in reality itself, to be convinced of the relevance of an intensely Jewish document? In a key strategic hermeneutical maneuver, Christian Alexandrian scholars turned to allegory to accomplish their apologetic, evangelistic, educational and homiletical task.

Origen

Origen represents both the strongest and the weakest aspects of Alexandrian exegesis. Probably a child prodigy of sorts, Origen demonstrated a lively faith from an early age as well as precocious intellectual abilities. In Origen we meet a man Karlfried Froehlich describes as "one of the great minds and probably the most influential theologian of the early Christian era."[27] Joseph Trigg writes that Origen is "the most influential early Christian interpreter of the Bible," whose "extant works comprise by far the largest body of work by a single author to survive from the first three centuries of the Christian church."[28] Whether in the last analysis we agree with Origen's hermeneutics, he remains a force to be reckoned with whose work deeply affected many fathers.

Throughout Origen's life the Scriptures remained the center of his existence, his spiritual food and drink. Origen possessed a deep reverence for the Hebrew Bible and the New Testament Scriptures, urging his students to set aside a significant part of each day for study, meditation and prayer. Harry Gamble observes that Origen presupposed the availability of the biblical text and the responsibility of students to ponder it carefully.

> Origen in various homilies speaks of the importance of reading the scriptures at home, recommending it as a daily exercise of at least a few hours. His admonitions were provoked by the indifference, indeed aversion, of some to the private reading of scripture; they complained

of the *taedium verbi divini*—the irksomeness of the private study of scripture. Origen certainly does not assume the literacy of all Christians, but he does presuppose the availability of texts to those who could read. For those who find the task difficult, he proposes a kind of graduated syllabus whereby one begins with the most intelligible books (Esther, Judith, Tobit, or the Wisdom of Solomon), moves on to the Gospels, Epistles, and Psalms, and only later tackles difficult and seemingly unrewarding texts like Leviticus or Numbers.[29]

Origen himself devoted much of his life to making the Bible in its entirety accessible to the church. While the Old Testament frequently troubled Origen when he attempted to interpret it literally, he affirmed, against Gnostic opposition, that the entire Bible was the book of the church. Thus, much of Origen's life was devoted to a study of the textual tradition and content of the Hebrew Scriptures. The church historian Eusebius was struck by Origen's unremitting labor:

> So earnest and assiduous was Origen's research into the divine words that he learned the Hebrew language, and procured as his own the original Hebrew Scriptures which were in the hands of the Jews. He investigated also the other translations of the Sacred Scriptures besides the Septuagint. And in addition to the well-known translations of Aquila, Symmachus, and Theodotion, he discovered certain others which had been concealed from remote times—in out-of-the-way corners I know not—and by his search he brought them to light.[30]

Procuring a reliable text of the Scriptures was only the first step for Origen. How, he asked, was one to interpret these holy texts in a sane, reliable and reverential manner? Origen explains his hermeneutical strategy in a well-known passage from his work *On First Principles*.

Origen begins by insisting that Christ, the Word of God, speaks throughout the biblical narrative recorded in the Bible. His words are not only those "which He spoke when He became man and tabernacled in the flesh; for before that time, Christ, the Word of God, was in Moses and the prophets." The words of Moses and of other prophets "were filled with the Spirit of Christ."[31] In turn, the revelation communicated by the Word in both Old and New Testaments has been faithfully preserved and transmitted by the church from generation to generation. As such, it can be used to gauge the validity of the various interpretations and opinions regarding the meaning of God's revelation.

[S]o, seeing there are many who think they hold the opinions of Christ, and yet some of these think differently from their predecessors, yet as the teaching of the Church, transmitted in orderly succession from the apostles, and remaining in the churches to the present day, is still preserved, that alone is to be accepted as truth which differs in no respect from ecclesiastical and apostolical tradition.[32]

How, Origen asks his reader, did the apostles communicate to their audience? Origen proposes a three-tiered apostolic revelation with each tier's accessibility gauged to the zealousness, discernment and wisdom of the interpreter. The deeper meaning of the Bible, Origen argues, "escapes the notice of most."

On the first tier the apostles spoke with the "utmost clearness" on subjects that all Christians needed to understand, "even to those who seemed somewhat dull in the investigation of divine knowledge." Origen describes this basic, universally accessible meaning of the Bible as "the 'flesh,' as it were, of the Scripture, for so we name the obvious sense."[33] "For it was intended that the covering also of the spiritual truths—I mean the 'bodily' part of Scripture—should not be without profit in many cases, but should be capable of improving the multitude, according to their capacity."[34]

The second tier of Scripture's meaning opens itself to those who have obtained the gifts "of language, of wisdom, and of knowledge." This tier reveals itself to a more limited, gifted group: those particularly graced in discerning the deeper meaning of texts through the power of the Spirit. In fact, Origen contends, biblical authors have implanted within the Bible different layers of meaning so that "the more zealous of their successors, who should be lovers of wisdom, might have a subject of exercise on which to display the fruit of their talents—those persons, I mean, who should prepare themselves to be fit and worthy receivers of wisdom."[35]

For those words which are written are the forms of certain mysteries, and the images of divine things. Respecting which there is one opinion throughout the whole Church, that the whole law is indeed spiritual; but that the spiritual meaning which the law conveys is not known to all, but to those only on whom the grace of the Holy Spirit is bestowed in the word of wisdom and knowledge.[36]

In the third tier, the Bible speaks to those who are "perfect" or "mature," as Paul puts it in 1 Cor. 2:6-7: "Yet among the mature we do speak wisdom, though it is not a wisdom of this age or of the rulers of this age, who are doomed to perish. But we speak God's wisdom, secret and hidden, which God decreed before the ages for our glory."

Origen springboards from Paul's division of humanity into body, soul and spirit to a similar division in Scripture itself, with the "spiritual law" as the summit of Scripture's deepest meaning. "For as man consists of body and soul and spirit, so in the same way does Scripture, which has been arranged to be given by God for the salvation of men."[37]

Origen gives at least three reasons for pursuing a deeper meaning in the Bible through allegorical interpretation. The first, as acknowledged by Jewish interpreters, is that many prophecies concerning the Messiah were never fulfilled literally by Jesus. Had, for example, Isaiah's prophecy of the wolf lying down with the lamb been literally fulfilled with the coming of Christ? "[S]eeing none of these things visibly accomplished during the advent of Him who is believed by us to be Christ, they did not accept our Lord Jesus."[38] For Origen, only a reading of Old Testament prophecies that perceives a deeper sense implanted by the Word will effectively overcome Jewish objections to a Christian interpretation of Scripture.

Second, whereas Jewish exegetes failed to see Jesus in their overly literalistic interpretation of the Hebrew Bible, Gnostic interpreters denigrated the Old Testament by branding it as the work of an inferior deity, the Demiurge. How could the Christian interpreter respond adequately to the Gnostic charge that many Old Testament texts presented a deity who was jealous, vengeful, apt to change, and in many instances responsible for evil itself? (See for example Jer 15:14; Ex 20:5; 1 Sam 15:11; Is 45:7; Amos 3:6; Mic 1:12; 1 Sam 16:14; 18:10.) Indeed, Origen argued, many in the church erred like the Gnostics in imagining God capable of "things as would not be believed of the most savage and unjust of mankind," a judgment Origen considers unavoidable if many biblical texts are accepted at face value.[39] We will return to this highly debatable point in our evaluation of Origen's hermeneutic at the end of this chapter.

Origen's third reason for the necessity of allegorical interpretation is closely related to his previous discussion of Gnostic exegesis. Origen argues strongly that many biblical texts are purposely obscure, rationally incoherent or morally repugnant in order to force the interpreter to discover their true, deeper meaning.

But since, if the usefulness of the legislation, and the sequence and beauty of the history, were universally evident of itself, we should not believe that any other thing could be understood in the Scriptures save what was obvious, the Word of God has arranged that certain stumbling blocks, as it were, and offenses, and impossibilities, should be introduced into the midst of the law and the history, in order that we may not, through being drawn away in all directions by the merely attractive nature of the language, either altogether fall away from the true doctrines, as learning nothing worthy of God, or, by not departing from the letter, come to the knowledge of nothing more divine.[40]

The biblical narrative for Origen is a tapestry woven with many threads: history, law and commandments, gospels, epistles and prophecy. In fact, Origen asserts, not all events portrayed as history by biblical writers actually occurred. Interspersed with genuine history are occasional accounts "of some event that did not take place, sometimes what could not have happened; sometimes what could, but did not."

Why would the Spirit of God speak in such a way, disguising deeper truths in historical garb? To drive "the more skillful and inquisitive" exegete to investigate the biblical text more carefully and reverently. For surely, Origen contends, many biblical texts in both the Old and New Testaments make little sense when interpreted literally. How, he asks, could the first and second days of Genesis be literal days if the sun, moon and stars have yet to be created? God is said to "walk" in the garden looking for Adam and Eve. Is this a literal walking? Hardly, Origen contends. Rather, "these things indicate certain mysteries, the history having taken place in appearance, and not literally."[41]

Origen strings together examples of texts from Genesis, Mosaic legislation and the Gospels that make little sense to him when interpreted literally. At times, however, he seems almost purposely blind to the possibility that his examples might be readily resolved through recognizing an author's use of well-known literary devices such as hyperbole. Although Origen rightly teaches that Jesus' words concerning an offending right eye (Mt 5:29) are "impossible to take literally," one can also argue that a "literal" interpretation of this text would include a recognition of hyperbole, a possibility Origen does not mention.

If we adopt Origen's methodology, how are we to know when the biblical narrative is genuine history and when the narrative is designed to lead beyond itself, a "stumbling block" to goad the interpreter to deeper musings? Origen readily acknowledges the difficulty of the task.

> The careful reader, however, will be in doubt as to certain points, being unable to show without long investigation whether this history so deemed literally occurred or not, and whether the literal meaning of this law is to be observed or not. And therefore the exact reader must, in obedience to the Savior's injunction to "search the Scriptures" [Jn 5:39], carefully ascertain how far the literal meaning is true, and how far impossible; and so far as he can, trace out, by means of similar statements, the meaning everywhere scattered through Scripture of that which cannot be understood in a literal sense.[42]

Perhaps a more detailed look at Origen's exegesis of the parable of the Good Samaritan (Lk 10:25-37) will clarify his approach and its relative strengths and weaknesses. Origen first acknowledges the literal meaning of the parable, one of the several senses he believes the passage possesses. "[Jesus] teaches that the man going down was the neighbor of no one except him who willed to keep the commandments and prepare himself to be a neighbor to every one who needs help."[43]

After quickly summarizing the literal meaning of the parable, Origen refers to a previous allegorical interpretation that he will modify slightly. The correspondences in the allegory are as follows:

The man going down to Jericho=Adam
Jerusalem=Paradise
Jericho=The world
The robbers=Hostile powers
The priest=The law
The Levite=The prophets
The Samaritan=Christ
The wounds=Disobedience
The beast=The Lord's body
The inn=The church
The two *denarii*=The Father and the Son
The innkeeper=The head of the church
The Samaritan's promise to return=The Lord's second coming[44]

Origen observes that "All of this has been said reasonably and beautifully." However, he desires to modify the allegory slightly. The man going down from Jerusalem, Origen believes, cannot represent all people, for not all go down from Jerusalem (paradise) to Jericho (the world). One has come down, he "who was sent on account of the lost sheep of the house of Israel." And what of the wounds? Yes, they represent disobedience, but more particularly "vices and sins."

Origen's reasoning for identifying Jesus as the Samaritan is particularly intriguing. Had not Jesus been called a Samaritan by his enemies (Jn 8:48)? And could not *Samaritan* be linked etymologically to *guardian*?

He is the one who "neither grows drowsy nor sleeps as he guards Israel." On account of the half-dead man, this Samaritan set out not "from Jerusalem into Jericho," like the priest and Levite who went down. Or, if he did go down, he went down to rescue and care for the dying man. The Jews had said to him, "You are a Samaritan and you have a demon." Though he denied having a demon, he was unwilling to deny that he was a Samaritan, for he knew that he was a guardian.[45]

Having thoroughly filled out the allegories in the parable, Origen develops the parable's homiletical possibilities. All "who are badly off" need this Samaritan's care. The oil and wine carried by the Samaritan are not only for the one man who had fallen into trouble, but for others "who, for various reasons, had been wounded and needed bandages, oil, and wine." The Samaritan places the wounded traveler on his own beast of burden, "that is, his own body, since he deigned to assume a man." Hence, the Samaritan "bears our sins" and "grieves for us."

He brings the fallen man to an inn, representing the church, a place of refuge "which accepts everyone and denies its help to no one. Jesus calls everyone to the church when he says, 'Come to me, all you who labor and are burdened, and I shall refresh you' [Mt 11:28]." Finally, the Samaritan leaves two *denarii* with the innkeeper, an attendant Origen believes is an angel. The two *denarii*, representing the Father and the Son, will care for the man in the Samaritan's absence.[46] Origen concludes his commentary by asserting that the Samaritan

showed that he was the man's neighbor more by deed than by word. According to the passage that says, "Be imitators of me, as I too am of Christ" [cf. 1 Cor 4:16], it is possible for us to imitate Christ and to pity those who "have fallen among thieves." We can go to them, bind their wounds, pour in oil and wine, put them on our own beasts, and bear their burdens. The Son of God encourages us to do things like this.[47]

While Origen's sermon is highly interesting and homiletically rich in its applications, the question remains whether Origen's interpretation of Jesus' parable is correct and ultimately satisfying. How do we know, for example, whether Jesus intended his parable to be interpreted allegorically? Even if this was shown to be the case, how can one know if Origen's allegories are Christ's? How would we know that the Samaritan is meant to represent Jesus? Or the inn the church? Or the traveler's wounds sins and vices?

Origen presents the biblical exegete with a number of paradoxes, possibilities, principles and problems. Think, for example, of Origen's view of inspiration. Origen is firmly convinced that every number, letter, line and sentence of the Bible is divinely inspired. His high view of Scripture is the motivating factor in Origen's continuing search for divine truth in the Bible, including the most surprising and seemingly unpromising places. His confidence in the Bible's inspiration causes him to pry the biblical narrative apart as though it were a walnut, with each story and character surely containing a hidden treasure, one readers can discern if they read the text of Scripture in the light of Christ and all he represents.

Ronald Heine sees a link between Origen's belief in divine inspiration and the Abraham narratives.

When the text of Genesis . . . relates that Abraham was standing under a tree, we ought not think, [Origen] asserts, that the Holy Spirit was concerned to tell us simply where Abraham was standing. Or, when Rebecca is said to come daily to the wells, he remarks that such details are significant, for the Holy Spirit is not just telling stories in the Scriptures. Even such minor details as Abraham's position and Rebecca's daily duties have been placed in the Scriptures by the Holy Spirit. We will not understand the way Origen reads the Bible if we miss this basic point, that it is always the Holy Spirit who speaks in the text of the Bible.[48]

At first glance, evangelicals and fundamentalists would seem to possess a friend and ally in Origen, for they too firmly insist that the Bible is divinely inspired. Yet, as Heine correctly notes, the conservative Protestant world has generally understood that a high view of Scripture guarantees "the accuracy of the historical and scientific information in the Bible." Origen, who holds a similarly high view of the Bible's inspiration, is untroubled by what he believes are occasional historical inaccuracies in the Scripture. He seems to have no trouble affirming the inspiration of the biblical text while simultaneously asserting that it occasionally errs in historical detail and scientific accuracy.

As we have already observed, Origen contends that some accounts of historical events in the Bible do contain discrepancies. For example, he clearly believes Jesus' cleansing of the temple as related in John cannot be reconciled with the description the Synoptic writers give of the same event.[49] And what should one make of the Bible's scientific statements? Are they really to be interpreted as communicating scientific truth? Origen would be open to the possibility that Scripture might speak in a scientific sense, but he also allows for the possibility of scientific error. He has, for example, grave doubts about the scientific accuracy of the Genesis creation story; at the same time, however, Origen remains convinced of the truthfulness of the biblical accounts.[50] How does he attempt to demonstrate the Holy Spirit's truthfulness in a narrative that might be historically or scientifically flawed?

Origen's central tactic is to make a distinction between spiritual truth and historical truth, a hermeneutical strategy not unlike that used by many theologians in the liberal tradition. Yes, the Bible does contain historical and scientific truth. Still, as Origen reads the Scripture, it seems clear that the biblical authors relate "what happened at this time as though it happened in another, or what happened at this time as though at another time, and they have composed what is reported in this manner with a certain degree of distortion."[51]

What does Origen see as the point of this purposeful distortion? How is it possible for the Holy Spirit to communicate truth infallibly through the use of purposeful distortion? Origen believed that when biblical authors realized historical accuracy could not convey the spiritual truth they desired to communicate, they felt free to modify history to communicate spiritual truth. Indeed, says Heine, Origen will sometimes argue that "historical problems were sometimes slipped into the text of Scripture to alert the reader to the fact that one must not depend on the literal meaning, but must search out the spiritual meaning."[52]

How would Origen teach us to read the Bible? What advice might Origen have to offer the modern exegete? Should evangelical and other conservative exegetes immediately discount Origen because of his hermeneutical approach?

First of all, we need to listen carefully to what Origen desires to say to us.

His first words of advice to all Christians would emphasize the importance of saturating our minds with Scripture itself, a saturation that must
take place in the context of prayer and worship. Origen contends that his
hermeneutic cannot function safely unless we are immersed in the biblical
narrative and praying that the Holy Spirit reveal the truth of the Bible to
us. Origen's own father had insisted that Origen spend time daily in
memorizing Scripture; by the time Origen began his scholarly work his
mind was a veritable biblical concordance. Heine comments that "One of
the criticisms that Origen directed at the majority of Christians later in
his life was that they lacked this long and diligent experience with the
Scriptures."[53]

A well-stocked biblical memory was only one of the requirements
Origen envisioned for the prepared exegete. Biblical insight only came
through knowledge conceived in the womb of prayer and worship. In his
well-known letter to Gregory the Wonderworker Origen urges Gregory
to ground his study of the Bible in prayer. Prayer "is most necessary for
understanding the divine Scriptures. . . . [T]he Saviour not only said,
'Knock and it will be opened to you,' and, 'Seek and you will find,' but he
also said, 'Ask and it will be given to you' [Mt 7:7]."[54]

Origen is convinced that Scripture possesses a deeper meaning that
opens itself to those filled with the Spirit. Did not Paul teach in 1 Corinthians 2:10 that "God has given us a revelation through his Spirit. For
the Spirit searches all things, even the depths of God"?[55] If so, the biblical
exegete must rely on the Holy Spirit to open the Scripture to her.

> It is the Spirit, he says, that is able to search "all things." The human
> soul cannot search all things, but the higher Spirit must come to be in
> us so that, when he who searches all things has come to be in us and
> has been united with us, we, together with him, may search "all things,
> even the depths of God."[56]

In a debatable hermeneutical maneuver, Origen contends that not all
Christians possess the insight to discern the Bible's deeper truths. Thus,
one must distinguish between "the simple" and those prepared to enter
the Bible's depths. Even the Spirit recognized that the church would
contain a mixture of believers—those able to plumb the depths of Scripture and those only able to understand on a simple, more literal level.[57]
Origen pictures the biblical interpreter as a miner who plumbs the depths
of the Bible for its hidden treasure and when possible presents this deeper

truth to the church at large in a more comprehensible form. Heine believes that in many of Origen's sermons he did this very thing, popularizing "those points of his thought which he considered most relevant to 'the simple' in his attempt to lead them to a higher level of understanding of the Christian faith."[58]

We must now explore more fully two key questions: Why did Origen believe there is a deeper truth contained within the literal sense of Scripture? What was his hermeneutic for discovering this deeper truth?

Heine mentions a group of Pauline texts that were fundamental in shaping Origen's interpretive method: Romans 7:14; 1 Corinthians 2:10-16; 9:9-10; 10:11; 2 Corinthians 3:6; 3:15-16 and Galatians 4:24. Origen's understanding of 1 Corinthians 2:10-16 in particular explains the rhyme and reason of his interpretive methodology.[59] Paul writes in verse 13, "This is what we speak, not in words taught us by human wisdom but in words taught by the Spirit, expressing spiritual truths in spiritual words" (NIV). Paul's words "provide Origen with one of his most used and most important techniques for discerning the spiritual meaning in a text. It is the principle which would later be called 'interpreting Scripture by Scripture.'"[60] Because Origen is convinced that the Holy Spirit has inspired all of the Bible, he feels free to exegete individual, separate passages in light of the whole, fully expecting the mysteries of one text to be illuminated by the clearer truth contained in another. According to Heine,

> Origen claims to have learned the principle from a Jewish teacher. The teacher compared Scripture to a house with many locked rooms. A key lies before each door, but it is not the key to that door. The difficulty in understanding the obscurities in the Scriptures is likened to the difficulty in discovering the right key for the right door. The proper procedure for unlocking the mysteries in a passage of Scripture is to search in other passages, since the Scriptures "hold the explanation themselves." Origen comments, "The apostle, I think, suggested such a way of coming to a knowledge of the divine words when he said, 'Which things also we speak, not in words taught by human wisdom, but in words taught by the Spirit, comparing spiritual things with spiritual'" [Selecta in Psalmos (PG 12: 1080C)].[61]

Through the comparison of texts inspired by the Spirit the interpreter recognizes and unlocks the truth of those same texts through the Spirit. "When, therefore, he arrives at a meaning for a text by comparing other Biblical texts containing similar terminology, it is the Spirit speaking in the auxiliary texts which teaches him the meaning of the text in question."[62]

This is the hermeneutical principle that Origen believes will prevent an overactive hermeneutical imagination from abusing the use of allegory in determining the deeper sense of Scripture. That is to say, the interpreter can build up a symbolic reservoir of meaning by soaking his mind in the biblical narrative as a whole. Scripture itself will provide the symbolic grid needed to discern and comprehend its deepest meaning.

This symbolism, once established, could then function without the continual repetition of the web of comparative texts from which it had been created. Particular persons, places and events in the Bible came to symbolize key persons, places and events in the drama of salvation being played out below the surface of the texts. The appearance of these indicators in a text immediately alerted the spiritual reader to this symbolic meaning.[63]

So, as both Origen and Heine believe, the search for a deeper symbolic or allegorical meaning in the biblical text is not a hermeneutical free fall in which anything can mean anything. Because the biblical narrative itself— from Genesis to Revelation—fills Origen's symbolic or allegorical reservoir, his interpretation results from the use of symbolic clues revealed through a comparison of text with text. This methodology is built on Origen's deeply held conviction that the Holy Spirit has inspired each syllable of the Bible. As Heine asserts, "Origen's allegorical reading of the Bible was a coherent and controlled reading. The principle of comparing Biblical texts, which he based on 1 Corinthians 2:13, was a primary factor in both the coherence and controlled nature of his reading."[64]

Clement of Alexandria, Origen's predecessor at Alexandria, applied a similar methodology in his interpretation of the Bible. Like Origen, Clement was firmly convinced of the entire Bible's inspiration by the Holy Spirit. Because the same Spirit is behind the entire text, one section can surely illuminate another. Clement likens the adept exegete to a honeybee, flying from flower to flower as it gathers nectar in "the meadow of Prophets and Apostles in order to produce pure knowledge in the souls of his hearers."[65]

Clement's hermeneutic enables him to group the Scripture's teaching on a given theme or concept. On the other hand, Clement tends, like Origen, to overlook the importance of context, wrenching verses out of their contextual setting in his desire to read all of Scripture in the light of the gospel. Exegesis becomes a sifting operation for Clement as he pans the riverbed of Scripture in search of the gold sprinkled there by Christ himself—a hidden vein of truth the Christian exegete can uncover through a discerning hermeneutic. Eric Osborn elaborates on this hermeneutic as practiced by Clement:

> His use of Scripture is distinctly theological, since he surmises that in Jesus Christ all truth has at once been communicated. This one truth of Jesus Christ must be discovered everywhere that it is hidden. Thousands of verses of Scripture, just like the quotations he draws from other sources, are uprooted from their old context so that they can be situated in the new context of Christ. Clement's theological method aims at recovering unity and truth in Christ by regathering the different elements of the truth; a concern for the unity of the whole body of truth presupposes the appreciation of its parts. Clement often assembles his quotations (as in Strom. 2.22) with an aesthetic sensibility that an attentive reader will pick up on. This sense of relations and connections comes from the fact that Clement lives within the Bible as did Origen and, much later, Luther.[66]

As we have seen, Origen's search for the symbolic sense of a text did not blind him to the literal meaning of many biblical passages. Origen felt it was his responsibility to use every tool available to him to grasp the literal sense. He was careful to study "textual variants, the geography of Palestine, the etymology of words, the general context, grammar, logic, and, when treating the Gospels, the parallel accounts."[67]

Origen, however, is continually waving his theological antennae over the literal sense of the biblical text. And if a text fails to satisfy or make sense to him on a literal reading, Origen will employ the larger symbolic field he has culled from Scripture as a whole to discern a deeper, allegorical sense. Greek philosophers had done so for years in studying Homer, and in what Heine calls "one of Origen's most significant borrowings from Greek philosophy," Origen does the same with the Bible itself.[68]

Because Origen was convinced of Scripture's inspiration, he was confident that the Bible's own symbolic range would prevent him from overstepping his bounds as he searched for the Bible's deeper sense. In addition, Origen argued that it is Scripture itself that drove him to seek this deeper meaning. He believed that too many texts remain inexplicable, nonsensical or morally repugnant if interpreted literally. The Bible's symbolic field functions "as a control on the possible range of meanings of a text," a symbolic field formed through the careful comparison of biblical texts.

Origen believed the goal of the biblical exegete, indeed of every Christian, was to read Scripture with the mind of Christ. That is, a mind filled with the Spirit of Christ, the Holy Spirit (cf. 1 Cor 2:12-16). Not all are able to read the Bible in this way. One must be trained to do so effectively. In particular, "simple" believers will need coaching and nudging to help them spot the deeper meaning of Scripture.

In the final analysis, as Heine explains, Origen's interpretation of the Bible entails a number of intersecting hermeneutical circles

> in which the whole is understood in terms of the details, and the details in terms of the whole. . . . There is the narrower circle of the comparison of texts in which the literal terminology is used to bring together texts which share words or ideas. From these texts which have elements in common, the key to the spiritual meaning of a word or concept in the text in question is established, and this meaning then functions to provide the symbolic significance wherever else the term may occur. This circle involves the text in relation to itself. The next larger circle involves the reader and the text. Only the spiritual person can discern the hidden meaning of the text, but the hidden meaning of the text itself plays a major role in the formation of the spiritual person. Finally, there is the circle that involves the Holy Spirit, the text, and the reader. Both the text and the spiritual reader are formed ultimately by the Holy Spirit. The Spirit works independently in both the text (by inspiration) and the reader (through prayer). But the Spirit also works conjointly in them in the illumination of the reader through the comparison of texts.[69]

As we will soon see, other fathers were quick to point out the dangers and weaknesses of Origen's hermeneutic. Scholars representing the rival exegetical school at Antioch critiqued sharply the allegorical methodology of Alexandria. Fathers such as Diodore, John Chrysostom, Basil the Great and Theodore of Mopsuestia advocated a hermeneutic that largely eschewed allegory. In Antiochene exegesis the "literal" meaning of the biblical text would be mined deeply. And yet fathers in Antioch were also open to a deeper sense they believed was embedded in a text's literal meaning. It is to these fathers' critique of Alexandria and their alternative approach to Scripture that we now turn.

SEVEN

THE FATHERS
& SCRIPTURE

The Response of Antioch

THE ALLEGORICAL METHODOLOGY SO POPULAR AT ALEXANDRIA was not without its critics among the church fathers, and rightly so, for the extended use of allegory is hermeneutical dynamite. At best, the use of allegorical interpretation requires great care and control. Clearly articulated rules governing its use and detecting its abuse are absolutely necessary. Without these safeguards exegetes can easily wrap their imaginations around the biblical text, importing into the text whatever their hermeneutical fancy desires the text to say. For these allegorical interpreters the Bible can become a lump of wax that they mold into a foreign shape, perhaps even into their own image.

Church fathers such as Irenaeus and Clement realized the need for tightly formulated rules for governing the use of allegory, but were less successful in formulating an adequate framework for the safe use of a hermeneutic so open to abuse. With the emergence of a rival school of interpretation at Antioch, a school that largely eschewed the allegorical exegesis practiced at Alexandria, the stage was set for a lively debate.

Should an exegete ever employ allegory in interpreting the Bible? Is there a difference between allegory and typology? If one discards allegory as too subjective a methodology, does this mean there is only one meaning a biblical text communicates? Can texts possess more than one level of significance? If so, how can we discern this deeper meaning? If not, how does one arrive at the literal meaning of a biblical text and discern its application for the daily life of the Christian? We have seen how Alexandrian interpreters tended to answer these questions. Now we shall examine how the fathers in Antioch responded to the same issues. Did they radically reject the Alexandrian perspective? Or, as Joseph Trigg suggests, do Alexandria and Antioch represent complementary rather than contradictory and competitive viewpoints?[1] We will explore a wide terrain to answer these questions adequately.

Joseph Trigg identifies the emergence of a distinctive Antiochene approach with the work of Theophilus of Antioch, a scholar from the late second century. It was not until the late fourth and early fifth centuries, however, that a significant flowering of Antiochene hermeneutics took place, with the work of well-known fathers such as Diodore of Tarsus, John Chrysostom, Theodore of Mopsuestia and Theodoret of Cyrrhus.

Karlfried Froehlich observes that "there can be little doubt that the hermeneutical theories of the Antiochene school were aimed at the excesses of Alexandrian spiritualism." He adds that Antioch was a scholarly environment well known for producing interpreters versed in "careful textual criticism, philological and historical studies, and the cultivation of classical rhetoric."[2] He warns, however, that to make a sharp distinction between Alexandrian and Antiochene exegesis, as though Alexandrian fathers were only allegorizers while Antiochene exegetes remained firmly planted in the literal meaning of the text, is to simplify matters.

Origen, the allegorizer par excellence, was well aware of the literal meaning of a biblical text. Similarly, exegetes formed by Antiochene hermeneutical methodology were not averse to viewing Scripture as a layered text. One could interpret the Bible in an anagogical fashion in which, as Froehlich explains, "the biblical text leads the reader upward into spiritual truths that are not immediately obvious and that provide a fuller understanding of God's economy of salvation."[3] An example is the interpretive method advocated by the fountainhead of Antiochene exegesis, Diodore of Tarsus.

Diodore of Tarsus (d. ca. 390)

Diodore, the bishop of Tarsus, had written a treatise entitled *What Is the Difference Between Contemplation and Allegory?* He had become suspicious of allegory because it seemed to impose a foreign meaning upon the biblical text. In contrast to the allegorical approach, Diodore advocated "contemplation" or "theoria," which, as Joseph Trigg defines it, is an interpretive disposition and device that identifies

> the spiritual meaning of a text which both inheres in the historical framework and also takes the mind of the reader of scripture to higher planes of contemplation. . . . *Theoria* was the disposition of mind, the insight, which enabled prophets to receive their visions in the first place; it was thus both the necessary condition for scripture and its highest interpretation. Diodore then could acknowledge the typological interpretation of the Old Testament which had long been a standard reading in the church without accepting an allegorical reading.[4]

This would suggest that the difference between Alexandria and Antioch might well be one of emphasis and priority, as Froehlich argues.

> In Antioch, the Hellenistic rhetorical tradition, and therefore the rational analysis of biblical language, was stressed more than the philosophical tradition and its analysis of spiritual reality. Moreover, in Alexandria, history was subordinated to a higher meaning; the historical referent of the literal level took second place to the spiritual teaching intended by the divine author. In Antioch, the higher *theoria* remained subject to the foundational *historia*, the faithful (or sometimes even fictional) account of events; deeper truth for the guidance of the soul took second place to the scholarly interest in reconstructing human history and understanding the human language of the inspired writers.[5]

Perhaps a closer look at Diodore's treatment of Psalms would be helpful in illustrating Froehlich's comment. In Diodore's prologue to his commentary on Psalms he writes that "Scripture teaches what is useful, exposes what is sinful, corrects what is deficient, and thus it completes the perfect human being."[6] The applicability of the psalms, Diodore rightly stresses, reveals itself to those reliving the situation of the psalmist, rather than to the person who simply chants them unreflectively. Therefore, Diodore argues,

> when our souls find in the psalms the most ready formulation of the concerns they wish to bring before God, they recognize them as a

wonderfully appropriate remedy. For *the Holy Spirit anticipated all kinds of human situations*, setting forth through the most blessed David the proper words for our sufferings through which the afflicted may find healing.[7] (emphasis added)

Because of this potential of the psalms for providing God-given remedies to the existential and spiritual quandaries all Christians face, Diodore is eager to explicate sound hermeneutical principles for understanding the Psalms well. He specifically explains that he will discuss the "plain text" of the psalms. He does not want his readers "to be carried away by the words when they chant, or to have their minds occupied with other things because they do not understand the meaning." Instead, Diodore wants his readers to comprehend "the logical coherence of the words."[8]

Diodore then provides a helpful classification of the psalms with major headings and subheadings. Some are ethical in nature while others are doctrinal. In turn, one can divide the ethical psalms into those that "correct the behavior of the individual" and those that address Israel as a whole.[9]

Diodore also identifies the Babylonian captivity, Israel's experience in Egypt and the journey of Israel through the wilderness as key events around which the psalms circulate and in a sense absorb their background themes. Varieties of new harmonies and melodies are built off these basic movements.

Some of these psalms seem to be spoken by people facing deportation, others by people already in captivity, others by people hoping to return, still others by people who have returned. There are also other psalms describing past events in which, for the benefit of later generations, the prophet recalls what happened in Egypt and in the desert. There are even Maccabean psalms, some spoken in the person of specific individuals such as Onias and leaders like him; others in the collective person of all Israelites enduring the sufferings of that time.[10]

Diodore covers "one more preliminary point" concerning the nature of biblical prophecy. "The entire prophetic genre," he writes, "is subject to the threefold division into future, present, and past." Moses' description of events concerning Adam and other primordial history is a type of prophecy that explains the inner divine meaning of past events to the reader. Peter's knowledge of the attempted deception of Ananias and Sapphira is an example of prophecy related directly to the present situation of the church in the book of Acts. And "most prominent" are prophecies concerning the future, "sometimes many generations in advance."[11]

Diodore clearly wants to explain the psalms within their own historical context, and the questions he asks of the texts reveal this concern. For example, are the psalms listed in chronological order? Evidently not is Diodore's conclusion, at least if the headings for individual psalms are trustworthy. The heading for Psalm 3 describes it as having been written while David was fleeing from Absalom, while Psalm 143 in Diodore's edition is headed "A song against Goliath." Thus, as Diodore analyzes matters, the psalms are chronologically out of order.

> The psalms suffered much displacement because the book was accidentally lost during the Babylonian captivity. Afterwards, about the time of Ezra, it was rediscovered, though not the whole book at once but piecemeal—one, two, or perhaps three psalms at a time. These were then reassembled in the order in which they were found, not as they were arranged originally. Hence, even the inscriptions are mostly incorrect; more often than not, the collectors tried to guess the context of the psalms they found but did not treat them according to a scholarly method.[12]

As Diodore closes his prologue to the psalms, he distinguishes between *historia* (the historical substance of a text), *lexis* (the plain literal sense), *theoria* (the elevated sense of a text gained from a careful exegesis of the literal sense) and allegory. Diodore desires to steer clear of allegory because it is divorced from the literal, historical sense of the Bible. It violates the historical substance of the text as the exegete creates meaning out of thin air. Those who introduce allegory as a hermeneutical device, then, "are careless about the historical substance, or they simply abuse it." They possess a "vain imagination, forcing the reader to take one thing for another."[13]

While Diodore rejects allegory he does not deny that the literal, historical meaning of a text can lead to a higher meaning, the anagogical sense Antiochene exegetes called *theoria*. Diodore argues that "history is not opposed to *theoria*. On the contrary, it proves to be the foundation and the basis of the higher senses." A key aspect of *theoria*, however, is that it never eliminates or ignores the underlying literal and historical sense. If it did so it "would then be no longer *theoria* but allegory. For wherever anything else is said apart from the foundational sense, we have not *theoria* but allegory."[14]

This fundamental distinction between *theoria* and allegory allows Diodore to perceive typologies created within the biblical narrative itself. Cain and Abel, for example, become types of Israel and the church: "[L]ike Cain's sacrifice the Jewish synagogue was rejected, while the offerings of the church are being well received as was Abel's offering at that time." Likewise, the sacrificial lamb of the Passover meal becomes Christ.[15]

Diodore insists that this kind of biblical cross-referencing does not violate the meaning of the Bible, but rather brings its higher meaning to light. It prevents a lapse into the interpretive free fall of allegory, while speeding the interpreter's hermeneutical lens beyond the shutter speed of Judaism. That is, the gospel itself—God's great redemptive act in Christ—demands that we read Scripture from a broader perspective.

> This method neither sets aside history nor repudiates *theoria*. Rather, as a realistic, middle-of-the-road approach which takes into account both history and *theoria*, it frees us, on the one hand from a Hellenism which says one thing for another and introduces foreign subject matter; on the other hand, it does not yield to Judaism and choke us by forcing us to treat the literal reading of the text as the only one worthy of attention and honor, while not allowing the exploration of a higher sense beyond the letter also.[16]

What of Paul's use of the term *allegoroumena* (speaking allegorically) in his Galatian epistle? Diodore acknowledges Paul used the term but denies that he employed it in its classical sense. "He was not ignorant of the term but was teaching us that, if the term 'allegory' is judged by its conceptual content, it must be taken in the sense of *theoria*, not violating in any way the nature of the historical substance."[17] He makes a similar point in the preface to his commentary on Psalm 118:

> Above all, one must keep in mind one point which I have stated very clearly in my prologue to the psalter: Holy Scripture knows the term "allegory" but not its application. Even the blessed Paul uses the term: "This is said by way of allegory, for they are two covenants" [Gal 4:24]. But his use of the word and his application is different from that of the Greeks.[18]

The distinction that Antiochene scholars made between allegory and *theoria* is of central importance. Diodore views allegory, forged in a Hellenistic furnace, as fundamentally foreign to a historically based *theoria*. Greek myths often demanded an allegorical interpretation, simply because they painted such an unattractive, bizarre picture of the Greek gods. Diodore relates the story of Zeus changing himself into a bull, seizing Europa and carrying her across the sea to foreign regions—hardly an attractive or flattering picture of the greatest Greek god. He emphasizes that a literal interpretation of the story makes little sense. Could, for instance, a real bull swim such a great distance?[19] The inherent improbability of the story demands that it be interpreted allegorically.

One is reminded of Origen's struggles with the literal sense of Scripture. Origen turned to allegory as a sort of hermeneutical rescue operation because when he read the biblical text literally it too often seemed implausible, confused or morally repugnant. Indeed, Origen is not reticent to declare certain biblical events as untrue, lacking historical basis and morally questionable if taken literally. Exegetes in Antioch were much more reluctant to take this hermeneutical escape route.

Again, take as an example Paul's "allegory" in Galatians 4. Diodore argues that Paul's treatment of this text is not true allegory because his comparison makes no sense if the exegete ignores the literal sense of the Genesis account of Hagar and Sarah. *Theoria*, the higher vision of the text, builds upon its literal and historical meaning but never ignores it.

> Based on the historical account of Isaac and Ishmael and their mothers, I mean Sarah and Hagar, Paul develops the higher *theoria* in the following way: He understands Hagar as Mount Sinai but Isaac's mother as the free Jerusalem, the future mother of all believers. The fact that the apostle "theorizes" in this way does not mean that he repudiates the historical account. For who could persuade him to say that the story of Hagar and Sarah was untrue? With the historical account as his firm foundation, he develops his *theoria* on top of it; he understands the underlying facts as events on a higher level. It was this developed *theoria* which the apostle calls allegory.[20]

Diodore's interpretation of Psalm 118, by way of contrast to an allegorical approach, refuses to bypass the literal and historical context of the psalm. Rather, he fully expects the psalm to be suited to the context of "those who first uttered it as well as those who come after them. . . . [T]his is not a case of allegory; rather, it is a statement adaptable to many situations according to the grace of him who gives it power."[21]

At this juncture Diodore's thinking is similar to the modern pastor who fully expects an Old Testament text to possess lasting relevance for a contemporary Christian audience. Conservative biblical interpreters trained in grammatical-historical exegesis will likely take a close look at historical and cultural context, political and theological background, and lexical and grammatical considerations. They will work hard to hear what the text might have said to its original audience. But they will also, particularly because of their high view of the inspiration and authority of all of Scripture, fully expect the Old Testament text still to speak today. Diodore would probably describe this last step, the reading of the Old Testament text in light of the New Covenant and the search for its present Christian relevance, as *theoria*.

After all, Diodore sees this layered meaning in Psalm 85:1-2 (Ps 84:1-2 LXX): "LORD, you were favorable to your land; you restored the fortunes of Jacob. You forgave the iniquity of your people; you pardoned all their sin."

> These words were certainly fitting at the time of Israel's return [from Babylon]; but they will be even more suitable at the resurrection when, freed from our mortality, we shall be liberated from all sins even more truly. . . . [In the same way, Psalm 118 can be applied to] those who first uttered it as well as those who come after them. . . . [I]t is a statement adaptable to many situations according to the grace of him who gives it power.
>
> Now, if this is the subject of the psalm and someone says that Psalm 118 fits all saints everywhere and that one should always pray to God for the general resurrection, as the exiles in Babylon prayed for their return to Jerusalem, this is no violation of propriety. Being so rich and lavish, the psalm adapted itself readily to the exiles in Babylon for their request and prayer, but it adapts itself even more precisely to those who fervently long for the general resurrection.[22]

Theodore of Mopsuestia (d. 428)

Theodore of Mopsuestia, another noteworthy Antiochene exegete, also had strong feelings about the shortcomings of the Alexandrian school and its reliance upon allegorical interpretation. Theodore's commentary on Galatians 4:21-31 is particularly enlightening in helping us to understand why exegetes in Antioch were so wary of allegory while simultaneously affirming the possibility of *theoria*.

Theodore first centers his attention on the wider context of Paul's apparent advocacy of allegory in his treatment of Hagar and Sarah. Theodore explains that two different principles are operative in the Galatian epistle. The principle of law "demands the hearer's obedience," "seems to offer righteousness . . . when it promises to offer these benefits to those who fulfill" its demands, but actually "defrauds many—virtually all, to be more precise," for "those who strive to fulfill the law find it impossible to do so."[23]

The second principle is that of grace. This principle accentuates "the giver's generosity":

[Paul] was eager . . . to establish the principle of grace firmly throughout. Therefore, he mentioned faith and the promises in one breath with those benefits we hope to obtain. . . . Paul therefore stresses very much that the righteousness coming through grace is better than the righteousness coming through law; God offers it in his natural generosity and no one is excluded because of his natural infirmity.[24]

How might the Hagar-Sarah narrative relate to these two fundamental principles in the Galatian letter? Ishmael, the son born by the slave woman Hagar, represents "the natural order," that which "takes part in a birth according to nature." Isaac, the son of the free woman, was born according to a different principle, "the promise, that is, according to grace, for all promises are normally made by grace." In some ways, Theodore argues, it is wrong to even consider Isaac's arrival a true birth. After all, Sarah suffered from both "sterility" and "was too old for childbirth." Yet Isaac was born according to the principle of promise and grace, "against all hope and against the order of nature by virtue of the power and generosity of the giver of the promise alone."[25]

Having used the Hagar-Sarah narrative to make his point, Paul must now face the methodological question. Was his interpretation a proper reading of the Old Testament account? He claims to be presenting an allegory (v. 24). Theodore, however, believes that Paul does not actually allegorize the Hagar-Sarah narrative, but instead uses it in the sense of a valid comparison. Theodore's defense of Paul springs from his arguments against the use of allegory.

There are people who take great pains to twist the senses of the divine Scriptures and make everything written therein serve their own ends.

... [T]hey dream up some silly fables in their own heads and give their folly the name of allegory. They (mis)use the apostle's term as a blank authorization to abolish all meanings of divine Scripture.[26]

Theodore insists that Paul is not treating Scripture as a wax nose to be shaped by the interpreter's whimsy. He is not practicing allegory in the sense in which meaning is created out of whole cloth. Instead, the apostle's reading of Genesis is rooted in history and context. "For the apostle neither does away with history nor elaborates on events that happened long ago. Rather, he states the events just as they happened and then applies the historical account of what occurred there to his own understanding."[27]

Theodore directs his reader's attention to Paul's use of "just as" in his comparison between Hagar and "the present Jerusalem." Would this comparison make sense if Paul were employing an allegorical device divorced from the Old Testament narrative's grounding in history? "For in saying 'just as' he pointed to a similarity; but similarity cannot be established if the elements involved do not exist."

Why is the historical grounding of the biblical narrative so important to Theodore? The allegorists, he maintains, act "as if the entire historical account of divine Scripture differed in no way from dreams in the night."[28] For example, when allegorists start interpreting Scripture "spiritually," how will they treat a figure such as Adam? Historical reality, Theodore contends, disappears completely as Adam suddenly "is not Adam, paradise is not paradise, the serpent not the serpent."

I should like to tell them this: If they make history serve their own ends, they will have no history left. But if this is what they do, let them tell us how they can answer questions such as these: Who was created the first human being? How did his disobedience come about? How was our death sentence introduced? ... [I]f their assertion is true, if the biblical writings do not preserve the narrative of actual events but point to something else, something profound which requires special understanding—something "spiritual" as they would like to say, which they have discovered because they are so spiritual themselves, then what is the source of their knowledge?[29]

Surely this is the key question, indeed, the most difficult question for the advocate of allegorical interpretation to answer convincingly. What central hermeneutical principle governs the use of allegory? Not only is the source of the allegorist's interpretation mysterious and illusive, but the search for meaning beyond history in a deeper "spiritual" sense threatens the gospel itself. Why, Theodore asks, would God become incarnate if the events related in the initial chapters of Genesis have no historical basis?

What were those events in the distant past to which he refers, and where did they take place, if the historical account relating them does not signify real events but something else, as those people maintain? What room is left for the apostle's words, "but I fear lest, as the serpent seduced Eve" [2 Cor 11:3], if there was no serpent, no Eve, nor any seduction elsewhere involving Adam?[30]

Theodore insists that Paul does not play fast and loose with history. Rather, he uses the historical events as the foundation for any deeper meaning he wishes to extrapolate. "In many instances the apostle clearly uses the historical account of the ancient writers as the truth and nothing but the truth. In our passage, he attempts to prove his assertion from actual events as well as from their written records."[31]

Theodore then proceeds to explain how the events concerning Hagar and Sarah are an apt comparison to the greater events and meanings brought to fulfillment in the work of Christ. Paul's fundamental goal in comparing these two women is to demonstrate "that even now the justification coming from Christ is far better than the other, because it is acquired by grace."[32]

Hagar represents the Old Covenant, the law given through Moses, the attainment of righteousness through the law, "with a great deal of effort and sweat." Theodore notes that "this is extremely hard, in fact impossible, if the standard of strict implementation of every command is applied. For it is impossible for a human being here on earth to live entirely without sin."[33] Hagar gives birth "according to the order of nature," representing "justification through the law." She correlates to those who live "in this life, in which a conduct regulated by law seems to have its place."[34]

Ishmael, Hagar's child, is born into slavery, as are Hagar's spiritual children. This is so "because those who live under the law experience precepts and law as the imposition of an order of slavery: They are punished mercilessly if they have sinned; they are praised if they have obeyed the law in all details. It is an arduous task requiring a great deal of effort."[35] This is the life of a slave, not a daughter or son.

Paul's comparison continues: Hagar-Mount Sinai-the Old Covenant-the present Jerusalem, "that is, Jerusalem regarded from the vantage point of this life." In sum, Hagar stands for the old aeon or old age and all it represents—law rather than gospel, slavery rather than freedom, the natural rather than the supernatural realm of grace. Hagar points to the freedom that Sarah signifies, but never attains it herself.[36]

Sarah represents the New Covenant, the new age, the "new existence in an immortal nature."[37] While Hagar gives birth to Ishmael according to the laws of nature, Sarah gives birth to Isaac against all hope. While the law "controls" those born naturally, the grace represented by Sarah signifies justification, "most truly implemented among those who have been raised once and for all and expect their second birth through grace against all hope."

Here is the reason for Paul's allegory, which according to Theodore turns out to be nothing more than a most appropriate comparison. Unlike allegory, the comparison is rooted and inseparable from the realities it represents on a higher level, "juxtaposing events of the past and present."[38]

Still, Theodore occasionally shows a surprising willingness to identify historical inaccuracies in the Old Testament narrative, at least when divorced from their greater fulfillment in Christ. Theodore believes comments made concerning Zerubbabel, for example, "are not true in terms of its immediate historical reference; but these things are found to be true, whenever they are interpreted in reference to the Lord Christ."[39] Scripture speaks of Zerubbabel "in a most exaggerated way," hyperbolically, in light of God's future purpose and action in Christ. Theodore explains that recognizing figures of speech such as hyperbole helps to clarify texts that at first glance are mysterious or confusing. In his commentary on Zechariah he gives three specific examples from the Old Testament of exaggerated or hyperbolic language. One example concerns the promises made to Abraham; two concern David.

In four different texts from Genesis (12:3; 22:18; 26:4; 28:14) appears a variation of the promise, "in you all the families of the earth shall be blessed." Theodore immediately affirms the reference of the text to Abraham. "It is clear that this refers to those immediately descended from him." Having said this, however, Theodore quickly adds that "the truth of the saying is to be understood with regard to Christ the Lord, in whom the nations have actually been blessed."[40] That is to say, the writer of Genesis spoke "hyperbolically" of Abraham. Was all the world blessed through Abraham? Only if one realizes that the promise to Abraham was wider than Abraham himself. Indeed, the promise must extend beyond Abraham if the Old Testament text itself is to make sense.

Psalm 89 repeats three times that God will establish David's line forever. "I will establish his line forever, and his throne as long as the heavens endure" (v. 29). "His line shall continue forever, and his throne endure before me like the sun. It shall be established forever like the moon, an enduring witness in the skies" (vv. 36-37). Was this prophecy fulfilled in "its immediate historical reference"? Theodore acknowledges that "it seems to refer to his successors," that is, to the immediate descendants of the king. Yet, because of the psalmist's use of hyperbolic language, "the truth of the matter is revealed in Christ the Lord."[41]

Psalm 16:10 illustrates the same point: "[Y]ou will not abandon me to the grave, nor will you let your Holy One see decay" (NIV). This was not true of David, for he was speaking hyperbolically. "What was said by the blessed David hyperbolically concerning the people of the Israelites has been seen, in the truth of the matter, to refer to Christ the Lord, in which sense the blessed Peter correctly cited it saying, 'For his soul was not abandoned to hell nor did his flesh see corruption'" [Acts 2:31].

Theodore understands hyperbolic language, then, as purposeful exaggeration by a biblical writer in light of God's future greater acts. In a strict interpretation, David's body experienced decay. His words in Psalm 16 appear to run aground. Theodore teaches, however, that "they are found to be true in so far as they were said concerning Christ the Lord."[42]

Theodore views the use of hyperbole as the key to understanding Zechariah 9. On the one hand, the passage speaks of Zerubbabel, "a man of David's succession who was, according to God's purpose, the leader of the Jews." In the passage's hyperbolic sense, Zechariah is referring to one much greater: "the uncontrovertible reality is that the truth refers to Christ the Lord."

> For the vengeance of the former against the nations was slight and salvation accomplished for the inhabitants of the land was paltry, whence it follows consistently that "He will cut off the chariot from Ephraim and the war horse from Jerusalem," showing that in reference to this he has contributed to them the removal of those making war upon them. But the true message was spoken about Christ the Lord, concerning whom it is really possible to rejoice with a steadfast and

perpetual joy, who is really just, seeing that, along with this, he is really
judging and saving for the sake of the whole world, who indeed sets all
free from destruction for salvation perpetually and surely.[43]
Both Zechariah's reference to Zerubbabel and the gospel writers' application of the same prophecy to Jesus are correct when Zechariah's use of
hyperbolic language is duly noted by the exegete. Theodore, again like all
fathers, ends up viewing the Scripture as a layered text. His methodology,
though, is significantly different from exegetes such as Origen. While
Origen is apt to leave history behind in his search for the deeper sense of
a text, Theodore believes he has preserved the significance of both history
and the gospel in his interpretation. He also avoids slicing Zechariah's
prophecy into bits and pieces, with this slice pertaining to Zerubbabel and
that slice to Christ.

> [T]o say that a part of it is said concerning Christ, but for those
> returning [from exile] to be changed to Zerubbabel, and back to Christ
> from him, and back to Zerubbabel from Christ the Lord, is nothing
> different, to begin with, from revealing the prophecy to be utterly
> bizarre, equally apportioning the written sayings to the steward and to
> the Lord. Using proof that the things spoken do not pertain to Zerub-
> babel—that the prophet says 'is coming,' and yet Zerubbabel had
> already returned from the exile with the rest—is a sign of extraordinary
> nonsense and lack of skill in interpreting the divine scriptures.[44]

Instead, in what Theodore argues is a "more consistent and more seemly"
exegesis, he has acknowledged both the historical sense of the text and its
typological significance. Or, to use slightly different language, Theodore
has rescued both the message and the vision of Zechariah. The message
pertains directly to the key role Zerubbabel played as a leader of the
southern kingdom after the Babylonian exile, though "the sense is limited." The vision looks ahead to its fulfillment in Christ. "The prophet is
speaking concerning Zerubbabel and prophesying present things concerning him, if also as a prophet himself he had a certain vision concerning
things to come."[45]

Zechariah's words in verse 10 clearly fall into this deeper category:
"His dominion shall be from sea to sea, and from the River to the ends
of the earth." Theodore understands Zechariah to speak hyperbolically about Zerubbabel to point purposely to a greater figure who is
yet to come.

170 READING SCRIPTURE WITH THE CHURCH FATHERS

Alexandria and Antioch on the Question of Wealth and Poverty

Perhaps one can best illustrate the similarities and differences between biblical interpretation in Antioch and Alexandria by comparing exegetes as they address a timely and difficult issue. In the following comparison we will also note the insights of Western exegetes such as Jerome, Augustine and Ambrose.

The question of wealth and poverty remained a burning issue for the early Christian community. Should Christians retain their possessions? Was the possession of property lawful or not? How much was too much? Was a rich Christian a contradiction in terms? Could one follow Christ wholeheartedly and not give up one's possessions to the poor? What was the Christian's responsibility to the poor?

These questions were particularly difficult to resolve because the Scriptures themselves seemed to be ambiguous. On the one hand, Jesus warned against the danger of riches and occasionally called individuals to give up all they possessed to follow him (Mk 10:17-22). Riches could clearly blur one's ability to perceive the kingdom of God. "Children, how hard it is to enter the kingdom of God. It is easier for a camel to go through the eye of a needle than for a rich man to enter the kingdom of God" (Mk 10:24-25 NIV).

On the other hand, Jesus freely ate and drank with the wealthy. He was not averse to accepting the financial support of close, well-to-do friends (Lk 8:1-3). Joseph Kelly asks, "If there were no Christians with money, how could the Church have aided the poor?"[46] But how did the fathers read Scripture as they attempted to deal with the difficult issue of wealth and poverty? Did Alexandrian exegesis differ significantly from exegesis in Antioch on this question?

Clement of Alexandria, the first great Alexandrian exegete, addressed the issue of wealth and poverty in his exegesis of Matthew 19:24, the difficult saying of Jesus concerning the plight of the rich: "Again I tell you, it is easier for a camel to go through the eye of a needle than for a rich man to enter the kingdom of God" (NIV). If this is so, Clement asks, what hope is there for the rich? Will not Jesus' teaching discourage them from even investigating the gospel? Some who hear this saying will

> give up all hope of attaining eternal life, surrender themselves totally to the world, cling to the present life as if it were the only thing left to them, and so move farther away from the path to the life to come, no

longer inquiring either whom the Lord and Master calls rich, or how that which is impossible to man becomes possible to God. . . . [The exegete] must first with good reasons relieve them of their groundless despair, providing them with satisfactory explanations of the Lord's sayings, and showing them that they are not quite cut off from inheriting the kingdom of heaven.[47]

Clement solves the seemingly impossible commandment of Christ, at least for many in his rich audience, by moving beyond the literal meaning of the text. Some people "hastily interpret it," limiting their interpretation to the literal command "that [the man of wealth] should throw away what he possesses and renounce his wealth." By keeping to the literal sense they bypass the more important meaning. "What he is told to banish from his soul are his notions about wealth, his attachment to it, his excessive desire for it, his morbid excitement over it, and his anxieties—those thorns of existence which choke the seed of true life."[48]

Poverty in and of itself, Clement writes, is no guarantee of sound character or of an open disposition to God's kingdom and priorities. If poverty itself were praiseworthy or "enviable," poor beggars by the roadside "would be the most blessed of men, the dearest to God, the sole possessors of eternal life, merely in virtue of their complete lack of any ways or means of livelihood and of their want of the smallest necessities."[49] And is the elevation of poverty itself as a sign of virtue a distinctly Christian characteristic? "Many did this before the Savior's coming, some to have leisure for the pursuit of dead wisdom, others to gain empty fame and vainglory—men like Anaxagoras, Democritus and Crates."

If so, why would Christ give such a command? Would the mere giving up of one's possessions open the door to perceiving the essence of Christ's kingdom? Clement thinks not. Other people of old had done this very thing without increasing their spiritual discernment and comprehension one whit. Getting rid of wealth does not mean that one will cease to "lust and hanker for it."[50] Hence, if the literal meaning of the text fails to make adequate sense, Clement believes, we must look beneath its surface. What do we find?

If there is something extraordinary that the new creation, the Son of God, reveals and teaches, then it cannot be the outward action that he is commanding; others have done that. It must be something else that is being indicated through it—something greater, more divine and more perfect. It is the stripping off of the passions from the soul itself and from its disposition; all that is alien must be uprooted and expelled from the mind.[51]

What good is it, Clement asks, to rid oneself of riches if one's internal life is a disaster? Might not the poor person be trapped by envy and greed while the rich person experiences genuine poverty of heart? That is, poverty continually tempts the poor person to meet his needs through whatever means present themselves. "For when someone lacks the necessities of life he cannot but be broken in spirit; he will have no time for better things since he will make every effort to procure what he needs however and whenever he can."[52] Clement's allegorical exegesis, he would contend, has uncovered the genuine meaning of Jesus' teaching.

Origen, the next great exegete of the Alexandrian school, first looks at Matthew's text on a literal level and then proceeds to an allegorical reading. Note, Origen instructs his readers, that Jesus does not say that a rich man will not enter the kingdom of God. If he had done so, the rich would have been excluded. Rather, Jesus makes it plain that salvation for the rich is "difficult." Why? It is only with great difficulty that the rich can "resist their passions and sinful inclinations and not allow themselves to be dominated by them."[53]

Origen then explores what he terms "the figurative sense" of the passage. If the rich man is interpreted figuratively, why is his salvation so difficult? Why is its difficulty compared to that of a camel passing through a needle's eye?

[T]he kingdom of heaven is likened to the eye of a needle to indicate how extremely narrow and tight the entrance into the kingdom of heaven is for the rich man. The Lord, then, declares that it is impossible for the camel to enter the eye of a needle; but since all things are possible with God, he makes such an entry possible either by trimming the fat of evil with his ineffable power or by widening the narrow entry.[54]

As the passions of the rich and their inordinate desire for more and more are trimmed by the power of the gospel, their entrance into the kingdom becomes a possibility, difficult though it may be.

How do other exegetes handle the same question? Jerome writes that Christ's command for the rich man to give away all that he possesses to obtain treasure in heaven is a call to "careful stewardship." The choice to give away one's possessions is up to the individual; "full freedom of choice is left to every individual, whether old or young."[55] Jerome views Christ's command as addressed to those who would pursue perfection.

> What he means is: I do not compel you. I do not command you, but I set the palm of victory before you, I show you the prize. It is for you to decide whether you will enter the arena and win the crown. . . . And when you have sold them, what then? "Give to the poor." Not to the rich, not to your relatives, not to minister to self-indulgence, but to relieve the needs of others. . . . Let your praises come from the stomachs of the hungry and not from the rich banquets of the overfed. . . . It is yours to clothe Christ in the poor, to visit him in the sick, to feed him in the hungry, to shelter him in the homeless.[56]

Jerome appears less concerned about the practical problems of Christ's command, solving its difficulties by assigning its intent to those who would pursue perfection through the exercise of their own free choice. By relegating the command to the counsels of perfection Jerome averts the need to allegorize the passage.

Augustine, too, sees a higher call to perfection issued to the rich young man by Christ. The rich who do not respond to this higher call can still enter the kingdom if they remain faithful in their adherence to the commandments. "Why, then, do we refuse to admit that the rich, although far from that perfection, nevertheless enter into life if they keep the commandments, and give that it may be given to them, forgive that they may be forgiven?" It is not so much riches as one's inner disposition toward them that points a person toward heaven or hell. The rich man, for example, who ignores the needs of the beggar at his gate, is blinded by his pride. "It was his pride, not his riches, that brought the rich man to the torments of hell, because he despised the good poor man who lay at his gate."[57] For Augustine, the seeming impossibility of Christ's command only accentuates the need for God's grace.

> [W]hether they retain their riches and do their good works by means of them, or enter into the kingdom of heaven by selling them and distributing them to provide for the needs of the poor, let them attribute their good works to the grace of God, not to their own strength. What is impossible for men is easy, not for men, but for God. . . . [L]et them not attribute this to their own strength, but to the same divine grace. For, what is impossible for men is easy, not for them, because they are men, but for God.[58]

Augustine and other fathers differ in their reliance upon allegory in making sense of Christ's command, but are one in the applications they draw from the text. All would be shocked, for example, by the idea that God promises to bless us materially if we are faithful to him in our giving. As Augustine comments disapprovingly, "there are many such who even think that the Christian religion ought to help them to increase their riches and multiply earthly delights."[59]

Ambrose takes a different tack in approaching Christ's command. Why should the rich be sorrowful over Christ's command to give their riches to the poor? Instead, he beckons the rich to remember that "your wealth may be snatched from you by death, wrested from you by the power of some greater one; consider too how you are asked to give little for much, the transitory for the eternal, treasure of money which is corruptible for the treasure of grace which lasts."[60]

Ambrose asks, Have not the rich lost all sense of proportion in their self-indulgence? Their riches have blinded them to the needs of the poor, daily paraded before their very noses.

You give coverings to walls and bring men to nakedness. The naked cries out before your house unheeded; your fellow-man is there, naked and crying, while you are perplexed by the choice of marble to clothe your floor. A poor man begs for money in vain; your fellow-man is there, begging bread, and your horse champs gold between his teeth. Other men have no corn; your fancy is held by precious ornaments. What a judgment you draw upon yourself! The people are starving, and you shut your barns; the people are groaning, and you toy with the jewel upon your finger. Unhappy man, with the power but not the will to rescue so many souls from death, when the price of a jewelled ring might save the lives of a whole populace.[61]

How might an exegete trained in Antioch interpret the story of the rich young man and its implications for the rich? Let us examine John Chrysostom's exegesis. In all likelihood, John will avoid the allegorical tendencies of the Alexandrian school. Will the applications he derives from the text, however, substantially differ?

Chrysostom asks, Why did the rich young man finally walk away from Christ? Why was he unable to give away his possessions? The problem, Chrysostom believes, is that the young man "had many possessions." He was trapped by what he possessed. As the stilted NPNF translation puts it, "as they that are overflowed with great affluence, for then the love of it becomes more tyrannical."[62] The young man's love for his many possessions tyrannizes him, blinding him to the treasure he would receive from Christ if only he would follow.

Jesus tells the young man that he will receive heavenly treasure if only he will release his hold on his earthly wealth. "He called it a treasure, showing the plenteousness of the recompense, its permanency, its security, so far as it was possible by human similitudes to intimate it to the hearer."[63]

The young man's many possessions, however, harden his spiritual eardrums and render him deaf to Christ's invitation. His riches are actually his poverty. "Which thing I cease not always saying, that the increase of acquisitions kindles the flame more, and *renders the getters poorer*, as it puts them in greater desire, and makes them have more feeling of their want" [emphasis added].[64] The problem, Chrysostom insists, is not riches themselves, "but them that are held in subjection by them."

Can the rich enter the kingdom of God? Only through the grace of God. "Whence it is shown, that there is no ordinary reward for them that are rich, and are able to practise self command. Wherefore also He affirmed it to be a work of God, that He might show that great grace is needed for him who is to achieve this."[65]

Up to this point in Chrysostom's explanation of the passage, he has avoided allegory. Yet his interpretation differs only slightly from that of Alexandrian fathers. Both they and he believe Jesus is warning his audience that riches are spiritual dynamite. Money and possessions too easily become the dominant focus of the wealthy as objects of devotion and allegiance; if one is to exercise an inordinate, unmeasured desire, let it be for God and nothing else.

Chrysostom, of all the fathers, is perhaps most practical and specific in the applications he draws from these texts. How can Jesus' impossible command become possible for the Christian? How can a person whose life has revolved around the acquisition of riches follow Jesus' advice to the rich young man? Chrysostom's advice is to take things in stages. Perhaps begin, John advises, by getting rid of what is "superfluous." In this way one will "advance further" and "run on his course more easily afterwards. . . . Do not then seek all at once, but gently, and by little and little, ascend this ladder, that leads thee up to heaven."[66]

Those who are rich are plagued by an insatiable thirst for more money and possessions. John suggests that we slowly choke off the desire for more by purposefully refraining from adding to what we already possess and genuinely do not need. Over time the desire for wealth will gradually diminish, just as a flame will flicker and finally die if its source of oxygen is cut off. Desire, John insists, can be changed as we shift the focus of our love from one form of treasure to another.

> Therefore that we may not have superfluous sorrows, let us forsake the love of money that is ever paining, and never endures to hold its peace, and let us remove ourselves to another love, which both makes us happy, and has great facility, and let us long after the treasures above.[67]

John also reminds his audience that God will judge those who pursue riches at the expense of more important priorities. Hell awaits. And yet is not the pursuit of wealth a kind of hell on earth? How many households have been "overthrown" through the unbridled pursuit of riches? How many wars have been "stirred up" by greed? How many souls have been deformed by envy and avarice? Yes, "silver is bright." The rich "possess many servants and live in grand houses. The eyes of all are upon them in the marketplace." They are the celebrities of the age. But what price do they pay for this homage?

> If you consider how these things affect your soul, how dark, and desolate, and foul they render it, and how ugly; if you consider how many evils were committed to obtain these things, and how much work it takes to keep them, with how many dangers; indeed, can they be kept at all? Death will come to you and remove all these things. They will end up in the hands of your enemies. . . . When you see any one resplendent outwardly with fine clothes and people in attendance, lay open his conscience. You will find many cobwebs within, and much dust.[68]

Can any possession or treasure be worth exclusion from Christ's kingdom? Lands? Gold? Mountains? Slaves? Baths? Chariots covered with silver or gold? The entire world? In comparison to Christ's kingdom all these things are no more than a "dung heap." In fact, John jokes, one can at least use dung for fertilizing a field or heating a bath. What purpose does buried gold serve? It is not only worthless, but actually can harm its possessor. Best to treat wealth with caution and store up lasting treasure in the kingdom of God.

E I G H T

MAKING SENSE OF
PATRISTIC EXEGESIS

N OW THAT WE HAVE SPENT THE PREVIOUS FIVE CHAPTERS READ-
ing Scripture with the church fathers, we must take the next step and ask
ourselves how we are to respond to patristic exegesis. An across-the-board
acceptance of the fathers' reading of Scripture seems less than wise. Even the
fathers, as we have seen in our comparison of Alexandrian and Antiochene
biblical interpretation, sometimes strongly disagreed with each other. Some
might be tempted to reject patristic exegesis altogether, particularly because
of the fathers' continual search for a deeper meaning in the text of Scripture.
This in itself, at least for some, will warrant leaving patristic exegesis behind
as a valid reading of the Bible.

Is there perhaps a middle path we can follow between a naive, uncritical
acceptance of all patristic exegesis and a peremptory rejection? If so, what
might characterize the interpreter choosing this middle way?

Preliminary Questions
Are there attitudes and dispositions any student of Scripture and the

history of interpretation must cultivate to best appreciate patristic interpretation? Are there theological underpinnings one can construct to support a healthy response to the fathers? What are the particular roadblocks modern Christians, whether they be Roman Catholic, Eastern Orthodox or Protestant, can expect to encounter as they read Scripture with the fathers? Are there specific influences in the modern environment that could cripple a pastor's or layperson's ability to enter effectively the world and mind of the fathers? Can we correlate or connect the approach of the fathers with a more modern hermeneutic? Are there hermeneutical blind spots in the modern theological retina that the fathers can help us recognize and remedy?

Knowledge, Attitudes and Dispositions

Perhaps as good a place as any to begin our response to these important questions is to take a closer look at our own hermeneutical and theological pedigree. Who are the key people—parents, friends, pastors, scholars, mentors, authors, even enemies—who have significantly shaped how we read and understand the Bible? Harold O. J. Brown reminds us that no one, including great Protestant reformers such as Calvin and Luther, came to the Bible "cold, as it were, but each had been exposed to the Christian message and to forms of Christian life before being 'reformed' by the text of Scripture."[1] Hence the importance of understanding how we have come to read and understand the Bible the way we do.

A move away from the first person plural might well raise the level of our self-awareness concerning key pastoral, scholarly and familial influences on our theological and spiritual formation. Why do I believe the things I do about God? How have I learned to read the Bible? Who have been the main interpreters of Scripture for me? To what extent have I accepted their reading of Scripture? Have I been teachable or unteachable, critical or uncritical in my responses, both to my teachers and biblical truth itself? Have I been allowed to ask questions of my teachers and the biblical text? Have I grown up in a more open or closed theological and church environment?

Further questions might probe the level of our knowledge of the Bible, theology and church history. If I were to grade myself on my knowledge of church history or historical theology, what grade would I receive? How familiar am I with the Christians who lived before my time? Have I read their books and pondered their thoughts? Why or why not? How would I describe my theological and spiritual diet over the past ten years? Are the books that I have read still in print? Were they faddish or substantial, a light dessert or a substantial repast? If I were to list the ten books that have most significantly shaped my understanding of the Bible, what would they be?

Am I tempted to take the road of least resistance in my study? If I am not immediately attracted to an author or find an author's vocabulary, worldview or thought patterns difficult or foreign, am I apt to give up the effort to read her or him? When was the last time I read a difficult book that genuinely challenged me, seemingly stretching my abilities to their limit? How quickly do I dismiss another Christian's point of view? Am I a good listener? Do I ask myself the same questions I am likely to ask other believers?

It is best to be ruthlessly honest here. As you read through the various examples of patristic exegesis in this book, did you find yourself becoming angry, dismissive, incredulous, irritated, bored, confused, excited, stimulated or frustrated? The list of possible responses appears endless. How might you relate your responses to your theological pedigree? Or are other influences affecting your ability and willingness, positively or negatively, to empathize with a father's reading of a biblical text?

These questions are important because patristic exegesis can be fanciful, frustrating and difficult. The fathers, just like us, were subject to a variety of influences, pressures, presuppositions, predilections and, occasionally, prejudices. If we are to bring our two worlds together, that of the ancient and modern exegete, we will have to build significant bridges. Most of the bridge-building will have to be done by us. While the fathers are still with us in the communion of the saints, at present they are observers rather than active participants in the exegetical task—apart from the words they have left for us to ponder. They invite us to enter their world and have left behind a significant body of work for us to explore. But for our exegetical and theological explorations to be successful, our own dispositions and attitudes, as well as those of the fathers, need to be kept in mind.

Recognizing the kinds of books we have read over the past ten years can be enlightening largely because the rhythms of our reading illustrate deeper habits of learning that either facilitate or disrupt our ability to read the fathers well. For example, the shelves of many Christian bookstores are lined with volumes that frequently promise easy solutions to difficult problems, whether the difficulty be spiritual, emotional or intellectual. Christian how-to books predominate for a reason: many North American Christians possess a short attention span. If authors do not quickly make their practical, exegetical or theological point, we are apt to set them aside in our search for easy, accessible, immediate solutions. We want answers and we want them quickly.

People bred by their culture to expect a text to address and immediately answer problems, questions or issues that by their intrinsic nature demand a slower, broader and deeper response will often find themselves frustrated by patristic writers. The quest for immediate spiritual or intellectual gratification is rarely successful; short-term solutions to long-term problems ultimately break down. The fathers are insistent that spiritual, theological and biblical insight does not appear overnight. Instead, they adamantly insist that the Bible opens itself to those who have immersed themselves in its riches and pondered it deeply within the context of prayer, worship and communal reflection.

Unlike most modern people, including too many Christians, the fathers are in no rush. You will not find them providing ten easy steps for spiritual fulfillment, nor evincing great sympathy for those who might find their writings difficult to grasp for the first time. The problems and realities Scripture addresses and elucidates—sin, evil, death, life, incarnation, redemption, creation, recreation—demand the attention of a mind and heart that has learned to be patient, to listen, to be silent, to study "with the mind in the heart."

Learning to Listen

So again we ask ourselves a difficult question. Would I classify myself as a good listener? When I encounter voices that are unfamiliar or foreign, does my attention lapse or my irritation increase? Do I fail to listen because of the threat of the unfamiliar or because I lack the time to listen attentively to another? Can I genuinely give a listening ear to a Jerome, Chrysostom, Ambrose or Augustine? Or can I, in my most honest moments, acknowledge a tendency to prejudge the texts I am reading because they fall outside my particular Christian worldview and experience? Am I willing to enter into a father's world, all the time cognizant of the differences between his time and culture and mine, in such a manner that I receptively begin to hear what he is trying to say to me? Am I open to being taught? Might a patristic writer have something to teach me, something perhaps earthshaking, if only I would open myself to his voice?

Recall Thomas Oden's words as he began to read Nemesius for the first time:

> I realized that I must listen intently, actively, without reservation. Listen in such a way that my whole life depended upon hearing. Listen in such a way that I could see telescopically beyond my modern myopia, to break through the walls of my modern prison, and actually hear voices from the past with different assumptions entirely about the world and time and human culture.[2]

Michael Casey mentions two characteristics or requirements of the student if patristic commentary is ever to be wisely appropriated: patience and instruction. Both are linked to the centrality of listening.[3] Brevard Childs speaks of the need for "special training, indeed an unusual empathy, to be able to overcome the initial sense of strangeness with the exegesis of the Early Fathers and the Medieval Schoolmen. One cannot pose to Chrysostom the questions of Gunkel, nor address Bultmann's problems to Calvin."[4]

A gifted listener is able to enter empathetically into another's world. While never able to leave her own world behind, the empathetic listener comes alongside another and asks the other to open a new world to her. She stands ready, receptive, open, eager to enter another's experience.

Gifted listening entails hard work. The insights and perspectives the empathetic listener seeks to receive from the fathers offer themselves only to those willing to enter a new linguistic, symbolic and cultural world. At first things will appear terribly strange. Symbolic, cultural and linguistic shock will set in. Less empathetic listeners will soon retreat, deeply threatened by unfamiliar sites, sounds, symbols, expressions, perspectives and actions.

The empathetic listener, though, because she is convinced that the other person has something valuable to offer, will resist the temptation to flee back to more comfortable and familiar surroundings. She will remain put, struggling to hear and comprehend the mysterious world offered to her, patiently allowing herself the time and effort required to adjust to another's home. At heart she is utterly convinced that the convergence between two worlds is possible, that communication and mutual understanding can be accomplished, that a merging of horizons is more than a pipe dream. Gradually she will feel more and more at home in her new environment. And in time she will have earned the right to respond to her teachers and even to criticize.

In the end we cannot with integrity analyze, criticize or reject a world that we refuse to enter. We cannot fairly judge or discard voices to which we have never bothered to listen deeply. One might then ask, But why these voices? I have found the examples of patristic exegesis to be interesting, surprising and occasionally enlightening, but also foreign to my life in the modern world. Are they worth the investment of time and energy they will ask of me? Are there not modern writers who can say the same things just as well and in a manner I can more readily understand?

All of us know that time is short in the modern world and should be invested in projects that seem to promise a high return. Are the fathers worthy of such an investment? For help in answering this question let us consider an essay written by C. S. Lewis, first published as an introduction to Athanasius's *The Incarnation of the Word of God* and later published as a separate essay.[5]

Lewis is determined to debunk the idea that old books are by definition boring, dense and irrelevant, accessible only to the professional scholar. The great thinkers remain great and in print, Lewis insists, precisely because they are much more accessible than the mound of secondary literature most students rely on to learn of them. Lewis does not fault his students for turning to secondary literature, knowing that they are often intimidated by the great thinkers.

> The student is half afraid to meet one of the great philosophers face to face. He feels himself inadequate and thinks he will not understand him. But if he only knew, the great man, just because of his greatness, is much more intelligible than his modern commentator. . . . It has always therefore been one of my main endeavours as a teacher to persuade the young that first-hand knowledge is not only more worth acquiring than second-hand knowledge, but is usually much easier and more delightful to acquire.[6]

The same can be said of many of the fathers. The Ancient Christian Commentary on Scripture purposely limits editorial comments, specifically because it is the commentary of the fathers themselves that the series wishes to highlight. The editors of the series are confident that those students willing to listen empathetically to the fathers will soon discover patristic commentary to be accessible, profitable, even delightful.

What, though, of the question of relevance? Do not modern Christian writers inhabit, understand and interpret a world utterly impossible for ancient commentators to comprehend? Not necessarily. Sexual insanity, for example, has a long history, as the reader of Augustine can testify.

Precisely because modern Christian writers inhabit the modern world, they will see clearly on certain issues but much less so on others. If, for example, I have always lived in a sexually insane society, might I not inadvertently identify sexual insanity as normal? Or even if I recognize its abnormalities, hearing a Christian writer from another time and place discuss issues of sexual sin and purity can throw new light on my own perspectives.

If I have grown up in a materialistic, self-indulgent culture, I might well fail to see how material self-indulgence can blind me to Christ's call to self-sacrifice and self-denial. Reading Christian authors who lived in other times and locales helps to provide a buffer against the self-delusions and blindness any culture generates within its inhabitants towards certain facets of the gospel. Perhaps there are elements of the gospel or aspects of human sin and error I can only identify and understand clearly by stepping outside my historical, cultural, political or linguistic environment. In the words of Lewis, "Every age has its own outlook. It is specially good at seeing certain truths and specially liable to make certain mistakes. We all, therefore, need the books that will correct the characteristic mistakes of our own period. And that means the old books."[7]

Lewis has no desire to deify the past: "People were no cleverer then than they are now; they made as many mistakes as we." However, they did not, generally speaking, make "the *same* mistakes" we make today: "They will not flatter us in the errors we are already committing; and their own errors, being now open and palpable, will not endanger us. Two heads are better than one, not because either is infallible, but because they are unlikely to go wrong in the same direction."[8]

Lewis is particularly concerned that the "ordinary reader" ground himself in older sources because the "amateur" is "less protected than the expert against the dangers of an exclusive contemporary diet."[9] How is the ordinary reader, Lewis asks, to judge the quality of a new book that purports to represent the Christian faith? Only by gaining a familiarity with "mere Christianity" through reading Christian authors writing outside of a modern context.

> A new book is still on its trial and the amateur is not in a position to judge it. It has to be tested against the great body of Christian thought down the ages, and all its hidden implications (often unsuspected by the author himself) have to be brought to light. . . . The only safety is to have a standard of plain, central Christianity ("mere Christianity" as Baxter called it) which puts the controversies of the moment in their proper perspective. Such a standard can be acquired only from the old books.[10]

The modern pluralistic cultural and theological flowering had only begun to bud when Lewis wrote his essay. Yet Lewis was deeply concerned that Christians only familiar with modern sources might "be tempted to think . . . that 'Christianity' is a word of so many meanings that it means nothing at all." The only remedy for this misperception, Lewis argued, was to step outside of a modern setting. A journey with older Christian writers would soon produce the familiar scent of "mere Christianity," a fragrance that varied in sweetness and strength among various writers, but remained unmistakable all the same. Here is the consensual Christianity of which Vincent of Lerins spoke, that "which has been believed everywhere, always, by everyone."

> Once you have been soaked in it, if you then venture to speak, you will have an amusing experience. You will be thought a Papist when you are actually reproducing Bunyan, a Pantheist when you are quoting Aquinas, and so forth. For you have now got on to the great level viaduct which crosses the ages and which looks so high from the valleys, so low from the mountains, so narrow compared with the swamps, and so broad compared with the sheeptracks.[11]

How can we most effectively access the consensual Christianity both Lewis and Vincent of Lerins see stretching across the ages? The first and most direct step is to broaden our knowledge base. We need to read widely and deeply, avoiding the temptation to study only modern authors and exegetes. Thomas Oden rightly insists that the Holy Spirit has a history. Christians have been reading and exegeting the Bible for centuries. This history of exegesis, too often the domain of professional historical theologians and historians of biblical interpretation, has largely been ignored by the broader Christian community. Many Roman Catholics have little idea of how Protestants have read the Bible over the past four hundred years. Many Protestants know little if anything of how Roman Catholics have exegeted the Scriptures. What they do know has often been communicated secondhand through skewed and prejudiced sources. Protestants and Catholics both remain widely unaware of the Greek and Russian Orthodox exegetical traditions, and vice versa.

Learning to Remember

How can the Christian community nurture a greater awareness of how other Christians in that same community read the Bible? Surely not by pretending that disagreements over the meaning of Scripture do not exist. At significant junctures Roman Catholic, Protestant and Orthodox Christians remain divided over the meaning of key biblical texts and their implications for the Christian community. Meaningful conversation between Christians should openly acknowledge these disagreements.

Simultaneously, though, Christians can concertedly learn to listen to one another, to seek to understand each other's position, to love other Christians enough to take their exegesis, theology and corporate life seriously. A step in the right direction would be for all three groups to again take a look at the fathers.

Of course, the Orthodox community would respond that they have been reading the fathers carefully for years. But what might take place if Orthodox, Roman Catholic and Protestant Christians attempted to read patristic texts together, listening with humility to the music each group was hearing the fathers sing?

The Rose Hill conference illustrates well the type and strength of theological cross-fertilization that can occur between Christian communions as believers work hard to listen to one another and to remember their common tradition. In 1995 a group of Orthodox, Roman Catholic and Protestant scholars gathered at Rose Hill College in Aiken, South Carolina "to test whether an ecumenical orthodoxy, solidly based on the classic Christian faith as expressed in the Scriptures and ecumenical councils, could become the foundation for a unified and transformative witness to the present age."[12]

James Cutsinger, editor of the collection of essays written for the conference, comments that "serious Christian scholars" known for the "tenacity with which they" held to their respective perspectives and positions were invited to offer papers at the conference. This group included J. I. Packer, Kallistos Ware, Richard John Neuhaus, Peter Kreeft, Harold O. J. Brown and Patrick Henry Reardon. Conference participants were clearly concerned for unity between Christians, but not at the expense of truth. Here was a conference where unity, if it was to be discovered and experienced, would be based on the heart of the Christian faith rather than its periphery. The conference aimed to produce a "traditionalist ecumenism," one that "at the very least" refuses "to compromise the integrity of the Christian tradition."[13]

We had what might seem a rather odd idea: if only each of us could be brought to confess with utter candor why precisely he is Orthodox and not Catholic or Protestant, or Protestant and not Catholic or Orthodox, or Catholic and not Orthodox or Protestant, these outwardly divergent confessions, far better than any list of agreements drafted by a task force or a committee, might together point to the very heart of our faith. Father Richard John Neuhaus captured the spirit of our thinking in the opening address when he observed that in many cases "our unity in the truth is more evident in our quarreling about the truth than in our settling for something less than the truth."[14]

The conferees were confident that there was indeed a body of revealed and received truth all could recognize and affirm as the Christian tradition. This truth would emerge in its clarity, though, only if the representatives of each communion were open, direct and clear in their perception of what Christianity was all about, in both its affirmations and denials. Cutsinger refers to Lewis's expectation, expressed in his introduction to *Mere Christianity*, that "It is at her center, where her truest children dwell, that each communion is really closest to every other in spirit, if not in doctrine. And this suggests that at the center of each there is something, or a Someone, who against all divergences of belief, all differences of temperament, all memories of mutual persecution, speaks with the same voice."[15]

The Rose Hill conference demonstrated that Christians from widely differing backgrounds could learn from each other and grow with one another if they were willing to extend to their neighbor the gift of a listening ear. They listened both to each other and to the tradition they held in common, though participants' understanding of that tradition occasionally varied. This was to be expected. What was somewhat less expected was the wide area of agreement that emerged as to what formed the heart of the church's tradition.

Certain themes kept reappearing as conferees talked to one another about what it meant to be a Christian and a member of Christ's church in the late twentieth century, themes occasionally developed by conference participants with the help of patristic exegesis. For example, near unanimity reigned among participants on the intimate connection between the Bible and the church. Participants acknowledged the fathers' consistent argument that one reads the Bible safely and effectively only within the context of Christ's body, the church.

Tradition?

Harold O. J. Brown, an evangelical theologian from Trinity Evangelical Divinity School, argued cogently that the relation between church, tradition and Scripture is dynamic. "Naive" Catholics may have argued "that the church—the Catholic church—gave us the Bible and that church authority authenticates it." Protestants, in turn, have contended that "the Scripture creates the church, which is built on the foundation of the prophets and apostles (that is, on their word)."[16]

In a striking move for an evangelical Protestant theologian, Brown acknowledged that "there is no way to make the New Testament older than the church." Does this mean that it is the church's authority that authenticates Scripture as the revealed word of God? "No," Brown responded, "that would be saying too much." And yet it was within the church that the Spirit acted to enable it to recognize God's voice and word.

New Testament books were accepted as the Word of God and placed in the New Testament canon because the churches of the time recognized them to be the Word of God; the work of the Holy Spirit enabled the human writers to write God's words, and it is this work of the Spirit that makes the Scriptures divinely authoritative and preserves them from error. In addition the Holy Spirit was active in the early congregations and councils, enabling them to recognize the right Scriptures as God's Word and to reject others, such as the apocryphal Gospel of Thomas, as inauthentic.[17]

If so, the completed canon of Scripture is younger than the church. This does not mean, however, that the Bible as God's Word is somehow under the church or in captivity to the church. Rather, as Brown pictures the relationship, it is the *"norma normans*, the 'norm that norms'" the church's teaching and life.

Once the authority of Scripture has been recognized by the church, the question of interpretation raises its head. Can the average, individual Christian understand the message of Scripture and interpret it well? The Roman Catholic Church has historically expressed doubts at this point and, as Brown observes, has occasionally attempted to keep the Bible out of the hands of laypeople.

Brown offers a nuanced response to the question of interpretation, one that Catholics, Orthodox and Protestants might do well to consider. First, he admits that the history of Protestant interpretation among "Bible-believing Christians" fails to sustain strongly the Protestant claim for the perspicuity of Scripture. "The way in which sects and heresies have proliferated among people who profess biblical inerrancy and assume that they understand the Bible correctly lends plausibility" to Catholic misgivings about the Bible's perspicuity.

On the one hand, many individuals have been led to a personal faith in Christ through the solitary study of the Bible. Think, Brown asks, of the person in a hotel room studying a Gideon Bible. Surely such an individual can understand the message of salvation as communicated in Scripture and respond in faith. On the other hand, "solitary study, cut off from the fellowship of believers seeking the guidance of the Holy Spirit and lacking any awareness of the faith of the church through the ages, is often a source of serious error."[18]

In what way, then, is Scripture sufficient and clear? Brown feels "it is fairly easy to defend the concept of scriptural teaching for salvation." That is, scores of people have read the Bible, understood with sufficient clarity its message of salvation and responded in faith. Things become more complex, though, after this initial step of faith. Brown asks rhetorically, "Where do they go from there?" The answer, of course, is "to church." In the church they will grow and mature as Christ's body nourishes them.

Let us think first of worship, then of the common life of the congregation. In using these terms we implicitly accept the notion that the Christian is called to membership in a body; that just as no baby is physically born solo, but always has at the very least a mother that it needs to nurture it and to permit it to grow, no one is born again as a child of God alone, but must always have a spiritual mother to bear and nourish him or her.[19]

The great Reformers on whose teaching much of the Protestant tradition is built were well aware of the blessings and dangers of church tradition. Few were stronger than Luther or Calvin in their trenchant critique of a papacy and tradition that appeared to have lost their moorings in the Bible. At the same time, Brown notes that Calvin would have found the highly individualized faith of many modern Christians to be a strange phenomenon at best. "Calvin would have considered the placing of Gideon Bibles in hotel rooms commendable but hardly sufficient."

All human communities, including those made up of Christians, create traditions. Tradition is inevitable. The Roman Catholic, Orthodox and Anglican communions have specific traditions they believe have their roots in the biblical narrative itself. But is not the same true for Protestant communions and even for the local independent Bible churches?

> If we look at the free churches in the Protestant communions, even those which claim to have "no creed but the Bible" show that they have plenty of tradition, though they may formally disdain the concept. Sunday school is not in the Bible, and Sunday school for all ages has become a virtual sign of fidelity to the Bible.... In many circles personal devotions, the "quiet time," is regarded as mandatory. Of course neither the Sunday evening service nor the prayer meeting is mandated in the Bible.[20]

These Protestant traditions are not wrong; they have been largely formed on principles gleaned from the Bible itself. The possibility does exist, as events surrounding the Reformation indicate, that tradition can lose its moorings. Jesus himself taught that human beings have a propensity to promulgate human ideas as the commandments of God (Mt 15:9). Brown lists a number of possible ways in which tradition can become distorted.

For example, tradition can be misunderstood or can actually conceal the essential truths of the gospel. "Where traditions lead the naive to trust in some human idea—a holy relic or particular pious devotion, for example—rather than the atoning sacrifice of Christ, they may imperil their own salvation. This is the personal danger of tradition."[21]

Brown also identifies an "organizational danger of tradition." While ecclesiastical traditions "help confessions to identify their members," they in turn can end up dividing one Christian communion from another, sometimes over trivial considerations or simply differences in emphasis. Other organizational distinctions based on tradition are not trivial; some, such as the "invocation and intercession of the saints, the understanding of the Eucharist, the teaching authority of popes, bishops and church councils," are based on profound theological differences.

The dilemma, as Brown rightly observes, is that despite the dangers of tradition, tradition cannot be avoided. No Christian reads the Bible in a hermetically sealed chamber shielded from familial, cultural, linguistic, political and ecclesiastical factors. The question then becomes, How can we wisely use tradition and hopefully avoid its personal and organizational dangers? Or, in Brown's words, "How can we maintain a rich community life, which necessarily develops traditions out of wnich it lives, without creating conflict with other Christian communities whose traditions develop differently?" Brown suggests the following safeguards and guidelines:

First, Protestants need to stop acting as if they are a traditionless community within Christendom. By recognizing the role of tradition in Protestant communities, Protestants will develop a greater "tolerance" for the traditions they find "in other communions." Brown counsels Protestants to admit the reality of tradition in all Christian communities, while also arguing that traditions must be critically analyzed, "lest they become the 'commandments of men' about which Jesus warns us."[22]

Second, "Catholics and Orthodox" would do well to examine more closely the "human element" in the formation of tradition. "Traditions do grow and proliferate, and they may be rich and helpful or rife and suffocating. Beware of placing the *mandata hominum* even alongside of the Word of God as though they were equal to it, and certainly never place them above it."[23]

Third, all Christian communions must be wary of forcing their traditions upon others as though they were the commandments of God. Brown reminds his listeners of Jesus' words in John 14:2. "In my Father's house are many mansions" (KJV). "Different mansions probably will have different furnishings. One can live in an Oriental palace; one can also live with Scandinavian modern furniture. It is hard, although not altogether impossible, to live without any furniture, and it certainly is not very nice."[24]

If we need furniture in order to live as Christians in community, how might we best construct it? Surely not by ignoring the tools, lumber and styles the fathers offer to us. They, like us, were faced with a number of interpretive possibilities, some more fruitful than others. They understood, as does Harold O. J. Brown, that it is impossible to do away with tradition and naive to think we can do so. The tradition of patristic exegesis provides us with a number of hermeneutical principles modern readers would do well to contemplate.

Read the Bible holistically. The fathers insist that the narrative of the Bible is a continuous, deeply connected story from Genesis through Revelation. The Old Testament is not discontinuous with the New. Rather, the themes presented in the Old Testament find their fulfillment in the narrative structure of the New Testament. Continuity and fulfillment characterize the entire story. Most importantly, the fathers insist that the biblical narrative reaches its culmination, its thematic climax, with the incarnation, crucifixion and resurrection of the Son of God. Indeed, the incarnational, soteriological and eschatological foci of the New Testament further clarify and deepen the Old Testament witness itself. We will read the Bible ineffectively and incorrectly, the fathers warn, if we fail to read its individual parts in the light of its overarching, unifying message. Echoing this sentiment, Robert W. Jenson asserts that

> All Scripture's detours and extensions and varieties of literary genre are to be read as moves within the telling of a single story. Therefore, for example, the single most important task of the preacher working on a parable-text is to ask what it means that Jesus told this parable, and that the one who told *this* parable is the risen Lord of all, and that it was *Israel* who heard and believed or did not believe, and that it is the *church* that retells it.[25]

None of these key words—*Jesus, Israel, church*—may be interpreted apart from their place in the biblical narrative's overarching storyline as presented by biblical authors. They find their meaning within that story. Thus, key terms such as *Israel* will develop in semantic significance as the story expands and moves towards its climax.

Hermeneutics, then, involves more than discovering and elucidating authorial intention. It encompasses a broader task, that of reading texts within the Bible's overall thematic structure, one that turns out to be fundamentally christological. Interpretive error will inevitably occur if only part of the story is accepted as authoritative or if earlier sections of the narrative are read in isolation from the story's final chapters. Gnostic interpreters such as Marcion, for example, read the New Testament in a skewed manner because they rejected the foundation of the biblical narrative laid out in the Old Testament. The New cannot be understood apart from the Old. In turn, the New Testament throws new light on the Old, unearthing hidden and unexpected treasures in its text.

Read the Bible christologically. All the fathers read Scripture through the prism of Christ's incarnation, crucifixion, resurrection and ascension. Unanimously they "held that the entire Old Testament—and most particularly the Psalms—is for the most part Christological."[26] As Irenaeus instructs,

> If one carefully reads the Scriptures, he will find there the word on the subject of Christ—*de Christo sermonem*—and the prefiguration of the new calling. He is indeed the hidden treasure in the field—the field in fact is the world—but in truth, the hidden treasure in the Scriptures is Christ. Because he is designed by types and words that humanly are not possible to understand before the accomplishment of all things, that is, Christ's parousia.[27]

Hilary, bishop of Poitiers around 350, sees Christ portrayed in a wide variety of Old Testament texts and contexts:

> Every part of Holy Writ announces through words the coming of Our Lord Jesus Christ, reveals it through facts and establishes it through examples. . . . For it is our Lord who during all the present age, through true and manifest adumbrations, generates, cleanses, sanctifies, chooses, separates, or redeems the Church in the Patriarchs, through Adam's slumber, Noah's flood, Melchizedek's blessing, Abraham's justification, Isaac's birth, and Jacob's bondage.[28]

Consider in the following comment how Hilary links together Adam's creation from the dust of the earth, Ezekiel's vision of the dry bones coming to life and Christ's resurrection from the dead.

> After the sleep of his Passion and upon awakening to his Resurrection, the celestial Adam recognized in the Church his bones and his flesh, no longer formed from the slime of the earth nor quickened by the breath of life, but having grown over the bones and gaining corporeity from a body, reaching completion by the flight of the Spirit. . . . For those who are in Christ shall rise according to Christ, in whom even now the resurrection of all flesh is accomplished, since he himself is born in our

flesh with God's power, in which his Father generated him before time began.[29]

At first glance Hilary's connections might seem puzzling. When we remember, though, that his reading of the Bible is guided by its central christological and soteriological events, his exegesis appears lively and insightful. Indeed, Metropolitan Timiadis asks what "was more natural than to interpret this Old Testament in light of the Christian revelation? It was natural for them to search in these writings as to how Christ, the accomplishment of the promises made to Israel, is already present in each page. For them, Jesus Christ was the key to opening the Old Testament."[30]

The interpretive rules of Tyconius, a Donatist exegete who significantly influenced Augustine's understanding of biblical exegesis, illustrate well how early Christian interpreters sought to understand and explain the relationship between Old and New Testament texts.[31] For example, in his first exegetical rule, titled *"De Domino et corpore eius* (on the Lord and his body)," Tyconius argues that Scripture does not clearly differentiate "between the person of Christ and his body, the church." Gerald Bray comments on Tyconius's distinction:

> Thus for example, when Daniel 2:34 speaks of the stone which destroys the kingdoms of the world, he is prophesying about the coming of Christ, but when this stone subsequently becomes a mountain filling the whole earth, it is no longer Christ who is meant but the church. Scripture passes from one to the other without hesitation or distinction.[32]

Bertrand de Margerie provides a helpful summary of how the fathers reread the Old Testament in light of its fulfillment in Christ, a technique de Margerie designates an "updated re-reading" within a new historical context. He breaks down the fathers' interpretation of the Old Testament into the following steps:

1. The original context—"a scriptural text may originally have been written in reference to a just individual, king or prophet."

2. Often later sections of the Old Testament have "reinterpreted" a text and viewed it as having "eschatological" relevance.

3. "Jewish interpretation" within the time of Jesus pushes the text "a bit further toward a messianic sense."

4. Jesus himself may have connected the text with "his own person and work."

5. The text is then "re-read" in the knowledge of the resurrection.

6. The church then reads the text as explaining further or illustrating "the person and function of the risen Christ."

7. If there is the need to use the text apologetically, the church will do so, particularly in debating with Jewish exegetes who fail to see the Old Covenant fulfilled in Christ.

8. Since the church is viewed as the "continuation of Christ" on earth—Christ's body—the text will be "read in relation to her and to the community."[33]

It is clear, as de Margerie indicates, that certain of these steps have already been accomplished for the fathers. The apostle Paul, for example, already read many Old Testament texts in light of the incarnation, crucifixion and resurrection of Jesus. "The fathers . . . in their exegesis resumed and carried forward the re-reading effort of the inspired authors themselves with respect to earlier biblical texts."[34] The fathers' re-reading project, guided by the apostle Paul and other apostolic interpreters, leads us to our third patristic hermeneutical principle.

Read the Bible communally within Christ's body, the church. As we have seen throughout this book, the fathers insisted that exegesis is an ecclesiastical task. It takes place within the church for the church. How, they would ask, could things be otherwise? The awareness of the communal nature of exegesis was particularly highlighted in the early church's encounter with the Gnostics, hermeneutical lone rangers who claimed to have received in secret both revelation and interpretive insight.

Irenaeus, the Gnostics' great opponent, rejected the possibility of secret revelation and interpretation because the meaning of Jesus and the narrative leading up to his coming can only be discovered and explained in the community he founded, the community whose very existence culminates the biblical narrative's plot structure. In effect, as Robert Jenson explains, "It is the *church* that knows the plot and *dramatis personae* of the scripture narrative, since the church is one continuous community with the story's actors and narrators, as with its tradents, authors, and assemblers."[35]

As the church pondered the message of the gospel and its relationship to the Old Testament narrative, it formulated a rule of faith—a sort of shorthand summary of the heart of the Christian message—to help its members understand the core of Christian belief and to read the Bible well. The fathers seemed to possess an innate awareness of the tendency of individual believers, especially those young in the faith, to attach themselves to minor themes and peripheral matters. Thus, as they summarized the gospel in the rule of faith they purposefully focused on the nonnegotiables, those truths that all Christians must believe if they were to bear the name of Christ.

For the fathers, then, hermeneutics is not an objective science that can be practiced by any scholar within any context. Rather, hermeneutics in Christ becomes a spiritual, communal, interpretive art. It can be safely, wisely and fruitfully exercised only by those whose minds and hearts have been soaked in and shaped by the gospel itself—within the Christian community's reflection, devotion and worship. For Brevard Childs

> This means that proper interpretation does not consist of an initial stance of seeking a purely objective or neutral reading to which the element of faith is added subsequently, but rather, from the start, the Christian reader receives a particular point of standing from which to identify with the apostolic faith in awaiting a fresh word from God through the Spirit.[36]

Patristic exegetes conducted their work in the church for the church, an idea foreign to many modern scholars who conduct their work in the academy and largely for the academy. Therefore, says Childs, the "challenge of reclaiming the Bible for the church is awesome, particularly at a time in which the academic guild is moving in exactly the opposite direction."[37]

Read the Bible within the context and practice of prayer, worship and spiritual formation. People reading the fathers for the first time need to keep in mind what the fathers can and cannot offer them in their exegesis of the Bible. Patristic exegetes had fewer linguistic, historical and theological tools available to them in their study of Scripture than the modern exegete. Students coming to patristic exegesis and expecting to encounter a modern commentary will walk away disappointed.

Yet patristic exegesis provides both an indispensable foundation and vital supplement for much modern commentary. The fathers' insistence on the connection between spiritual health, life in the church and commentary on the church's book rebukes the modern tendency to separate scholarship from spirituality and worship. Metropolitan Emilianos Timiadis admits the need for modern critical scholarship, but argues strongly that exegesis is not the sole prerogative of the modern academic. [E]xegesis has so many other very important aspects. The fathers help us tremendously in finding the counterweight to the emptiness and spiritual poverty found in many modern commentaries which under the pretext of appearing scientific, strictly critical and historical pass over the fundamental dimension of our salvation in the Scripture. Today we are nearly twenty centuries distant from the New Testament authors, but the fathers were much nearer to the salutary events and more competent to seize the spirit behind the scriptural records.[38]

As noted at the close of chapter two, the hermeneutical and historical proximity of the fathers to the New Testament church and its apostolic tradition demands that we listen carefully to their exegetical insights, advice and intuitions. The music they hear as they listen to biblical authors is often different from the melodies and rhythms modern scholars enjoy. It contains notes, patterns, harmonies and movements to which the modern ear is tone-deaf. According to Timiadis, the fathers

are more apt to seize the key ideas and challenge the true meaning of the fundamental themes of the New Testament than authors of the twentieth century trained in the school of structuralism or rational criticism, thinking in different categories and animated by a quite different mentality. Of course, we do not suggest the exclusion of a critical exegesis, and there is no damage in an acceptable method of approaching the Scriptures. But it is very important to recognize that the patristic exegesis brings forth an indispensable corrective, indicating to us by a sure intuition the profound sense of the biblical text.[39]

Almost all the fathers were pastors; many were bishops. As leaders of the church they did not have the luxury of pursuing biblical scholarship as an academic exercise. Their exegetical work was done in the context of the preparation of sermons or the instruction of catechumens. As they read a text they asked themselves, What is the word of Christ in this text to my congregation? How can I shepherd my flock more effectively through preaching this text well? How is it addressing my heart as well as my mind? Where is this text calling me and my congregation to listen? To change? To repent? To grow?

The pastoral heart reflected in patristic literature remains a rich and largely unexplored field for pastors and teachers. Because the fathers were so well-grounded in the biblical narrative and its implications for spiritual health and growth, they refused to allow their students to treat biblical study in an abstract fashion, as an intellectual stimulant unrelated to the daily call to reflect Christ in word and deed.

Consider, for example, Augustine's struggle with the Bible as a young man just beginning to blossom intellectually. He wanted to study Scripture, but at a distance. In his *Confessions* Augustine links his skeptical attitude towards the Bible to his pride. "They [the Scriptures] were indeed of a nature to grow in your little ones. But I could not bear to be a little one; I was only swollen with pride, but to myself I seemed a very big man." In a later sermon he recalls his skewed perspective as a young man:

> I who speak to you, I was deluded in the past when, while still in my childhood, I tried to start by applying to the divine Scriptures critical discussion rather than pious research. Through my lax morals, I closed off my own access to the Lord. . . . In my pride, I dared to seek that which no man can find unless he practices humility.[40]

Bertrand de Margerie also observes that in *De utilitate credendi*, written a number of years before the *Confessions*, Augustine's recollection of reading the Bible wrongly remained seared in his memory.

> [W]e brilliant young men and wondrous searchers-out of reason, not even having opened these books, without having looked for teachers, without directing the least accusation at our own dullness, and, finally, not even conceding an average understanding to those men who for so long had wished books of this kind to be read and guarded and expounded throughout the entire world, we thought that no confidence should be placed in these men; and we were moved to this opinion by the words of those who were their enemies and foes and among whom we would be forced to cherish and believe, under the false-pretense of reason, untold thousands of fables.[41]

From his conversion to his call to ordained ministry to the end of his life, Augustine was to insist on the inseparable link between the knowledge of Scripture, the community of faith, humility, and constant prayer for guidance in the interpretation of the Bible. A letter to his bishop Valerius written shortly after his ordination catches well his dramatic change in perspective. He was clearly reading Scripture with new eyes and a new attitude. Gone was his pride and self-assurance.

> I ought to study all his remedies in the scriptures, and by praying and reading, so to act that strength sufficient for such perilous duties may

be granted to my soul. I did not do this before, because I did not have time, but as soon as I was ordained, I planned to use all my leisure time in studying the Sacred Scriptures. . . . Help me . . . with your prayers. . . . I know that the Lord does not despise the charity of prayers in such cause, but perhaps he will accept them as a sacrifice of sweetness, and will restore me in a shorter time than I had asked, armed with saving knowledge from the Scriptures.[42]

Origen also warned against a misguided approach to exegesis, fearing that familiarity with Scripture can breed a pride that distorts our ability to read the Bible well.

Let us beware also, because often we are near the well of living water. . . . This is why, we need many tears and unceasing prayers in order that the Lord may open our eyes. . . . But why use such a metaphor: to open the eyes? They are already open. Because Jesus came down to open the eyes of the blind and the veil of the Law was taken away.[43]

Consider too Jerome's exhortation to the monk Rusticus: "Make your cell your paradise, gather there the varied fruits of Scripture, delight in these holy books, and enjoy their intimacy. . . . Never take your hand or your eyes off your book; learn the psalms word for word, pray without ceasing."[44] Ponder as well Jerome's counsel to two close friends: "If there is anything, O Paula and Eustochium, where here below can keep us steady and hold our soul in balance, amid the tribulations and the bustle of this world, I believe it is first and foremost meditation on and knowledge of the Scriptures."[45]

Ambrose also exposes his deep insight into the relationship between the state of his heart and his ability to read Scripture well in the prayer found near the end of his exegesis of Psalm 119 (118 LXX). The last verse of the psalm is a prayer for the Lord to seek the psalmist, who has wandered away. "I have strayed like a lost sheep. Seek your servant, for I have not forgotten your commands" (v. 176 NIV). Ambrose prays in response:

Come therefore, Lord Jesus, to look for your servant, to search for the tired sheep. Come, O shepherd, and look for me as Joseph sought his brethren [Gen 37:16]. Your sheep has gone astray, while you dwelt in the mountains. Leave there the ninety-nine other sheep, and come after the one which strayed away. Come without the dogs, without the bad workers, without the hirelings too uncouth to enter through the door.

Come without seeking help or being announced: long have I awaited
your arrival. I know that you will come, "because I have not forgotten
your commandments." Come, not with a whip, but with charity and
gentleness of heart. . . . Come to me, for I am disturbed by the
incursions of the ravening wolves. Come to me, for I have been cast out
of Paradise. . . . I have wandered far from the herd grazing on the
heights. . . . You had placed me there, but the wolf roaming by night
drove me away from the fold. Come to look for me, for I too am seeking
you. Search for me, find me, gather me to you, carry me. You can find
the one you seek: deign to welcome the one you find, and to place him
on your shoulders. . . . Come yourself to look for your sheep, rather
than send servants or hirelings to do the searching. Draw me to you in
this flesh which failed in Adam; draw me to you, not from Sarah, but
from Mary. . . . Carry me to your cross, which is the salvation of the
lost and the only rest of the weary, to your cross by which whoever dies
can live again.[46]

These extensive quotations from Augustine, Origen, Jerome and Ambrose
can help us enter more deeply into their hearts. Perhaps by listening to
their hearts we can learn to trust them, even love them. Michael Casey
suggests that one way to overcome the difficulties in communication we
experience in encountering the fathers is to "become 'emotionally involved' with one of the figures of the ancient Church. This may lead us to
read a biography that will help the person come alive. Reading letters is
another way to become acquainted with someone."[47]

An Invitation

Casey's words ring true as I reflect on my own study of John Chrysostom.
Until I began my doctoral work at Drew University I had had little contact
with the church fathers. I had read Augustine's *Confessions* and *The City
of God*, as had most theological students, but had little other exposure to
patristic perspectives. I had heard of Chrysostom, knew that he was well
known as a preacher and that he had a special concern for the poor and
destitute. That was about it.

At Drew I was attracted to graduate seminars on patristic writings,
partly because they were entirely new to me and seemed somewhat novel,
and partly because I felt embarassed that I was almost entirely ignorant
of theologians and exegetes many other Christians admired deeply. Why

were these people still in print? I asked myself. What did people find in their writings that was of such lasting value? Would they feed me or lead me astray? Could the fathers be trusted?

Seminars on Augustine and on other post-Nicene fathers helped me begin to answer these questions. I learned that exegetes, theologians and pastors I trusted—John Calvin, Martin Luther, John Wesley—had read deeply in patristic sources. I was intrigued by the spiritual and theological pilgrimage of Thomas Oden, my mentor and adviser at Drew. I had come to trust these teachers, who were all pointing their fingers at the fathers as people worth studying—for the sake of my theological education, my spiritual life and my call to the ministry.

As I immersed myself in the life and work of Chrysostom in preparing my doctoral dissertation, I realized that my teachers had been right. But it was only through coming to know Chrysostom himself, through reading biographies of him, through reading his sermons and treatises, through seeing his responses to the deep suffering and trials he encountered through much of his life, that the world of the fathers opened up to me. I realized Chrysostom was calling me to listen to both his words and his life. In him I saw the integrity too often missing in my own Christian experience. His words and life dramatically fit together.

My encounter with Chrysostom led to a deeper exposure to other fathers. As the days and months passed, a world that had once appeared foreboding, alien and intimidating began to feel more like home. But the first step in this process, what I see as the formation of new and lasting friendships, was the choice to study one father in some detail.

And so I invite you to read Scripture with the fathers—not to the neglect of the exegetical riches your own tradition offers, nor to the denigration of the resources much modern biblical interpretation provides. I invite you to read the fathers because they are part of your family, relatives perhaps long forgotten who long to be remembered as part of the family tree. For too long they have been shut out of the family circle. Welcome them home.

Notes

Abbreviations

ACW	Ancient Christian Writers
ANF	Ante-Nicene Fathers
CSEL	Corpus Scriptorum Ecclesiasticorum Latinorum
FC	Fathers of the Church
NPNF	Nicene and Post-Nicene Fathers
PG	Patrologia Graeca
PL	Patrologia Latina
SC	Sources Chrétiennes

Chapter 1: Why Read the Fathers?

[1] Martin Luther, *The Bondage of the Will*, in *Martin Luther's Basic Theological Writings*, ed. Timothy F. Lull (Minneapolis: Fortress, 1989), p. 200.

[2] Martin Luther, *Concerning the Letter and the Spirit*, in *Martin Luther's Basic Theological Writings*, ed. Lull, p. 81. Luther does not explicitly identify the father's exegetical error, wirting that "at the moment I shall ignore how and why" Jerome and Origen's mistake occurred (p. 81).

[3] Ibid., p. 75.

[4] Anthony N. S. Lane, "Sola Scriptura? Making Sense of a Post-Reformation Slogan," in *A Pathway into the Holy Scripture*, ed. Philip E. Satterthwaite and David F. Wright (Grand Rapids, Mich.: Eerdmans, 1994), p. 324.

[5] Cf. Calvin's interaction with the church fathers in his discussion of the Trinity: John Calvin, *Institutes of the Christian Religion*, ed. John T. McNeil (Philadelphia: Westminster Press, 1975), p. 158 (1.14.29).

[6] Cited in Lane, "Sola Scriptura?" p. 311.

[7] Robert L. Wilken, *Remembering the Christian Past* (Grand Rapids, Mich.: Eerdmans, 1995).

[8] David Tracy, *Blessed Rage for Order: The New Pluralism in Theology* (New York: Seabury Press, 1975), p. 6.

[9] Wilken, *Remembering the Christian Past*, p. 170.

[10] Much of the following material on Oden's spiritual pilgrimage is based on my interview of Oden for *Christianity Today* 34, no. 13 (September 24, 1990), and Oden's own biographical remarks in the second volume of his systematic theology, *The Word of Life* (San Francisco: Harper & Row, 1989).

[11] Oden, *Word of Life*, p. 219.

[12] Christopher A. Hall, "Back to the Fathers," *Christianity Today* 34, no. 13 (September 24, 1990): 28.

[13] Oden, *Word of Life*, pp. 219-20.

[14] Ibid., p. 220.

Chapter 2: The Modern Mind & Biblical Interpretation

[1] William J. Abraham, "Oh God, Poor God—The State of Contemporary Theology," *The Reformed Journal* 40, no. 2 (February 1990): 19.

[2] Ibid.

[3] Ibid., p. 20.

[4] Ibid.

[5]Ibid., p. 23.

[6]Ibid.

[7]Cited in Guenter Lewy, *Why America Needs Religion: Secular Modernity and Its Discontents* (Grand Rapids, Mich.: Eerdmans, 1996), p. 26.

[8]Cited in ibid., p. 25.

[9]Voltaire, "The Questions of Zapata," in *Les Philosophes*, ed. Norman L. Torrey (New York: Capricorn Books, 1960), p. 282.

[10]Voltaire, "On Absurdities and Atrocities," in *Les Philosophes*, p. 277.

[11]I am indebted to the helpful insights and analysis of Stanley J. Grenz, Roger E. Olson and Richard Tarnas in my discussion of Enlightenment developments and effects. Cf. Stanley J. Grenz and Roger E. Olson, *20th-Century Theology: God & the World in a Transitional Age* (Downers Grove, Ill.: InterVarsity Press, 1992), pp. 15-23; Richard Tarnas, *The Passion of the Western Mind: Understanding the Ideas That Have Shaped Our World View* (New York: Ballantine, 1991), pp. 248-323.

[12]Richard Tarnas, *The Passion of the Western Mind: Understanding the Ideas That Have Shaped Our World View* (New York: Ballantine Books, 1991), p. 301.

[13]Cited in ibid.

[14]Grenz and Olson, *20th-Century Theology*, p. 23.

[15]Clark Pinnock, *Tracking the Maze: Finding Our Way Through Modern Theology from an Evangelical Perspective* (San Francisco: Harper & Row, 1990), p. 83.

[16]Ibid., p. 84.

[17]Mark A. Noll, *The Scandal of the Evangelical Mind* (Grand Rapids, Mich.: Eerdmans, 1994).

[18]Ibid., p. 97.

[19]Nathan O. Hatch, *The Democratization of American Christianity* (New Haven, Conn.: Yale University Press, 1989), p. 182, cited in Noll, *Scandal of the Evangelical Mind*, p. 97.

[20]Cited in Noll, *Scandal of the Evangelical Mind*, p. 98.

[21]Cited in ibid.

[22]Lewis Sperry Chafer, *Systematic Theology*, 1:x, xiii (2d and 32d quotations), xix, xx, 115, 119, cited in Noll, *Scandal of the Evangelical Mind*, p. 128.

[23]Noll, *Scandal of the Evangelical Mind*, p. 127.

[24]Cited in C. F. Lincoln, "Biographical Sketch of the Author," in Chafer, *Systematic Theology*, 8:5-6, cited in Noll, *Scandal of the Evangelical Mind*, p. 128.

[25]Craig A. Blaising, "Dispensationalism: The Search for Definition," in *Dispensationalism, Israel and the Church: The Search for Definition*, ed. Craig A. Blaising and Darrell L. Bock (Grand Rapids, Mich.: Zondervan, 1992), pp. 29-30, 22 n. 28, cited in Noll, *Scandal of the Evangelical Mind*, p. 129.

[26]Cited in Noll, *Scandal of the Evangelical Mind*, p. 129.

[27]Roger Lundin, *The Culture of Interpretation* (Grand Rapids, Mich.: Eerdmans, 1993), p. 88.

[28]Ibid., p. 89. I have found Roger Lundin's analysis of postmodern thought in *The Culture of Interpretation* to be extremely helpful and am indebted to him in my own intrpretation of postmodernism and its effects.

[29]Robert L. Wilken, *Remembering the Christian Past* (Grand Rapids, Mich.: Eerdmans, 1995), p. 171.

[30]Ibid., pp. 170-71.

[31]Thomas C. Oden, *The Living God* (San Francisco: Harper & Row, 1987), p. 1.

[32]Wilken, *Remembering the Christian Past*, p. 174.

[33]Lundin, *Culture of Interpretation*, p. 35.

[34]Cf. Alasdair MacIntyre, *Whose Justice? Which Rationality?* (Notre Dame, Ind.: University of

Notre Dame Press, 1989), p. 353, cited in Lundin, *Culture of Interpretation*, p. 89.

[35]Lundin, *Culture of Interpretation*, p. 33.

[36]C. Stephen Evans, "Postmodernism with a Twang," *Books and Culture*, May-June 1997, p. 6.

[37]Ibid.

[38]Lundin, *Culture of Interpretation*, p. 25.

[39]Stanley Fish, *Doing What Comes Naturally: Change, Rhetoric and the Practice of Theory in Literary and Legal Studies* (Durham, N.C.: Duke University Press, 1989), p. 11, cited in Lundin, *Culture of Interpretation*, p. 15.

[40]Richard Rorty, *Contingency, Irony and Solidarity* (Cambridge: Cambridge University Press, 1989), pp. 60-61, cited in Lundin, *Culture of Interpretation*, p. 15.

[41]Lundin's summary of MacIntyre (Lundin, *Culture of Interpretation*, p. 98).

[42]Tertullian, "The Prescriptions Against the Heretics," chap. 7 in *Early Latin Theology*, ed. S. L. Greenslade (London: SCM Press, 1956), p. 36, cited in Anthony N. S. Lane, "*Sola Scriptura?* Making Sense of a Post-Reformation Slogan," in *A Pathway into the Holy Scripture*, ed. Philip E. Satterthwaite and David F. Wright (Grand Rapids, Mich.: Eerdmans, 1994), p. 301.

[43]Tim Stafford, "Getting Serious About Lust in an Age of Smirks," *Christianity Today*, January 10, 1994, p. 29.

[44]Augustine, *Confessions*, trans. R. S. Pine-Coffin (New York: Penguin, 1961), p. 55 (3.1).

[45]Michael Grant, *The Twelve Caesars* (New York: Scribner's, 1975), p. 198.

[46]Suetonius *Vitellius* 13.2, trans. R. Graves, cited in Grant, *Twelve Caesars*, p. 199.

[47]Grant, *Twelve Caesars*, p. 199.

[48]Clement of Alexandria *The Tutor* 2.3.38 (SC 108.82), cited in *Social Thought*, trans. Peter Phan, Message of the Fathers of the Church 20 (Wilmington, Del.: Michael Glazier, 1984), p. 66.

[49]Michael Casey, *Sacred Reading: The Ancient Art of Lectio Divina* (Ligouri, Mo.: Triumph Books, 1995), pp. 104-5.

[50]Ambrose, PL 16, cols. 28.2.5—29.7, cited in Aelred Squire, *Asking the Fathers* (New York: Morehouse-Barlow, 1973), p. 130.

[51]*De Vitis Patrum, Liber V: Verba Seniorum*, 72, PL 73, 966ab, cited in Casey, *Sacred Reading*, p. 44.

[52]Cf. Francis Young, "Patristics," in *A New Dictionary of Christian Theology*, ed. Alan Richardson and John Bowden (London: SCM Press, 1983), pp. 431-35.

[53]Casey, *Sacred Reading*, p. 109.

[54]This and the quotations that follow are from a lecture by Dale C. Allison Jr., delivered at the Billy Graham Center, Wheaton College, for the first annual meeting of the Society for the Study of Eastern Orthodoxy and Evangelicalism, September 28, 1991.

[55]Athanasius, *On the Incarnation* (Crestwood, N.Y.: St. Vladimir's Seminary Press, 1982), p. 96.

[56]Gregory of Nazianzus, "The First Theological Oration," in *Christology of the Later Fathers*, ed. Edward R. Hardy, Library of Christian Classics (Philadelphia: Westminster Press, 1954), p. 129.

Chapter 3: Who Are the Fathers?

[1]I have borrowed the phrase "models and mentors" from Elizabeth A. Clark, *Women in the Early Church*, Message of the Fathers of the Church 13 (Collegeville, Minn.: Liturgical Press, 1983), p. 204.

[2]Jerome, Epistle 127, CSEL 56.146, cited in Clark, *Women in the Early Church*, pp. 207-8.

[3]Jerome, Epistle 108, CSEL 55.308, cited in Clark, *Women in the Early Church*, p. 209.

[4]Ibid., pp. 211-12.

[5]Jerome, Epistle 108, CSEL 55.344, cited in Clark, *Women in the Early Church*, p. 164.

[6]Palladius, *The Lausiac History of Palladius*, ed. C. Butler (1898; reprint, Hildesheim, Germany:

Georg Olm, 1967), p. 149, cited in Clark, *Women in the Early Church*, pp. 164-65.

[7]Palladius, *Lausiac History of Palladius*, p. 149, cited in Clark, *Women in the Early Church*, p. 224.

[8]Cited in Christopher A. Hall, "Letters from a Lonely Exile," *Christian History* 13, no. 4 (1994): 44.

[9]Anonymous, *Life of Olympias*, SC 13 bis. 408, cited in Clark, *Women in the Early Church*, p. 229.

[10]Clark, *Women in the Early Church*, p. 15.

[11]Ibid., p. 20.

[12]I am indebted to Elizabeth A. Clark's analysis of women and Christian asceticism found in Clark, *Women in the Early Church*, pp. 15-25.

[13]Cf. *The Letters of St. Jerome*, trans. Charles Christopher Mierow, ACW 33 (New York: Paulist Press, 1963), p. 12.

[14]Jerome, Epistle 45, CSEL 54.325, cited in Clark, *Women in the Early Church*, pp. 220-21.

[15]Clark, *Women in the Early Church*, p. 176.

[16]Jaroslav Pelikan, *Christianity and Classical Culture: The Metamorphosis of Natural Theology in the Christian Encounter with Hellenism* (New Haven, Conn.: Yale University Press, 1993), p. 8.

[17]Ibid.

[18]Gregory of Nyssa, *Life of St. Macrina*, SC 178.136, para. 3, cited in Clark, *Women in the Early Church*, p. 238.

[19]Ibid., para. 6, cited in Clark, *Women in the Early Church*, p. 241.

[20]Ibid., para. 17, cited in Clark, *Women in the Early Church*, pp. 242-43.

[21]Basil, Epistle 223.3, cited in Pelikan, *Christianity and Classical Culture*, p. 303.

[22]Clark comments that "we have almost no materials remaining from ancient Christianity that were composed by women (*Women in the Early Church*, p. 165).

[23]Cf. "The Sayings of the Fathers" in *Western Asceticism*, ed. Owen Chadwick, Library of Christian Classics (Philadelphia: Westminster Press, 1958), pp. 120-21.

[24]Cf. Clark, *Women in the Early Church*, pp. 165-68.

[25]Cf. "Father" and "Fathers of the Church," in *Encyclopedia of the Early Church*, 2 vols. (New York: Oxford University Press, 1992), 1:320; "Fathers of the Church," in *Encyclopedia of Early Christianity* (New York: Garland, 1990), p. 345.

[26]1 Clement 62:2 in *The Apostolic Fathers*, trans. J. B. Lightfoot and J. R. Harmer, ed. and rev. Michael W. Holmes (Grand Rapids, Mich.: Baker, 1989), p. 63.

[27]Irenaeus *Adversus Haereses* 4.41.2, cited in *Encyclopedia of the Early Church*, p. 320.

[28]Clement of Alexandria, *Stromateis* 1.1.2-2.1, cited in Johannes Quasten, *Patrology*, 4 vols. (Westminster, Md.: Christian Classics, 1986), 1:9.

[29]Quasten, *Patrology*, 1:9.

[30]Augustine *Contra Julian* 1.7.34, cited in Quasten, *Patrology*, 1:9.

[31]Vincent of Lerins *Commonitory*, chap. 41, cited in *Encyclopedia of Early Christianity*, p. 345.

[32]Vincent of Lerins *Commonitory*, chap. 41, cited in Quasten, *Patrology* 1:9-10.

[33]Boniface Ramsey, *Beginning to Read the Fathers* (New York: Paulist Press, 1985), p. 4.

[34]Ibid.

[35]Pier Franco Beatrice, *Introduction to the Fathers of the Church* (Vicenza, Italy: Edizioni Istituto San Gaetano, 1987), p. 14.

[36]Ramsey, *Beginning to Read the Fathers*, p. 4.

[37]Ibid., p. 5.

[38]Origen *De principiis* 1.6.1, ANF, cited in Quasten, *Patrology*, 2: 87.

[39]Origen *De principiis* 3.6.3, ANF, cited in Quasten, *Patrology*, 2:89.

[40]Ramsey, *Beginning to Read the Fathers*, p. 6.

[41]Ibid., pp. 6-7.

[42]Beatrice, *Introduction to the Fathers*, p. 11.

[43]Michael Casey, *Sacred Reading: The Ancient Art of Lectio Divina* (Ligouri, Mo.: Triumph Books, 1995), p. 105.

[44]Henry Chadwick, *Early Christian Thought and the Classical Tradition* (Oxford: Oxford University Press, 1984), p. 123.

[45]Origen *Commentary on Genesis*, cited in the preface to Pamphilus's Apology (24.296 Lommatzsch), cited in Chadwick, *Early Christian Thought*, p. 123.

[46]Quasten, *Patrology*, 1:10.

Chapter 4: The Four Doctors of the East

[1]Robert Payne, *The Fathers of the Eastern Church* (New York: Dorset Press, 1989), p. 67.

[2]I believe I borrowed this illustration from either Alister McGrath or Thomas Marsh, but I have been unable to find the reference.

[3]Thomas Marsh, *The Triune God: A Biblical, Historical and Theological Study* (Mystic, Conn.: Twenty-Third Publications, 1994), p. 104. I have found Marsh's discussion of the Arian controversy to be quite helpful and have drawn upon it in my discussion of the conflict between Athanasius and Arius. I have also found Alister McGrath's *Studies in Doctrine* (Grand Rapids, Mich.: Zondervan, 1997) to be helpful.

[4]Athanasius, *Four Discourses Against the Arians*, Discourse 3, NPNF Second Series, vol. 4 (Peabody, Mass.: Hendrickson, 1994), p. 408.

[5]Athanasius *Contra Gentes* 9, cited in Alvyn Pettersen, *Athanasius* (Harrisburg, Penn.: Morehouse Publishing, 1995), p. 91.

[6]Pettersen, *Athanasius* p. 91.

[7]Athanasius *Ad Adelph.* 8, cited in Pettersen, *Athanasius*, p. 91.

[8]Athanasius *De Incarnatione* 7, cited in Pettersen, *Athanasius*, p. 91.

[9]Pettersen, *Athanasius*, p. 91.

[10]Athanasius *De Incarnatione* 14-15, cited in Pettersen, *Athanasius*, p. 68.

[11]C. S. Lewis, "Introduction to St. Athanasius," in Athanasius, *On the Incarnation* (Crestwood, N.Y.: St. Vladimir's Seminary Press, 1982), p. 9.

[12]Ibid.

[13]Athanasius, *Four Discourses Against the Arians*, p. 408.

[14]Ibid.

[15]Ibid., p. 409.

[16]Ibid., p. 410.

[17]Ibid.

[18]Ibid., p. 411.

[19]St. Athanasius, *On the Incarnation* (Crestwood, N.Y.: St. Vladimir's Seminary Press, 1982).

[20]Athanasius, *The Life of Antony and the Letter to Marcellinus* (New York: Paulist Press, 1980).

[21]Athanasius, *Four Discourses Against the Arians*, pp. 306-447.

[22]*Letters of Athanasius*, NPNF Second Series, vol. 4 (Peabody, Mass.: Hendrickson, 1994), p. 551.

[23]Johannes Quasten, *Patrology*, vol. 3 *The Golden Age of Greek Patristic Literature* (Westminster, Md.: Christian Classics, 1986), p. 54.

[24]Payne, *Fathers of the Eastern Church*, p. 170.

[25]Frederick Norris, "Gregory of Nazianzus," in *Encyclopedia of Early Christianity* (New York: Garland 1991), p. 397.

[26]Gregory of Nazianzus Oratio 4.10, cited in Payne, *Fathers of the Eastern Church*, p. 174.

[27]Payne, *Fathers of the Eastern Church*, p. 174.

[28]Quasten, *Patrology*, 3:236.

[29]Cf. Gregory of Nazianzus, "In Defence of His Flight to Pontus," in *Orations and Letters*, NPNF Second Series, vol. 7 (Peabody, Mass.: Hendrickson, 1994), pp. 204-27.

[30]Norris, "Gregory of Nazianzus," p. 398.

[31]Gregory of Nazianzus, Epistle 80, cited in Anthony Meredith, *The Cappadocians* (Crestwood, N.Y.: St. Vladimir's Seminary Press, 1995), p. 50.

[32]Norris, "Gregory of Nazianzus," p. 398.

[33]Gregory of Nazianzus, Oratio 42.27, cited in Payne, *Fathers of the Eastern Church*, pp. 192-93.

[34]Edward R. Hardy, ed., *Christology of the Later Fathers*, Library of Christian Classics (Philadelphia: Westminster Press, 1954), p. 117.

[35]Ibid.

[36]Gregory of Nazianzus, "The First Theological Oration," in *Christology of the Later Fathers*, ed. Hardy, p. 128.

[37]Ibid., p. 129.

[38]Ibid.

[39]Anthony Meredith believes that Gregory's reliance upon Origen and through him to Plato is apparent in Gregory's insistence that "God can only be a true light to those who are pure of heart." According to Meredith, this means that "the preliminaries to full salvation are moral purity leading to vision. In this also Gregory shows himself a follower of Origen, and through him of Plato, for both of whom access to the highest mysteries is only gained by those who have been purified through the necessary training of morality and mind. The spirit, therefore, of *Republic* 7 and *On First Principles* 2.11.7 is clearly discernible." (Anthony Meredith, *The Cappadocians*, p. 43.)

[40]Gregory of Nazianzus, "First Theological Oration," p. 130.

[41]Jaroslav Pelikan, *Christianity and Classical Culture: The Metamorphosis of Natural Theology in the Christian Encounter with Hellenism* (New Haven, Conn.: Yale University Press, 1993), p. 174; cf. Gregory of Nazianzus, Oratio 21.5, SC 270:118-20.

[42]Gregory of Nazianzus, Oratio 21.24, SC 270:160, cited in Pelikan, *Christianity and Classical Culture*, p. 175.

[43]Gregory of Nazianzus, "First Theological Oration," p. 131.

[44]Ibid., p. 130.

[45]Ibid., p. 131.

[46]Ibid., p. 132.

[47]Ibid.

[48]Gregory of Nazianzus, "The Third Theological Oration—On the Son," in *Christology of the Later Fathers*, ed. Hardy, p. 173.

[49]Ibid., pp. 174-75.

[50]Ibid., p. 180.

[51]Gregory of Nazianzus, "The Fifth Theological Oration—On the Spirit," in *Christology of the Later Fathers*, ed. Hardy, p. 207.

[52]Ibid., p. 208.

[53]Ibid., p. 209.

[54]Ibid.

[55]Ibid., p. 210.

[56]Ibid., p. 211.

[57]Ibid., p. 214.

[58]Frederick Norris, "Gregory Nazianzen: Constructing and Constructed by Scripture," in *The Bible in Greek Christian Antiquity*, ed. Paul M. Blowers (Notre Dame, Ind.: University of Notre Dame Press, 1997), p. 152. My analysis of Gregory's exegesis at this point is a summary of

Norris's essay and highly dependent upon his expertise and insight.

[59]Ibid., p. 153.

[60]Ibid., p. 149.

[61]Ibid., p. 155.

[62]Ibid.

[63]Ibid.

[64]Ibid.

[65]Ibid.

[66]The discussion that follows is from Norris, "Gregory Nazianzen," pp. 155-56.

[67]Ibid., p. 156

[68]Ibid.

[69]Ibid., p. 157.

[70]Gregory Nazianzen, *Orations and Letters*, NPNF Second Series, vol. 7 (Peabody, Mass.: Hendrickson, 1994), pp. 203-482.

[71]Hardy, ed., *Christology of the Later Fathers*, pp. 128-214.

[72]St. Gregory Nazianzen, *Funeral Orations*, trans. Martin R. P. McGuire, FC 22 (Washington: The Catholic University of America Press, 1953).

[73]St. Gregory of Nazianzus, *Three Poems: Concerning His Own Affairs, Concerning Himself and the Bishops, Concerning His Own Life*, trans. Denis Molaise Meehan, FC 75 (Washington: The Catholic University of America Press, 1987).

[74]Payne, *Fathers of the Eastern Church*, p. 113.

[75]Gregory of Nyssa, *Life of St. Macrina*, cited in Clark, *Women in the Early Church*, p. 241.

[76]St. Basil, *Letters*, vol. 2, trans. Sister Agnes Clare Way, FC 28 (Washington: The Catholic University of America Press, 1955), p. 127. Johannes Quasten refers to this letter in his *Patrology*, 3:204-5.

[77]Ibid., pp. 127-28.

[78]Cited in Quasten, *Patrology*, 3:205.

[79]Basil the Great, *Homily Delivered in Times of Famine and Drought*, cited in *Social Thought*, trans. Peter Phan, Message of the Fathers of the Church, vol. 20 (Wilmington, Del.: Michael Glazier, 1984), p. 118.

[80]Norris, "Basil of Caesarea," in *Encyclopedia of Early Christianity*, p. 140.

[81]St. Basil, *Letters*, p. 39.

[82]Ibid.

[83]Gregory of Nazianzus, Epistle 50, cited in Payne, *Fathers of the Eastern Church*, p. 182.

[84]Blomfield Jackson, "Introduction to the *Hexaemeron*," NPNF Second Series, vol. 7 (Peabody, Mass.: Hendrickson, 1994), p. 51.

[85]Gregory of Nazianzus, Oratio 43.67 (PG 36:585), cited in Pelikan, *Christianity and Classical Culture*, p. 7.

[86]Pelikan, *Christianity and Classical Culture*, p. 226.

[87]Basil, *The Hexaemeron*, trans. Blomfield Jackson, NPNF Second Series, vol. 7 (Peabody, Mass.: Hendrickson, 1994), Homily 9:101.

[88]Ibid., Homily 3:71.

[89]Ibid., Homily 9:102.

[90]Ibid., Homily 2:61.

[91]Ibid., Homily 2:62.

[92]Ibid., Homily 1:52.

[93]Ibid., Homily 6:89.

[94]Ibid., Homily 1:52.

[95]Ibid., Homily 3:65.

[96]Ibid.

[97]Ibid., Homily 4:72.

[98]Ibid., Homily 6:82.

[99]Ibid., Homily 1:55.

[100]Ibid., Homily 4:75.

[101]Ibid., Homily 5:76.

[102]Ibid., Homily 5:76-77.

[103]Ibid., Homily 5:78.

[104]Ibid., Homily 6:88.

[105]Ibid., Homily 6:89.

[106]Ibid., Homily 7:91.

[107]Ibid., Homily 7:93.

[108]Ibid., Homily 8:95.

[109]Ibid., Homily 8:100.

[110]Ibid.

[111]Ibid., Homily 9:106.

[112]Ibid. Cf. Gen 1:27; Jn 10:30; 14:9; Col 1:15; Heb 1:2-3. I have modified the translation slightly.

[113]St. Basil, The Letters, trans. Roy J. Deferrari, 4 vols., Loeb Classical Library (Cambridge, Mass.: Harvard University Press, 1930; reprinted 1953, 1962, 1986).

[114]Basil, Letters and Select Works, trans. with notes by Blomfield Jackson, NPNF Second Series, vol. 8 (Peabody, Mass.: Hendrickson, 1994).

[115]St. Basil the Great, On the Holy Spirit, trans. David Anderson (Crestwood, N.Y.: St. Vladimir's Seminary Press, 1980).

[116]Robert A. Krupp has written a brief but excellent description of the major events and influences in Chrysostom's life. See Robert A. Krupp, "Golden Tongue and Iron Will," Christian History 13, no. 4. For years the definitive biography of Chrysostom was that of F. Chrysostomos Baur, John Chrysostom and His Time, 2 vols. (Philadelphia: Westminster Press, 1959-1960). The dominance of Baur's biography will surely be challenged by J. N. D. Kelly's Golden Mouth: The Story of John Chrysostom, Ascetic, Preacher, Bishop (Ithaca, N.Y.: Cornell University Press, 1995).

[117]Payne, Fathers of the Eastern Church, p. 195.

[118]Cited in John Chrysostom, On the Priesthood, trans. Graham Neville (Crestwood, N.Y.: St. Vladimir's Seminary Press, 1984), pp. 38-40.

[119]Payne, Fathers of the Eastern Church, p. 197.

[120]Quasten, Patrology, 3:433.

[121]Cf. J. A. Sawhill, "The Use of Athletic Metaphors in the Biblical Homilies of St. John Chrysostom" (Th.D. diss., Princeton University, 1928).

[122]John Chrysostom, On the Priesthood, pp. 114-15.

[123]Ibid., pp. 115-16.

[124]Isidore of Pelusium, Epistle 5:32, cited in Quasten, Patrology, 3:442.

[125]John Chrysostom, On the Priesthood, p. 123.

[126]John Chrysostom, Homilies on Colossians, NPNF First Series, vol. 13 (Grand Rapids, Mich.: Eerdmans, 1988), Homily 9:300-301. I have modernized and slightly paraphrased the passage.

[127]The only English translation available is my own, completed as part of my doctoral dissertation, John Chrysostom's "On Providence": A Translation and Theological Interpretation (Ann Arbor, Mich.: University Microfilms International, 1991).

[128]Ibid., p. 155.

[129]Ibid., p. 156.

[130]Ibid., pp. 333-34.

[131]Ibid., p. 334.

[132]John Chrysostom, *Homilies on Galatians, Ephesians, Philippians, Colossians, Thessalonians, Timothy, Titus and Philemon*, NPNF First Series, vol. 13 (Grand Rapids, Mich.: Eerdmans, 1988), Homily 9:512.

[133]John Chrysostom, *Letters of St. Chrysostom to Olympias*, trans. W. R. W. Stephens, NPNF First Series, vol. 9 (Grand Rapids, Mich.: 1988), p. 297. I have modernized the translation somewhat.

[134]Ibid., p. 293. I have modernized the translation somewhat.

[135]Cf. Christopher A. Hall, "Letters from a Lonely Exile," *Christian History* 13, no. 4, pp. 30-32.

[136]John Chrysostom, *Homilies on the Gospel of St. John and the Epistle to the Hebrews*, NPNF First Series, vol. 14 (Grand Rapids, Mich.: Eerdmans, 1988), Homily 62:231. I have modernized the translation.

[137]John Chrysostom, *Homilies on the Epistles to the Corinthians, First Corinthians*, NPNF First Series, vol. 12 (Grand Rapids, Mich.: Eerdmans, 1988), Homily 28:166.

[138]John Chrysostom, *Homilies on the Acts of the Apostles and the Epistle to the Romans*, NPNF First Series, vol. 11 (Grand Rapids, Mich.: Eerdmans, 1988), Homily 22:507. I have modified the translation slightly.

[139]Ibid., Homily 23:266.

[140]John Chrysostom, "*On Providence*," p. 361 (20:5-6).

[141]Ibid., p. 376 (22:8).

[142]Ibid., p. 377 (22:10).

[143]Ibid., p. 320 (14:9).

[144]Ibid.

[145]Quasten, *Patrology*, 3:429.

Chapter 5: The Four Doctors of the West

[1]Gerald Bray, *Biblical Interpretation: Past and Present* (Downers Grove, Ill.: InterVarsity Press, 1996), p. 91.

[2]Robert Payne, *The Fathers of the Western Church* (New York: Dorset Press, 1989), p. 60.

[3]Charles Kannengiesser, *Early Christian Spirituality* (Philadelphia: Fortress Press, 1986), p. 26.

[4]Cf. Maria Grazia Mara, "Ambrose of Milan," in *Patrology*, ed. Angelo Di Berardino (Westminster, Md.: Christian Classics, 1988), 4:144.

[5]Bertrand de Margerie, S.J., *An Introduction to the History of Exegesis*, vol. 2, *The Latin Fathers* (Petersham, Mass.: Saint Bede's Publications, 1995), p. 76n.2.

[6]Ibid.

[7]Augustine *Confessions*, trans. R. S. Pine-Coffin (New York: Penguin, 1961), p. 159 (8.2).

[8]Ibid., p. 107 (5.13).

[9]Ibid.

[10]Ibid., p. 108 (5.14); pp. 115-16 (6.4).

[11]De Margerie, *Introduction to the History of Exegesis*, 2:79.

[12]Ambrose, *Letters to Bishops*, FC 26 (Washington: The Catholic University of America Press, 1987), p. 77.

[13]Ibid., p. 78.

[14]Ibid., p. 79.

[15]Ibid., pp. 264-65.

[16]Ibid., p. 227.

[17]Ambrose *De Paradiso*, 10.47, cited in de Margerie, *Introduction to the History of Exegesis*, 2:81.

[18]Ibid., p. 82.

[19]Ambrose, *Select Works and Letters*, NPNF Second Series, vol. 10 (Peabody, Mass.: Hendrickson, 1994).

[20]Jan L. Womer, ed., *Morality and Ethics in Early Christianity*, Sources of Early Christian Thought (Philadelphia: Fortress Press, 1987).

[21]Charles Kannengiesser, ed., *Early Christian Spirituality* (Philadelphia: Fortress Press, 1986).

[22]Payne, *Fathers of the Western Church*, p. 90.

[23]Cited in Payne, *Fathers of the Western Church*, p. 89. Payne does not list the original reference, and I have been unable to locate it.

[24]Jerome, Letter 107.4, cited in Payne, *Fathers of the Western Church*, p. 131.

[25]Ibid., p. 132.

[26]De Margerie, *Introduction to the History of Exegesis*, 2:115.

[27]Jean Gribomont, "The Translations: Jerome and Rufinus," in *Patrology*, ed. Angelo Di Berardino (Westminster, Md.: Christian Classics, 1988), 4:226.

[28]To speak anachronistically, Jerome embraced H. Richard Niebuhr's Christ against culture stance.

[29]Jerome, *The Letters of St. Jerome*, vol. 1, trans. Charles Christopher Mierow, ACW 33 (New York: Newman Press, 1963), p. 165.

[30]Ibid., p. 166.

[31]Ibid., p. 97.

[32]Ibid., p. 111.

[33]Ibid., p. 81.

[34]Ibid., p. 82.

[35]Ibid., p. 84.

[36]Ibid., p. 85.

[37]Ibid., p. 90.

[38]Ibid., pp. 85-86.

[39]Readers using modern translations such as the NIV and NRSV, both based on the Masoretic Text (MT), will no doubt be confused by Jerome's comment that the wings of the seraphim cover God's face and feet rather than their own. Jerome is working from a Latin text that reads, "Et duabus quidem velabant faciem et duabus velabant pedes et duabus volabant." ("With two wings they covered [his] face and with two wings [his] feet and with two wings they flew.") The Vulgate supplies the third person singular personal possessive pronoun "ejus" following both "faciem" and "pedes." The pronoun is ambiguous. Does it refer to the angels' own feet and face, viewing each angel individually, or to God's? Exegetes following this Latin textual tradition, then, could validly understand Isaiah to mean that the angels covered God's face and feet rather than their own. Cf. Jerome, *Letters of St. Jerome*, p. 215.

[40]Jerome, *Letters of St. Jerome*, p. 86.

[41]Ibid.

[42]Ibid., pp. 86-87.

[43]Joseph W. Trigg, *Biblical Interpretation*, Message of the Fathers of the Church, vol. 9 (Wilmington, Del.: Michael Glazier, 1988), p. 251.

[44]Jerome, *Letters and Select Works*, trans. W. H. Fremantle, NPNF Second Series, vol. 6 (Peabody, Mass.: Hendrickson, 1994).

[45]Jerome, *The Letters of St. Jerome*, vol. 1, trans. Charles Christopher Mierow, with introduction and notes by Thomas Comerford Lawler, ACW 33 (New York: Newman Press, 1963).

[46]Joseph W. Trigg, *Biblical Interpretation*, Message of the Fathers of the Church, vol. 9 (Wilmington, Del.: Michael Glazier, 1988).

[47]Augustine, *Confessions*, p. 45 (2.3).

[48]Ibid., p. 43 (2.2).

[49]Ibid., p. 47 (2.4).

[50]Augustine *Confessions* 2.2, cited in Benedict J. Groeschel, *Augustine: Major Writings* (New York: Crossroad, 1995), p. 21.

[51]Augustine *Confessions* 2.10, cited in Groeschel, *Augustine: Major Writings*, p. 22.

[52]Roland J. Teske, S.J., introduction to *On Genesis*, by Augustine, FC 84 (Washington: The Catholic University of America Press, 1991), p. 9.

[53]Peter Brown, *Augustine of Hippo* (Berkeley and Los Angeles: University of California Press, 1969), pp. 42-43.

[54]Ibid., p. 42.

[55]Teske, introduction to *On Genesis*, p. 12.

[56]Augustine, *Confessions*, pp. 62-63 (3.7).

[57]Brown, *Augustine of Hippo*, p. 43.

[58]Teske, introduction to *On Genesis*, p. 8.

[59]Augustine, *Confessions*, p. 103 (5.10).

[60]Pheme Perkins, "Mani, Manichaeism," in *Encyclopedia of Early Christianity* (New York: Garland Publishing, 1990), p. 563.

[61]Ibid.

[62]Ibid., pp. 562-63.

[63]Brown, *Augustine of Hippo*, pp. 43-44.

[64]Augustine, *Confessions*, p. 108 (5.14).

[65]Ibid., pp. 114-15 (6.3-4).

[66]Augustine, *Two Books on Genesis Against the Manichees*, trans. Roland J. Teske, S.J., pp. 74-75 (1.17).

[67]Ibid., pp. 75-76 (1.17).

[68]Augustine *Confessions* 7.18, cited in Groeschel, *Augustine: Major Writings*, p. 27. I have modified the translation slightly.

[69]Ibid., 8.11, cited in Groeschel, *Augustine: Major Writings*, p. 28.

[70]Augustine, *Confessions*, p. 176 (8.11).

[71]Ibid., p. 178 (8.12).

[72]Cf. Payne, *Fathers of the Western Church*, p. 179.

[73]Augustine, *Christian Instruction*, trans. John J. Gavigan, FC 2 (Washington: The Catholic University of America Press, 1947).

[74]St. Augustine, *On Christian Teaching*, trans. R. P. H. Green (Oxford: Oxford University Press, 1997).

[75]Augustine, *The Literal Meaning of Genesis*, 2 vols., trans. John Hammond Taylor, ACW 41-42 (New York: Paulist Press, 1982).

[76]Augustine, *On the Psalms*, 2 vols., trans. Dame Scholastica Hebgin and Dame Felicitas Corrigan, ACW 29-30 (New York: Paulist Press, 1960, 1961).

[77]Augustine, *Tractates on the Gospel of John*, trans. John W. Rettig, FC 78, 79, 88, 90, 92 (Washington: The Catholic University of America Press, 1988, 1988, 1993, 1994, 1995).

[78]Joseph W. Trigg, *Biblical Interpretation*, Message of the Fathers of the Church, vol. 9 (Wilmington, Del.: Michael Glazier, 1988), pp. 250-95.

[79]Grover A. Zinn Jr., "Gregory I the Great, in *Encyclopedia of Early Christianity*, pp. 393-98, has been a helpful source in the discussion that follows.

[80]Gregory the Great, *Register of the Epistles of Saint Gregory the Great*, NPNF Second Series, vols. 12-13 (Peabody, Mass: Hendrickson, 1994).

[81]Payne, *Fathers of the Western Church*, p. 201.

[82]Ibid., p. 203.

[83]Zinn, "Gregory I the Great," p. 394.

[84]Gregory the Great, *Register of the Epistles*, 12:75.

[85]Ibid.

[86]Ibid., p. 142.

[87]Gregory the Great, *Forty Gospel Homilies*, trans. Dom David Hurst (Kalamazoo, Mich.: Cistercian Publications, 1990).

[88]Ibid., Homily 12:89.

[89]Ibid., Homily 13:97-98.

[90]Ibid., Homily 19:140-41.

[91]Ibid., Homily 21:160.

[92]Payne, *Fathers of the Western Church*, p. 212.

[93]*Moralia*, 25, p. 39, cited in Payne, *Fathers of the Western Church*, p. 213. I have modernized the translation slightly.

[94]Gregory the Great, *Register of the Epistles*, vols. 12-13.

[95]St. Gregory the Great, *Pastoral Care*, trans. Henry Davis, ACW 11 (New York: Paulist Press, 1978).

[96]Thomas C. Oden, *Care of Souls in the Classic Tradition* (Philadelphia: Fortress Press, 1984).

[97]Gregory the Great, *Forty Gospel Homilies*, trans. Dom David Hurst (Kalamazoo, Mich.: Cistercian Publications, 1990).

[98]Trigg, *Biblical Interpretation*, p. 42.

[99]Ibid., pp. 223-38.

Chapter 6: The Fathers & Scripture: Exegesis at Alexandria

[1]Boniface Ramsey, *Beginning to Read the Fathers* (New York: Paulist Press, 1985), p. 25.

[2]James L. Kugel and Rowan A. Greer, *Early Biblical Interpretation* (Philadelphia: Westminster Press, 1986), p. 80.

[3]Ibid., p. 81.

[4]Manlio Simonetti, *Biblical Interpretation in the Early Church: An Historical Introduction to Patristic Exegesis* (Edinburgh: T & T Clark, 1994), p. 12.

[5]Ibid.

[6]Ibid.

[7]Irenaeus, *Against Heresies*, 4.26.1, cited in *The Church Fathers on the Bible*, ed. Frank Sadowski (New York: Alba House, 1987), p. 38.

[8]Justin Martyr *Dialogue with Trypho* 68, cited in Sadowski, *Church Fathers on the Bible*, p. 15. I have modified the translation slightly.

[9]Irenaeus *Against Heresies* 4.26.1, cited in Sadowski, *Church Fathers on the Bible*, pp. 38-39.

[10]Irenaeus *Against Heresies* 4.32, cited in Sadowski, *Church Fathers on The Bible*, p. 44.

[11]Origen, *De principiis* 1, praef. 8, cited in Ramsey, *Beginning to Read the Fathers*, p. 25.

[12]Simonetti, *Biblical Interpretation in the Early Church*, pp. 2-6.

[13]Joseph F. Kelly, *The World of the Early Christians*, FC 1 (Collegeville, Minn.: Liturgical Press, 1997), p. 119.

[14]Joseph W. Trigg, "Allegory," in *Encyclopedia of Early Christianity* (New York: Garland, 1990), p. 23.

[15]Simonetti, *Biblical Interpretation in the Early Church*, p. 7.

[16]Trigg, "Allegory," p. 24.

[17]Simonetti, *Biblical Interpretation in the Early Church*, p. 7.

[18]Ibid.

[19]Justin Martyr *Dialogue with Trypho*, ANF 1 (Grand Rapids, Mich.: Eerdmans, 1987), p. 268.

[20]Simonetti, *Biblical Interpretation in the Early Church*, p. 21; cf. Irenaeus, *Against Heresies*, 5.8.3.

[21]Ibid., p. 22.

[22]Irenaeus *Against Heresies* 4.19.1, ANF 1 (Grand Rapids, Mich.: Eerdmans, 1987), p. 486.

[23]Simonetti, *Biblical Interpretation in the Early Church*, pp. 14-15.

[24]Irenaeus *Against Heresies* 5.33.3, p. 562.

[25]Ibid., 4.19.1, pp. 486-87.

[26]Simonetti, *Biblical Interpretation in the Early Church*, p. 24.

[27]Karlfried Froehlich, ed., *Biblical Interpretation in the Early Church* (Philadelphia: Fortress Press, 1984), p. 16.

[28]Joseph W. Trigg, *Biblical Interpretation*, Message of the Fathers of the Church, vol. 9 (Wilmington, Del.: Michael Glazier, 1988), p. 23.

[29]Harry Y. Gamble, *Books and Readers in the Early Church: A History of Early Christian Texts* (New Haven, Conn.: Yale University Press, 1995), p. 232.

[30]Eusebius *Ecclesiastical History* 6.16, cited in Sadowski, *Church Fathers on the Bible*, p. 105.

[31]Origen *On First Principles*, Preface.1, cited in Sadowski, *Church Fathers on the Bible*, p. 108.

[32]Ibid., cited in Sadowski, *Church Fathers on the Bible*, p. 109.

[33]Ibid., 4.11, cited in Sadowski, *Church Fathers on the Bible*, p. 116.

[34]Ibid., 4.14, cited in Sadowski, *Church Fathers on the Bible*, p. 120.

[35]Ibid., Preface.4, cited in Sadowski, *Church Fathers on the Bible*, p. 109.

[36]Ibid., Preface.8-9, cited in Sadowski, *Church Fathers on the Bible*, pp. 111-12.

[37]Ibid., 4.11, cited in Sadowski, *Church Fathers on the Bible*, p. 116.

[38]Ibid., 4.8, cited in Sadowski, *Church Fathers on the Bible*, p. 114.

[39]Ibid., cited in Sadowski, *Church Fathers on the Bible*, p. 115.

[40]Ibid., 4.15, cited in Sadowski, *Church Fathers on the Bible*, p. 121.

[41]Ibid., 4.16, cited in Sadowski, *Church Fathers on the Bible*, p. 122.

[42]Ibid., 4.19, cited in Sadowski, *Church Fathers on the Bible*, p. 125.

[43]Origen *Homilies on Luke*, trans. Joseph T. Lienhard, S.J., FC 94 (Washington: The Catholic University of America Press), Homily 34:138.

[44]Ibid.

[45]Ibid., Homily 34:139.

[46]Ibid., pp. 139-40.

[47]Ibid., p. 141.

[48]Ronald Heine, "Reading the Bible with Origen," in *The Bible in Greek Christian Antiquity*, ed. Paul M. Blowers (Notre Dame, Ind.: University of Notre Dame Press, 1997), p. 132. In many ways the following pages are my summary of Heine's article, to which I am highly indebted.

[49]Cf. Heine, "Reading the Bible with Origen," p. 133.

[50]Ibid.

[51]Origen, *Comm. in Joannem*, 10.19-20, cited in Heine, "Reading the Bible with Origen," p. 133.

[52]Heine, "Reading the Bible with Origen," p. 133.

[53]Ibid., p. 131.

[54]Origen, *Ep. ad Gregorium* 4 (*Origenis Philocalia* 13, ed. J. A. Robinson [Cambridge: Cambridge, 1893]), p. 67, cited in Heine, "Reading the Bible with Origen," p. 144.

[55]Cited in Heine, "Reading the Bible with Origen," p. 140.

[56]Cited in Heine, "Reading the Bible with Origen," p. 140.

[57]Heine, "Reading the Bible with Origen," p. 134.

[58]Ibid.

[59]Ibid., p. 136.

[60]Ibid.

[61]Ibid.

[62]Ibid., p. 137.

[63]Ibid., pp. 137-38.

[64]Ibid., p. 139.

[65]Clement of Alexandria, Strom. 1.1.11, cited in Eric Osborn, "The Bible and Christian Morality in Clement of Alexandria," in The Bible in Greek Christian Antiquity, ed. Blowers, p. 113.

[66]Osborn, "The Bible and Christian Morality," pp. 113-14.

[67]Heine, "Reading the Bible with Origen," p. 135.

[68]Ibid.

[69]Ibid., pp. 144-145.

Chapter 7: The Fathers & Scripture: The Response of Antioch

[1]Joseph W. Trigg, Biblical Interpretation, Message of the Fathers of the Church, vol. 9 (Wilmington, Del.: Michael Glazier, 1988), p. 31.

[2]Karlfried Froehlich, ed., Biblical Interpretation in the Early Church (Philadelphia: Fortress Press, 1984), p. 20.

[3]Ibid.

[4]Trigg, Biblical Interpretation, p. 32.

[5]Froehlich, ed., Biblical Interpretation in the Early Church, pp. 20-21.

[6]Diodore of Tarsus, Commentary on the Psalms: Prologue, in Biblical Interpretation in the Early Church, ed. Froehlich, p. 82.

[7]Ibid., pp. 82-83.

[8]Ibid., p. 83.

[9]Ibid.

[10]Ibid., p. 84.

[11]Ibid., pp. 84-85.

[12]Ibid., p. 85.

[13]Ibid., pp. 85-86.

[14]Ibid., p. 85.

[15]Ibid., p. 86.

[16]Ibid.

[17]Ibid.

[18]Diodore of Tarsus, Preface to the Commentary on Psalm 118, in Biblical Interpretation in the Early Church, ed. Froehlich, p. 87.

[19]Ibid.

[20]Ibid., p. 88.

[21]Ibid., p. 93.

[22]Ibid.

[23]Theodore of Mopsuestia Commentary on Galatians 4:22-31, in Biblical Interpretation in the Early Church, ed. Froehlich, p. 95.

[24]Ibid.

[25]Ibid., p. 96.

[26]Ibid.

[27]Ibid.

[28]Ibid., p. 97.

[29]Ibid.

[30]Ibid.

[31]Ibid., pp. 97-98.

[32]Ibid., p. 99.

[33]Ibid., p. 98.

[34]Ibid., p. 99.

[35]Ibid., p. 100.

[36]Ibid.

[37]Ibid., p. 98.

[38]Ibid., p. 99.

[39]Theodore of Mopsuestia *Commentary on Zechariah*, cited in Trigg, *Biblical Interpretation*, p. 168.

[40]Ibid.

[41]Ibid.

[42]Ibid.

[43]Ibid., pp. 168-69.

[44]Ibid., p. 169.

[45]Theodore of Mopsuestia *Commentary on Zechariah*, cited in Joseph F. Kelly, *The World of the Early Christians*, Message of the Fathers of the Church, vol. 1 (Collegeville, Minn.: Liturgical Press, 1997), pp. 169-70.

[46]Kelly, *The World of the Early Christians*, p. 167.

[47]Clement of Alexandria, *Who Is the Rich Man That Is Saved?* in *Social Thought*, ed. Peter C. Phan, Message of the Fathers of the Church, vol. 20 (Wilmington, Del.: Michael Glazier, 1984), p. 71.

[48]Ibid., p. 72.

[49]Ibid.

[50]Ibid., p. 73.

[51]Ibid., p. 72.

[52]Ibid., p. 73.

[53]Origen *Commentary on Matthew* 15.20, cited in *Social Thought*, ed. Phan, p. 78.

[54]Ibid., p. 79.

[55]Jerome, Letter 130.14, cited in *Social Thought*, ed. Phan, p. 187.

[56]Ibid.

[57]Augustine, Letter 157 to Hilarious, cited in *Social Thought*, ed. Phan, p. 211.

[58]Ibid., p. 212.

[59]Ibid., p. 213.

[60]Ambrose *On Naboth* 58, cited in *Social Thought*, ed. Phan, p. 175.

[61]Ibid.

[62]John Chrysostom, *The Gospel of St. Matthew*, Homily 63.2, NPNF First Series, vol. 10 (Grand Rapids, Mich.: Eerdmans, 1986), p. 388.

[63]Ibid.

[64]Ibid.

[65]Ibid., p. 389.

[66]Ibid.

[67]Ibid., p. 390.

[68]Ibid. I have modified the translation slightly.

Chapter 8: Making Sense of Patristic Exegesis

[1]Harold O. J. Brown, "Proclamation and Preservation: The Necessity and Temptations of Church Tradition," in *Reclaiming the Great Tradition: Evangelicals, Catholics and Orthodox in Dialogue*, ed. James S. Cutsinger (Downers Grove, Ill.: InterVarsity Press, 1997), p. 78.

[2]Thomas C. Oden, *The Word of Life* (San Francisco: Harper & Row, 1989), pp. 219-20.

[3]Michael Casey, *Sacred Reading: The Ancient Art of Lectio Divina* (Liguori, Mo.: Triumph Books, 1995), p. 110.

[4]Brevard Childs, "On Reclaiming the Bible for Christian Theology," in *Reclaiming the Bible for the Church*, ed. Carl E. Braaten and Robert W. Jenson (Grand Rapids, Mich.: Eerdmans, 1995), p. 16.

[5]C. S. Lewis, "On the Reading of Old Books," in *God in the Dock: Essays on Theology and Ethics*, ed. Walter Hooper (Grand Rapids, Mich.: Eerdmans, 1970), pp. 200-207.

[6]Ibid., p. 200.

[7]Ibid., p. 202.

[8]Ibid.

[9]Ibid., p. 201.

[10]Ibid.

[11]Ibid., p. 204.

[12]James S. Cutsinger, introduction to *Reclaiming the Great Tradition*, p. 8.

[13]Ibid, p. 9.

[14]Ibid. p. 8.

[15]C. S. Lewis, *Mere Christianity* (New York: Macmillan, 1943), p. viii, cited in Cutsinger, *Reclaiming the Great Tradition*, p. 9.

[16]Brown, "Proclamation and Preservation," p. 78.

[17]Ibid., p. 79.

[18]Ibid., p. 80.

[19]Ibid., p. 81.

[20]Ibid., p. 83.

[21]Ibid., p. 84.

[22]Ibid., p. 85.

[23]Ibid.

[24]Ibid.

[25]Robert W. Jenson, "Hermeneutics and the Life of the Church," in *Reclaiming the Bible for the Church*, ed. Braaten and Jenson, p. 97.

[26]Bertrand de Margerie, *An Introduction to the History of Exegesis*, vol. 2, *The Latin Fathers* (Petersham, Mass.: Saint Bede's Publications, 1995), p. 54.

[27]Irenaeus *Adversus Haereses* 4.26.1, cited in Metropolitan Emilianos Timiadis, *The Relevance of the Fathers* (Brookline, Mass.: Holy Cross Orthodox Press, 1994), p. 57.

[28]St. Hilary *Traite des Mysteres*, I Pref., ed. Brisson, SC 19 bis (Paris: Editions du Cerf, 1967), pp. 73-75, cited in de Margerie, *Introduction to the History of Exegesis*, 2:55.

[29]Ibid., 1.5, SC 19, cited in de Margerie, *Introduction to the History of Exegesis*, 2:71-72.

[30]Timiadis, *Relevance of the Fathers*, p. 56.

[31]I am dependent upon Gerald Bray's summary of Tyconius's seven exegetical rules found in Bray, *Biblical Interpretation: Past and Present* (Downers Grove, Ill.: InterVarsity Press, 1996).

[32]Bray, *Biblical Interpretation*, p. 107.

[33]De Margerie, *Introduction to the History of Exegesis*, 2:3.

[34]Ibid.

[35]Jenson, "Hermeneutics and the Life of the Church," pp. 97-98.

[36]Childs, "On Reclaiming the Bible," p. 10.

[37]Ibid., p. 17.

[38]Timiadis, *Relevance of the Fathers*, pp. 55-56.

[39]Ibid., p. 56.

[40] Augustine *Sermo* 51.4-5 (PL 38.336), cited in Bertrand de Margerie, *An Introduction to the History of Exegesis*, vol. 3, *Saint Augustine* (Petersham, Mass.: Saint Bede's Publications, 1991), p. 10.

[41] Augustine *De utilitate credendi* 6.13, cited in de Margerie, *Introduction to the History of Exegesis*, 3:11.

[42] Augustine, Epistle 21 to Bishop Valerius, par. 3ff., PL 33.88, cited in de Margerie, *Introduction to the History of Exegesis*, 3:14.

[43] Origen Homily on Genesis 7.6, cited in Timiadis, *Relevance of the Fathers*, p. 57.

[44] St. Jerome, Epistle 125, 7.3, 11.1, cited in de Margerie, *Introduction to the History of Exegesis*, 2: 142.

[45] St. Jerome, Prologue to the Commentary on the Letter to the Ephesians, PL 26.439, cited in de Margerie, *Introduction to the History of Exegesis*, 2:142.

[46] St. Ambrose, Expositio in Ps. 118, Sermo 22, 28-30, PL 15, 1520-1521, cited in de Margerie, *Introduction to the History of Exegesis*, 2:112-13.

[47] Michael Casey, *Sacred Reading: The Ancient Art of Lectio Divina* (Liguori, Mo.: Triumph Books, 1996), p. 113.

General Index

Index of Biblical Texts